D0844807

Bloom's Modern Critical Views

Bloom's Modern Critical Views

T. S. ELIOT
New Edition

Edited and with an introduction by
Harold Bloom
Sterling Professor of the Humanities
Yale University

BLOOM'S
LITERARY CRITICISM
An imprint of Infobase Publishing

Bloom's Modern Critical Views: T.S. Eliot—New Edition

Copyright © 2011 by Infobase Publishing
Introduction © 2011 by Harold Bloom

Bloom's Literary Criticism
An imprint of Infobase Publishing
132 West 31st Street
New York NY 10001

Library of Congress Cataloging-in-Publication Data
T.S. Eliot / edited and with an introduction by Harold Bloom. — New ed.
    p. cm. — (Bloom's modern critical views)
    Includes bibliographical references and index.
    ISBN 978-1-60413-879-5 (hardcover)
    1. Eliot, T. S. (Thomas Stearns), 1888–1965—Criticism and interpretation.
I. Bloom, Harold.
    PS3509.L43Z872433 2010
    821'.912—dc22   2010019960

You can find Bloom's Literary Criticism on the World Wide Web at
http://www.chelseahouse.com.

Contributing editor: Pamela Loos
Cover designed by Takeshi Takahashi
Composition by IBT Global, Troy NY
Cover printed by IBT Global, Troy NY
Book printed and bound by IBT Global, Troy NY
Date printed: October 2010
Printed in the United States of America

10 9 8 7 6 5 4 3 2 1

This book is printed on acid-free paper.

All links and Web addresses were checked and verified to be correct at the time of publication. Because of the dynamic nature of the Web, some addresses and links may have changed since publication and may no longer be valid.

Contents

Editor's Note

My introduction asserts the perpetual freshness of "Prufrock" and the less unified efforts of *The Waste Land*, an American self-elegy masking as a mythological romance.

Hugh Kenner opens the volume with a discussion of Eliot's wrangling with the personal ghosts of history, after which Cleo McNelly Kearns examines the religious and doctrinal influences in *Four Quartets*.

John Paul Riquelme turns to the same work in an exploration of Eliot's disjunctive style, followed by A.D. Moody's query: Was Eliot an American poet after all?

Anthony L. Johnson broaches the similarities and differences in "Gerontion" and "The Journey of the Magi," and Lee Oser listens for Prufrock's puritan underpinnings.

Denis Donoghue looks at Eliotic origins giving rise to Prufrock's spiritual panic, while Ronald Bush examines the poet in the context of modernism and the aesthetic energies of the 1890s.

Joseph Jonghyun Jeon traces the tension between privacy and revelation in "The Hollow Men," after which John H. Timmerman addresses the presence of the Aristotelian in *The Waste Land*.

Introduction

One can fight a long war against T.S. Eliot's criticism and still confess a lifelong fascination with his best poems: *The Waste Land* and a group that certainly includes "The Love Song of J. Alfred Prufrock," "La Figlia Che Piange," "The Hollow Men," and "The Journey of the Magi." Probably one could add "Gerontion" and "Little Gidding" to any short list of Eliot's most lasting poetry, but the five poems initially listed can be called his essential achievement in verse.

The perpetual freshness of "Prufrock" is a surprise each time I return to the poem. Actually, reading "Prufrock" (preferably out loud to oneself) is never quite the experience I expect it to be. Christopher Ricks charmingly demonstrates the incongruity of "Love Song" and the outrageous name J. Alfred Prufrock, and yet this dramatic monologue remains something of a defeated erotic reverie. In his very useful *Inventions of the March Hare* (1996), Ricks gives us a richly annotated version of Eliot's poems of 1909–17 and includes an unpublished passage of the "Love Song." The missing middle, "Prufrock's Pervigilium," plays in its title on the Latin poem *Pervigilium Veneris* (fourth century CE), the "Eve of Venus," which had a great vogue in the era of the splendid critic Walter Pater. Eliot had nothing good to say of Pater, probably because his own sensibility was essentially Paterian, but Prufrock seems to have read Pater's historical novel, *Marius the Epicurean*. Pater, the prophet of the Aesthetic movement in England, exalted perception and sensation and deprecated dogmatic belief of any sort. *Marius the Epicurean* has a memorable scene in which the authorship of the Pervigilium is ascribed to Marius's dying friend, Flavian. Ricks shrewdly notes Pater's hint that Flavian's illness is venereal, and something otherwise obscure in Prufrock's dramatic monologue is illuminated when we intuit that J. Alfred's erotic timidity is allied to his obsessive fear of venereal infection.

The "Love Song" is a perpetual "dying fall," its "hundred indecisions" a series of erotic evasions. Brooding on the arms of women, which have for him an overwhelming sexual power, Prufrock will never bring any of his incipient relationships to the moment of crisis. His poem continues to pulsate with a barely repressed energy and may be the most remarkable instance in the language of a deferred eroticism transfiguring itself into a sublime eloquence.

2

Even as a boy, I fell in love with "La Figlia Che Piange," which remains one of Eliot's incantory triumphs and the poem he chose to conclude the volume *Prufrock and Other Observations* (1917). Eliot's weeping girl is far more intense than the alluring women of the "Love Song," but the chanter of "La Figlia" is very like Prufrock: another obsessed evader of the sexual experience. Nearly 60 years of reciting the lyric to myself have only enhanced its aura for me; few poems in the language so evoke erotic longing, the sense of an unrealized relationship.

And yet the voice of this lyric is in one respect not Prufrockian; its imaginative sympathy adheres to the weeping girl and hardly at all to her departing lover. Something very like a Paterian privileged moment, or secularized epiphany, is being celebrated, even as the voice retreats into detachment, the autumn weather of the soul. The Paterian flesh of radiance against a darkening background is the sunlight woven in the girl's hair. Eliot, notoriously unsympathetic to John Milton's poetry, vies with Milton as the poet in English most celebratory of the erotic glory of a woman's hair.

Despite himself, Eliot always remained a High Romantic lyric poet, with profound affinities to Shelley (whom he professed to dislike) and Tennyson (to whom he condescended). Any vision of romantic love poetry would be impoverished if it excluded "La Figlia Che Piange."

3

"The Hollow Men" (1925) is the culmination of early (and major) Eliot, a grim and permanent achievement, indeed a parodic masterpiece. Though the chant is overtly Dantesque, I hear in it Shakespeare's Brutus of *Julius Caesar*, a drama replete with "hollow" Roman patriots, who protest their endless sincerity, only to be subtly exposed by the playwright. Brutus, no Hamlet, but dominated by a Macbeth-like proleptic imagination, kills himself, still blind to his own hollowness. Eliot, who perhaps unconsciously was more affected by *Julius Caesar* than his beloved *Coriolanus*, parodies saints as well as "patriots." The power of "The Hollow Men" is its universality. Though some critics interpret the poem as a portrait of a world without belief, waiting for the return of Christian revelation, scarecrows hardly seem candidates for any redemption. Eliot himself was moving toward conversion (two years later, in 1927), but nothing in "The Hollow Men" intimates that such movement is possible.

Eliot's poetry of belief—in "Ash Wednesday," "The Rock," and *Four Quartets*—seems to me considerably less persuasive than his visions of the waste land. "The Journey of the Magi" is Eliot's most effective "religious" poem because its speaker dramatizes the poignance of exile, always Eliot's true mode. The Magus speaks for Eliot the poet and not for Eliot the Anglo-Catholic. Like Tennyson, whom Eliot had praised for the quality of his doubt, the Magus stands between two worlds, never to be at home in either. At his best, the poet Eliot remained dispersed.

4

The Waste Land, though something less than a unified poem, is Eliot's masterwork, by common agreement. Where few agree is on the question as to just what *The Waste Land* is doing as a poetic performance. Is it a lament for Western cultural decline, for a Europe in retreat from Christianity? Or is it a very American elegy for the self, in direct descent from Walt Whitman's magnificent "When Lilacs Last in the Dooryard Bloom'd." Clearly the second, I would insist, though mine remains a minority view.

Eliot's own "Notes" to *The Waste Land* are frequently outrageous, never more so than when they explicate the song of the hermit thrush by remarking, "Its 'water-dripping song' is justly celebrated." Why, yes, particularly when the hermit thrush sings its song of death in Whitman's "Lilacs" elegy. Ostensibly mourning the martyred Lincoln, "Lilacs" more pervasively both celebrates and laments the Whitmanian poetic self. Eliot's poethood, and not Western civilization, is the elegiac center of *The Waste Land*. Personal breakdown is the poem's true subject, shrewdly masked as the decline and fall of Christian culture in post–World War I Europe.

Such a judgment, on my part, hardly renders *The Waste Land* a less interesting or aesthetically eminent poem (or series of poems, or fragments). Hardly an escape from either emotion or from personality, *The Waste Land*, 90 years after its publication, seems a monument to the emotional despair of a highly individual romantic personality, one in full continuity with Shelley, Tennyson, and Whitman, who are far closer to the poem than are Eliot's chosen precursors: Dante, Baudelaire, and Jules Laforgue.

Northrop Frye followed Eliot himself in reading *The Waste Land* as a poem of Christian redemption. I think that Eleanor Cook is more accurate in her subtle emphasis on the poem as a representation of exile and of private grief. No one is saved in *The Waste Land*, any more than Lincoln or Whitman is saved in "When Lilacs Last in the Dooryard Bloom'd." Both grand elegies for the self are American songs of death, including the death-in-life of poetic crisis.

The Waste Land is an American self-elegy masking as a mythological romance, a romantic crisis poem pretending to be an exercise in Christian irony. Mask and pretence, like the invention of more congenial fathers and ancestors, are customary poetic tropes and certainly not to be censured. They are part of any poet's magic, or personal superstition, and they help to get authentic poems written. *The Waste Land*, rather than *Four Quartets* or the verse dramas, is Eliot's major achievement, a grand gathering of great fragments and indisputably the most influential poem written in English in our century. I read it, on evidence internal and external, as being essentially a revision of Whitman's final great achievement, "When Lilacs Last in the Dooryard Bloom'd," ostensibly an elegy for Lincoln but more truly the poet's lament for his own poethood. Elegy rather than brief epic or quest romance, *The Waste Land* thus enters the domain of mourning and melancholia, rather than that of civilization and its discontents.

Many of the links between Eliot's and Whitman's elegies for the poetic self have been noted by a series of exegetes starting with S. Musgrove and continuing with John Hollander and myself and younger critics, including Gregory S. Jay and Cleo McNelly Kearns. Rather than repeat Cleo Kearns, I intend to speculate here on the place of *The Waste Land* in romantic tradition, particularly in regard to its inescapable precursor, Whitman.

In his essay, "The *Pensées* of Pascal" (1931), Eliot remarked upon Pascal's adversarial relation to his true precursor, Montaigne:

> One cannot destroy Pascal, certainly; but of all authors Montaigne is one of the least destructible. You could as well dissipate a fog by flinging hand-grenades into it. For Montaigne is a fog, a gas, a fluid, insidious element. He does not reason, he insinuates, charms, and influences.

Walt Whitman, too, is "a fluid, insidious element," a poet who "insinuates, charms, and influences." And he is the darkest of poets, despite his brazen self-advertisements and his passionate hopes for his nation. *Song of Myself*, for all its joyous epiphanies, chants also of the waste places:

Of the turbid pool that lies in the autumn forest,
Of the moon that descends the steeps of the soughing twilight,
Toss, sparkles of day and dusk—toss on the black stems that
decay in the muck,
Toss to the moaning gibberish of the dry limbs.

No deep reader of Whitman could forget the vision of total self-rejection that is the short poem "A Hand-Mirror":

Hold it up sternly—see this it sends back, (who is it? is it you?)
Outside fair costume, within ashes and filth,
No more a flashing eye, no more a sonorous voice or springy step,
Now some slave's eye, voice, hands, step,
A drunkard's breath, unwholesome eater's face, venerealee's flesh,
Lungs rotting away piecemeal, stomach sour and cankerous,
Joints rheumatic, bowels clogged with abomination,
Blood circulating dark and poisonous streams,
Words babble, hearing and touch callous,
No brain, no heart left, no magnetism of sex;
Such from one look in this looking-glass ere you go hence,
Such a result so soon—and from such a beginning!

Rather than multiply images of despair in Whitman, I turn to the most rugged of his self-accusations, in the astonishing "Crossing Brooklyn Ferry":

It is not upon you alone the dark patches fall,
The dark threw its patches down upon me also,
The best I had done seem'd to me blank and suspicious,
My great thoughts as I supposed them, were they not in reality
meagre?
Nor is it you alone who know what it is to be evil,
I am he who knew what it was to be evil,
I too knotted the old knot of contrariety,
Blabb'd, blush'd, resented, lied, stole, grudg'd,
Had guile, anger, lust, hot wishes I dared not speak,
Was wayward, vain, greedy, shallow, sly, cowardly, malignant,
The wolf, the snake, the hog, not wanting in me,
The cheating look, the frivolous word, the adulterous wish, not
wanting,
Refusals, hates, postponements, meanness, laziness, none of these
wanting,

Was one with the rest, the days and haps of the rest,
Was call'd by my nighest name by clear loud voices of young men
   as they saw me approaching or passing,
Felt their arms on my neck as I stood, or the negligent leaning of
   their flesh against me as I sat,
Saw many I loved in the street or ferry-boat or public assembly,
   yet never told them a word,
Lived the same life with the rest, the same old laughing, gnawing,
   sleeping,
Play'd the part that still looks back on the actor or actress,
The same old role, the role that is what we make it, as great as we
   like,
Or as small as we like, or both great and small.

The barely concealed allusions to Milton's Satan and to *King Lear* strengthen Whitman's catalog of vices and evasions, preparing the poet and his readers for the darker intensities of the great *Sea-Drift* elegies and "Lilacs," poems that are echoed everywhere in Eliot's verse but particularly in "The Death of Saint Narcissus," *The Waste Land*, and "The Dry Salvages." Many critics have charted these allusions, but I would turn consideration of Eliot's agon with Whitman to the question: Why Whitman? It is poetically unwise to go down to the waterline or go to the headland with Walt Whitman, for then the struggle takes place in an arena where the poet who found his identifying trope in the sea drift cannot lose.

An answer must be that the belated poet does not choose his trial by landscape or seascape. It is chosen for him by his precursor. Browning's quester in "Childe Roland to the Dark Tower Came" is as overdetermined by Shelley as Eliot is overdetermined by Whitman in *The Waste Land*, which is indeed Eliot's version of "Childe Roland," as it is Eliot's version of Percivale's quest in Tennyson's "The Holy Grail," a poem haunted by Keats in the image of Galahad. "Lilacs" is everywhere in *The Waste Land*: in the very lilacs bred out of the dead land, in the song of the hermit thrush in the pine trees, and most remarkably in the transumption of Whitman walking down to where the hermit thrush sings, accompanied by two companions walking beside him, the thought of death and the knowledge of death:

Then with the knowledge of death as walking one side of me,
And the thought of death close-walking the other side of me,
And I in the middle as with companions, and as holding the
   hands of companions,

I fled forth to the hiding receiving night that talks not,
Down to the shores of the water, the path by the swamp in the
dimness,
To the solemn shadowy cedars and ghostly pines so still.

The "crape-veil'd women" singing their dirges through the night for Lincoln are hardly to be distinguished from Eliot's "murmur of maternal lamentation," and Whitman's "tolling tolling bells' perpetual clang" goes on tolling reminiscent bells in *The Waste Land* as it does in "The Dry Salvages." Yet all this is only a first-level working of the influence process, of interest mostly as a return of the repressed. Deeper, almost beyond analytical modes as yet available to criticism, is Eliot's troubled introjection of his nation's greatest and inescapable elegiac poet. "Lilacs" has little to do with the death of Lincoln but everything to do with Whitman's ultimate poetic crisis, beyond which his strongest poetry will cease. *The Waste Land* has little to do with neo-Christian polemics concerning the decline of Western culture and everything to do with a poetic crisis that Eliot could not quite surmount, in my judgment, since I do not believe that time will confirm the estimate that most contemporary critics have made of *Four Quartets*.

The decisive moment or negative epiphany of Whitman's elegy centers on his giving up of the tally, the sprig of lilac that is the synecdoche for his image of poetic voice, which he yields up to death and to the hermit thrush's song of death. Eliot's parallel surrender in "What the Thunder Said" is to ask "what have we given?" where the implicit answer is "a moment's surrender," a negative moment in which the image of poetic voice is achieved only as one of Whitman's "retrievements out of the night." In his essay on Pascal, Eliot says of Montaigne, a little resentfully but with full accuracy, that "he succeeded in giving expression to the skepticism of *every* human being," presumably including Pascal, Shakespeare, and even T.S. Eliot. What did Whitman succeed in expressing with equal universality? Division between "myself" and "the real me" is surely the answer. Walt Whitman, one of the roughs, an American, is hardly identical with "the Me myself" who:

Looks with its sidecurved head curious what will come next,
Both in and out of the game, and watching and wondering at it.

Thomas Stearns Eliot, looking with side-curved head, both in and out of the game, has little in common with Walt Whitman, one of the roughs, an American, yet almost can be identified with that American "Me myself."

The line of descent from Shelley and Keats through Browning and Tennyson to Pound and Eliot would be direct were it not for the intervention of the genius of the shores of America, the poet of *Leaves of Grass*. Whitman enforces on Pound and Eliot the American difference, which he had inherited from Emerson, the fountain of our eloquence and of our pragmatism. Most reductively defined, the American poetic difference ensues from a sense of acute isolation, both from an overwhelming space of natural reality and from an oppressive temporal conviction of belatedness, of having arrived after the event. The inevitable defense against nature is the Gnostic conviction that one is no part of the creation, that one's freedom is invested in the primal abyss. Against belatedness, defense involves an immersion in allusiveness, hardly for its own sake, but in order to reverse the priority of the cultural, pre-American past. American poets from Whitman and Dickinson onward are more like Milton than Milton is, and so necessarily they are more profoundly Miltonic than even Keats or Tennyson was compelled to be.

What has wasted the land of Eliot's elegiac poem is neither the malady of the Fisher King nor the decline of Christianity, and Eliot's own psychosexual sorrows are not very relevant either. The precursors' strength is the illness of *The Waste Land*; Eliot, after all, can promise to show us "fear in a handful of dust" only because the monologist of Tennyson's *Maud* already has cried out: "Dead, long dead, / Long dead! / And my heart is a handful of dust." Even more poignantly, Eliot is able to sum up all of Whitman's extraordinary "As I Ebb'd with the Ocean of Life" in the single line: "These fragments I have shored against my ruins," where the fragments are not only the verse paragraphs that constitute the text of *The Waste Land* but crucially are also Whitman's floating sea-drift:

> Me and mine, loose windrows, little corpses,
> Froth, snowy white, and bubbles,
> (See, from my dead lips the ooze exuding at last,
> See, the prismatic colors glistening and rolling,)
> Tufts of straw, sands, fragments,
> Buoy'd hither from many moods, one contradicting another.
> From the storm, the long calm, the darkness, the swell,
> Musing, pondering, a breath, a briny tear, a dab of liquid or soil,
> Up just as much out of fathomless workings fermented and thrown,
> A limp blossom or two, torn, just as much over waves floating,
> drifted at random,
> Just as much for us that sobbing dirge of Nature,
> Just as much whence we come that blare of the cloud—trumpets,

We, capricious, brought hither we know not whence, spread out
before you,
You up there walking or sitting,
Whoever you are, we too lie in drifts at your feet.

"Tufts of straw, sands, fragments" are literally "shored" against Whitman's ruins, as he wends "the shores I know," the shores of America to which,
Whitman said, Emerson had led all of us, Eliot included. Emerson's essays,
Eliot pugnaciously remarked, "are already an encumbrance," and so they
were, and are, and evermore must be for an American writer, but inescapable
encumbrances are also stimuli, as Pascal learned in regard to the overwhelming Montaigne.

HUGH KENNER

Eliot and the Voices of History

Eliot preferred to be anonymous; it's said that on being recognized on a London bus he'd crisply get off at the next stop. One time, though, it was a cab-driver who recognized him, and he chose not to make a scene. The dialogue, by his account, went as follows:

> "You're T. S. Eliot, aren't you?"
> "Ah."
> "Just last week, do you know who was sitting where you're sitting now? Bertrand Russell!"
> "Ah."
> "So I said, 'Well, Lord Russell, what's it all about?' And do you know, he couldn't tell me!"

That was too good not to be recounted again and again; Eliot's widow says it was one of his favorite stories. For its theme is how self-assumed Omniscience got confronted by a man with a simple wish for one clarifying sentence . . . which Omniscience was powerless to formulate. It's like having the Voice from the Burning Bush struck dumb.

Had Russell possessed the wit he might have responded in the Voice of the Eliotic Thunder: DA *Datta Dayadhvam Damyata*, which is more or

From *T. S. Eliot: Man and Poet*, Volume 1, edited and introduced by Laura Cowan, pp. 71–81. © 1990 by the National Poetry Foundation.

less What It's All About, and would be especially persuasive from the back of a cab (CPP 49). Perhaps he did think of it but feared being asked to translate, which would have consumed an evening while the meter ran. (I mean the meter of the taxi.) Eliot's impish mind would not have missed the analogy between the taxi-driver and the Quester of *The Waste Land*, who in Jessie Weston's rescension of the myth finds relics in a ruined chapel and wants to know what they are: whereupon the heavens open and rain falls. The heavens have been shut up in wait for someone—anyone—with merely the desire to know.

It had been part of Eliot's implication, perhaps, that by 1921 England no longer contained that desire. For its literati read the *Times Literary Supplement* and could not be stumped. If you wrote, "Those are pearls that were his eyes," they murmured smartly, "*Tempest!*" If you wrote, "The Army of unalterable law," they responded, "Meredith: 'Lucifer in Starlight'"; then they hissed "plagiarist!" (Yes, that did get said, when Eliot built Meredith's line into a minor poem, "Cousin Nancy.") And if you put *The Waste Land* before them they knew on what prior wealth this "poem" was drawing, and could be relied on to find its "parodies" "cheap," its "imitations" "inferior." (F. L. Lucas, the bookman's bookman, said so, in '22. And Jack Squire, a bookman who stood for Traditional Values, added that a grunt would have served about as well. [118].)

And if you'd asked, "What's it all about?" meaning not *The Waste Land* but our circumambient "it," they'd have invoked Rural Certainties, Traditional Values, even Iambic Pentameter. (Bertrand Russell, to his credit, hadn't resorted to that.)

But such "cultivation" reduces Literature, our communal memory, to the status of Trivial Pursuit. It's noteworthy how it's now the theme of a relentless weekly contest in the *TLS*, where people who can Spot the Author gain Book Coupons. But the Thunder's words to the Quester would earn no coupons. Far from filling a quizmaster's "Aha!" slots, they ravel down from prehistory through history to our present consciousness, and never are they neat, no, simply omnipresent. Their syllables come literally from prehistory and are all but impenetrable.

Eliot had drawn on the great discovery we identify now with Sir William Jones, a man Dr. Johnson had known. It was not true, thought Sir William Jones, that etymologies lie inert in a tidy field, Greek deriving from Hebrew, Latin from Greek, English from all of the above. No, what we now call the Indo-European tongues descend from a lost speech to which our best clue is the Sanskrit of India. In 1882, the year James Joyce was born, Walter Skeat, one pioneer in the tradition of Jones, published the final volume of his *Etymological Dictionary*, with a list of 461 Aryan (Sanskrit) roots. Skeat's book was just a short generation old when Eliot, a graduate student, undertook Sanskrit at Harvard, knowing that beyond Sanskrit stretched the unknowable, "that vanished mind of which our mind is a continuation." By another decade he was making his Thunder speak Sanskrit.

So the DA root is from prehistory, and utters the bestowing impulse. Then one compound, *Datta* says "Give," and other words specify what is to be given: *Dayadhvam*, "Give Sympathy," *Damyata*, "Give Guidance." In a world now infinitely more bureaucratized, English has borrowed "data" from dead Latin to signify items given, just scraps like the fact that Shakespeare wrote *The Tempest*. We consign them to a computer program we call a Data Base Manager, and perish amid their proliferation.

And that's not all; we can further persuade ourselves that *Dayadhvam* and *Damyata* command an encompassing force that leaves "Give Sympathy" and "Give Guidance" sounding pedantic. That may well be an illusion derived from our ignorance of Sanskrit; Eliot once alluded to the pleasure he took, in his student days, from repeating to himself passages of Dante he did not yet know how to construe or translate. Still, those English phrases are but ways to analyze, and they use unproducible abstractions, "sympathy," "guidance," such glibness as Bertrand Russell under pressure from the taxicab driver had failed to conjure up. Nor are the "Sympathize" and "Control" of Eliot's own note much better: words, words, words. What *The Waste Land* strives to isolate is the starkly inarticulable: what can't be explained if you don't know it already: so to speak, F. H. Bradley's Immediate Experience, no longer Immediate once we try to think "about" it.

For such is the way our deepest certainties are, according to Eliot, who by Jeffrey Perl's showing was in a strict sense a Radical Skeptic. For Knowing, the opposite of Skepticism, is the art of isolating what is knowable. Your Practical Cat you can perhaps make shift to isolate (though does anyone *know* a cat?). But try to isolate some object of profounder knowledge, and lo, it disappears. That hints at flower-child, countercultural lore, an unsettling thought if your degree is from the old Harvard.

(It follows, by the way, that Eliot's verse can't be explained; the best the explainer can offer is such hinting as may help reposition a reader's mind. It's odd indeed that Eliot of all poets became the New Criticism's patron saint; less odd, then, that John Crowe Ransom didn't greatly care for his work, or that Yvor Winters liked it very much less.)

So Eliot talks of a poet's usable knowledge being in his bones; "the historical sense compels a man to write not merely with his own generation in his bones, but with a feeling that the whole of the literature of Europe from Homer and within it the whole of the literature of his own country has a simultaneous existence and composes a simultaneous order" (SE 4). Having something "in your bones" and having a complex "feeling," those appear to be synonymous; two pages later Eliot is distinguishing it (or them) from "erudition," which he also calls "pedantry" (SE 6). Another time he said, "At the moment one writes, one is what one is, and the damage of a lifetime, and of having been born into an unsettled society, cannot be repaired at the moment of composition." No use, at that moment, resolving to be "classical"; no use signing up for an extension course.

So we've a moral obligation not to be ignorant, but what we've learned in partially freeing ourselves from ignorance we cannot really say. Pound, with his gift for being less mysterious, once said that real knowledge begins when one has "forgotten which book." Repeatedly, in "Tradition and the Individual Talent," Eliot brushes aside "Blue-book" knowledge: the kind that helps you on examinations, and later with those *TLS* competitions. Not that he'd have willingly been without such knowledge, else he'd not have been able to write the Notes to *The Waste Land*, those few enigmatic pages which, as he once remarked, were to achieve "greater popularity than the poem itself." But the knowledge that had fed the poem itself was of a different, unformulable order.

Some of the notes do offer Blue-book facts, as when they tell us in what older book this or that detail of *The Waste Land* may also be found. As information goes, that is information, or perhaps data-base management. But the connection of "The Chair she sat in, like a burnished throne" with *Antony and Cleopatra*, II, ii, 190, is a perfectly pointless tit-bit to offer any reader who doesn't already know it (CPP 39). Such notes tell us what we don't need if we know it already but can't use if we don't, and insofar as the notes are part of the poem their poetic force lies in their enactment of futility. Everyone who has tried to "teach" *The Waste Land* knows that.

And if it seems elementary, it's to Eliot's credit that he has made it seem so. That issue at least he forced into a corner, that sharp distinction between what you have in your bones (having perhaps even "forgotten which book") and what you're just now snacking up, or just now regurgitating ("Ah, yes, *Antony and Cleopatra*; Enobarbus' speech"). He had come to England from what he once called "a large flat country which nobody wants to visit;" in that, he said, America resembled Turgenev's Russia. Eliot coined the phrase apropos of Henry James; we may remember how when James in 1904 revisited the flat land of his birth, he rode the ferry to New Jersey and watched shore houses

> waiting, a little bewilderingly, for their justification, waiting for the next clause in the sequence, waiting in short for life, for time, for interest, for character, for identity itself to come to them, quite as large spread tables or superfluous shops might wait for guests and customers. . . . (8)

—waiting, in short, to be haunted by the voices of history.

But that phrase has a romantic ring, not an Eliotic. Henry James can talk as though all that America has lacked is time. For buildings and furniture to marinate in time is what makes them of interest, and here time has been in insufficient supply. Moreover, Americans—especially New Yorkers—tend to pull down an edifice well before time has begun to soak into its pores. James does seem susceptible to the romance of old houses that have stayed in place for centuries. It's an endearing susceptibility. By now, were he alive, he might judge the time just ripening for a coy sidle toward the Flatiron Building.

Eliot, though: when he writes of "old stones that cannot be deciphered" one detects little romance (CPP 128). The journey to a sacred place leads "behind the pig-sty to the dull façade / And the tombstone" (CPP 139). If history, as he says, may be freedom, it may also be servitude, unless we realize the truth that

> We cannot revive old factions
> We cannot restore old policies
> Or follow an antique drum. (CPP 143)

That's pretty plain speaking, in an idiom close to that of a *Times* leader. Though when Eliot's verse speaks plainly there are generally reservations close to the surface. Plain speech is apt to be a practical compromise. And his way of speaking profoundly, on one occasion, was to quote the Thunder which can barely be understood. "Intolerable," indeed, was the "wrestle / With words and meanings," its issue, at best, ways of putting it, "not very satisfactory" (CPP 125).

A genre to which he was drawn in the 1930s was that defined by Thomas Gray, the genre of the "Elegy in a Country Churchyard." Fully nine Eliot poems take their titles from a place, and voice meditations which the place helps to compose; they are the five short "Landscapes" and the four ambitious "Quartets." One thing curious about all nine poems is the absence of other people, other voices. The virtual Babel of *The Waste Land* has been superseded by circumambient silence in which the poet hears only his own low voice; and when, exceptionally, *Little Gidding* does assign a long speaking part to another voice, it is the voice of an ambiguously identified ghost.

Of the "Landscapes," three are American—"New Hampshire," "Virginia," "Cape Ann"—and two from Great Britain—"Usk" and "Rannoch, by Glencoe." "Virginia" moves like an incantation:

> Red river, red river,
> Slow flow heat is silence

No will is still as a river
Still. Will heat move
Only through the mocking-bird
Heard once? Still hills
Wait. Gates wait. Purple trees,
White trees, wait, wait,
Delay, decay. Living, living,
Never moving. Ever moving
Iron thoughts came with me
And go with me:
Red river, river, river. (CPP 94)

It's notable how this small poem closes in on itself; of its fifty-eight words fully eight occur twice, two thrice, one ("wait") four times, one ("river") six times. It hears its own words, and it hears a mocking bird, once; all else simply waits. Apart from "me" and "iron thoughts," which I brought here and will take away again, the only hint of human presence is the one word, "gates." We might expect an American poet to hear, in the Virginia of Washington and Jefferson, quickening voices out of American history: the more striking, then, is this sheer depopulated silence, amid which the colors of the flag can be barely collected from a red river, white and purple trees. It was in Virginia, in 1933, that Eliot spoke to a lecture audience of Landscape: "a passive creature," he said, which "lends itself to an author's mood." That was also where he called the American Civil War "a disaster from which the country has never recovered, and perhaps never will." He remarked, too, on human over-readiness to assume that ill effects are obliterated by time. Virginia, the poem hopes we'll remember, was not only the forging place of the Union but the heart of the Secession. They canceled: hence a vacancy of "wait, wait / Delay, decay."

Then in "Rannoch by Glencoe," a place he visited shortly after returning from Virginia, Eliot found what Elisabeth Schneider finely calls "the dark side of unity of culture, the moment of time none can redeem, a Waste Land contracted into the single scene of a present indelibly but invisibly marked by the past" (163). Rannoch was the site of the massacre that terminated Jacobite hopes; that foreclosed, so to speak, the English Civil War:

Here the crow starves, here the patient stag
Breeds for the rifle. Between the soft moor
And the soft sky, scarcely room
To leap or soar. Substance crumbles, in the thin air
Moon cold or moon hot. The road winds in

Listlessness of ancient war
Languor of broken steel,
Clamour of confused wrong, apt
In silence. Memory is strong
Beyond the bone. Pride snapped,
Shadow of pride is long, in the long pass
No concurrence of bone. (CPP 94–95)

Stags breed but to be shot; the very scavengers starve. Truly, "[i]f all time
is eternally present / All time is unredeemable" (CPP 117), and history is
the nightmare Stephen Dedalus called it, a nightmare from which we can
foresee no awakening.

The broken steel, the clamour of confused wrong, are constituents of
knowledge we must bring to Glencoe; a visitor deprived of that knowledge
would see only the soft moor, the soft sky. (It can be tenuous knowledge, by
the way; the *Encyclopedia Britannica*'s entry on Glencoe gives the location of
the district and its dimensions and reports a monument to a Gaelic school-
teacher, but omits all mention of the only compelling reason to go there.)

The *Quartets*, of course, bear the names of places, moreover, places we
are unlikely to have heard of save as students of T. S. Eliot. In that, they
resemble the Churchyard at Stoke Poges, where Gray chose to locate meditations Westminster Abbey couldn't have prompted. Burnt Norton: a manor in
the Cotswolds, at one time "burnt"; unlike Rannoch or Canterbury or Saint
Paul's, it has escaped being claimed by "history," which is not to say that it
doesn't possess a history. Not only have I never visited it, I have known only
two people who had, of whom one was Eliot himself. He was there in 1934
and found empty gardens, an alley bordered by trees, a drained lily-pool. He
saw, the poem tells us, the pool mysteriously filled "with water out of sunlight" (CPP 118). "Then a cloud passed, and the pool was empty": nothing as
dramatic as thunder giving tongue, just a trick of the light, but it seemed to
take away hidden presences. One theme of the poem is the presence of those
presences—

      dignified, invisible,
Moving without pressure, over the dead leaves,
In the autumn heat, through the vibrant air, . . .

Meanwhile the very roses "[h]ad the look of flowers that are looked at," a
tricky line that can collapse into tautology, since if flowers have a "look" they
are being "looked at," but a line that somehow conveys the possibility of other
lookers-on than ourselves. The unknown dead? Partly. Partly too, denizens of

"what might have been," in the infinity of worlds we never entered, through that door "we did not open," because we elected to open whatever door led us to our Now. One door Eliot had opened was the one that led to residence in England. So among the "dignified, invisible" presences will have been an Eliot who might have stayed in America, might even have joined the faculty at Harvard. He'd have sparred with that phantom in 1932, when he gave the Norton Lecture at Harvard and even stayed in Eliot House. That American visit did unleash much poetry. He published *Burnt Norton* in 1935.

For Eliot, Burnt Norton was a chance encounter. East Coker, though, was part of his personal history: the place from which his American ancestor departed for America, leaving behind the stay-at-home Eliots to whom Sir Thomas Elyot belonged, whose "Boke Named the Governour" the poem quotes. (That Boke, as Eliot would not have failed to notice, got reprinted in Everyman's Library, a series to which he himself had gained admission not as his time's most influential poet but as introducer of the *Pensées* of Pascal.) And the Dry Salvages—*Les Trois Sauvages* "off the N.E. Coast of Cape Ann, Massachusetts"—(here Eliot did for once supply a note) sport a "beacon" (as he specifies) by which he'd sailed in his youth, long ago when

> The boat responded
> Gaily, to the hand expert with sail and oar.... (CPP 49)

Last, Little Gidding, back in England, is a place of pilgrimage for British and Anglican Eliot; also a place where Charles I sought refuge amid the wreckage of his fortunes. Though it comes closest of the four to involvement in formal History, it's by no means a tourist trap, with obvious associations such as Eliot wanted above all to avoid.

So, as he'd done in "Virginia" and "Rannoch," he can import his own associations, for delicate entangling with an obduracy of place. By contrast, Henry James, yearning for those Jersey houses to offer a producible past, can seem not just romantic but nearly blatant. Yet Eliot, being aware of being James' countryman, conjured in his fourth quartet that most Jamesian of apparitions, a ghost. Of Jamesian ghosts, the most famous is perhaps one that Eliot alludes to in *The Family Reunion*, the specter that haunts the Jolly Corner back in New York, to personify the crippled thing New York has come to, the impaired being New York would have made of the protagonist had he stayed there. Its impairment is theatrical: missing fingers, a covered face. Having spelled this out, we recognize that in *Burnt Norton* we've already encountered a theme from "The Jolly Corner": the footfalls of "What might have been," echoing through passages, towards doors. And as long ago as the "Gerontion" of 1919 Eliot had likened history to a Jamesian haunted house, with

> many cunning passages, contrived corridors
> And issues, [where it] deceives with whispering ambitions,
> Guides us by vanities. (CPP 22)

So now, after the "American" quartet—the one that wrestles with Mark Twain on his own ground, the shores of the great River—it is time for Eliot in England, fire-watching in an "English" war he'd not have known had he stayed in Harvard, to encounter, after deaths by air, earth, water and fire, the ghost his longest poem has been aching to produce: the "other" voice for so long so conspicuously silent. It has, as in "The Jolly Corner," a down-turned face, and proves to be "some dead master,"

> Whom I had known, forgotten, half recalled
> Both one and many; in the brown baked features
> The eyes of a familiar compound ghost
> Both intimate and unidentifiable. (CPP 140)

Horace Gregory once told me something Eliot had confided to him, that the "dead master" was principally Yeats, another ghost-specialist who had "left his body on a distant shore" (the French Riviera) early in 1939. But—Eliot had added to Gregory—it was "also myself":

> So I assumed a double part, and cried:
> And heard another's voice cry: 'What! are *you* here?'
> Although we were not. I was still the same,
> Knowing myself, yet being someone other—
> And he a face still forming. (CPP 141)

Another ghost in this compound is the ghost of Dante, whose specialty was confronting the dead, and whose measure haunts a passage which, as we know by Eliot's own word, embodies a prosodist's contradiction in terms, unrhymed *terza rima*: phantom rhymes, in short. Like Hamlet's father, the ghost has come from a place of fire, and the fire-bombing of the place he's come to makes the two worlds, he remarks, "much like each other." And he goes on to paraphrase the most general lesson of human experience, of history: the gifts life reserves for the old age of whoever lives to grow old.

> First, the cold friction of expiring sense
> Without enchantment, offering no promise
> But bitter tastelessness of shadow fruit
> As body and soul begin to fall asunder. (CPP 142)

That harks back to Tantalus, to the grapes Apelles painted, and to Tennyson's Percivale, questing for the Grail, who drank from a clear brook and ate
goodly apples, whereupon "all these things at once / Fell into dust": a detail
Eliot had recalled in *Ash Wednesday*, where his protagonist

> cannot drink
> There, where trees flower, and springs flow, for there is
> nothing again. (CPP 60)

So we've known already hints of these disappointments, but in old age we
may expect to know them continually. And the ghost presses on:

> Second, the conscious impotence of rage
> At human folly, and the laceration
> Of laughter at what ceases to amuse. (CPP 142)

—where "laceration" remembers the epitaph Swift wrote for himself.

> And last, the rending pain of re-enactment
> Of all that you have done, and been; the shame
> Of motives late revealed, and the awareness
> Of things ill done and done to others' harm,
>   Which once you took for exercise of virtue.
>   Then fools' approval stings, and honour stains.
> From wrong to wrong the exasperated spirit
>   Proceeds, unless restored by that refining fire
>   Where you must move in measure like a dancer.

That remembers Dante, and the Yeats of the play Eliot so admired, *Purga-
tory*, and the far younger Yeats whose vision of the afterworld was an eternity
of being "busied by a dance." It all remembers fairy tales too, where injunc-
tions and admonitions come in threes.

Once again it is James whose vision seems trivial by comparison: merely
a complaint that its post–Civil-War obsession with bankable gold has kept
his native land from cultural maturity. James, who Eliot greatly admired, had
brought from the large flat country a subtlety, an authority, against which
Eliot habitually measured his own. "Ghost psychology of New England old
maid," Wyndham Lewis once wrote of James, and there's justice in that, as
there is in Lewis' companion phrase: "Stately maze of imperturbable analogies." And here we're up against James' great limitation, that in his subtle

explorations of the social and the psychological he had, it seems, save as a nasty smell, no intimation of the spiritual.

"History" Eliot's ghost subsumes into human experience: nothing specifically Greek nor English nor American: no Spenglerian Rise and Fall but a destiny we all share. The man who was born a century ago in St. Louis was at various times many things—schoolmaster, banker, publisher, essayist, editor, London Clubman, vicarious archdeacon—and might have been many more—I've suggested Harvard Professor. Easily, he might have been locked into a ready fate: the American Unitarian, primly broadminded. He evaded that; evaded, too, dogmatic adhesions; developed a mind like the one he ascribes to James, "so fine no idea could violate it" ("In Memory of Henry James" 856–57). An "Idea" was what the cabby had hoped for from Bertrand Russell, that incarnate belfry aswarm with symbolic logic and dry slogans. What Eliot gave the cabby was his proximity; what the cabby gave Eliot resembles what the ghost in *Little* Gidding gave him: on a street in London, inexhaustible testimony.

WORKS CITED

Perl, Jeffrey M. *Skepticism and Modern Enmity: Before and After Eliot.* Baltimore: Johns Hopkins UP, 1989.

Schneider, Elisabeth W. *T. S. Eliot: The Pattern in the Carpet.* Berkeley: U of California P, 1975.

Wilson, Edmund, ed. *The Shock of Recognition.* New York: Farrar, Straus, Cudahy, 1943.

CLEO MCNELLY KEARNS

Doctrine and Wisdom in Four Quartets

No modern poet is so anthologized in collections of devotional and religious verse as T. S. Eliot, and no poet would have been more ambivalent about this mode of reception. This response is not one Eliot actively solicited for his work, nor one to which his poetry is always as conveniently suited as it may appear. The ambiguity ancient and well-preserved monuments represent, at once occasions of living worship and testaments to a desire to fetishize as past what we cannot quite assent to as present, often attends as well a devotional use of Eliot's work. Hence his poems function uneasily, if at all, as a kind of modern day simulacrum of the kind of traditional religious and inspirational art to which they are so often compared.

Eliot was, I would argue, fully aware of this slight disjuncture between his poetry and that of other, less secular, cultures and times. Rather than waste energy in deploring it, however, he made of it part of the substance of his reflections. He thus contributed far more than a mere lesson in nostalgia to the religious sensibility of his time. The poems of his Christian period are in this respect at once devotional and modern not only in the literary, but in the religious senses of the term. While clearly designed to evoke more than a merely aesthetic response, they are at the same time fully reflective of that essential relativizing and reformulating of Christian tradition which stemmed, at the end of the nineteenth century and the beginning of the twentieth, from

From *T. S. Eliot: Man and Poet*, Volume 1, edited and introduced by Laura Cowan, pp. 205–18. © 1990 by the National Poetry Foundation.

a greater knowledge of other faiths, from Biblical criticism, and from the rise of science. (The term *modern* in this context refers, of course, specifically, to the efforts in and around the Roman Catholic church to open its teaching to the insights of the new Biblical scholarship. Baron von Hügel, whose thought so attracted and repelled Yeats, was perhaps its best-known Roman Catholic exponent, one of the few moderates to survive the repressive reaction. Eliot himself sometimes made use of the term in this sense. See for instance his syllabus for a course of lectures given to adult students in London reprinted in A. D. Moody's *T. S. Eliot*, Poet [124].)

Some such modern stance was widely felt, in Eliot's day, to be the necessary consequence, both for Roman Catholics and for Protestants, of three major factors: the rediscovery of other, notably Eastern, religious and spiritual traditions; the entirely new view of Christian history and of Biblical truth required by the development of the Higher Criticism in Germany, with its emphasis on the role of changing interpretation in constituting the Christian community; and the need to formulate a non-defensive and intellectually respectable response to the growing prestige of science. Eliot's interest in all of these fields of inquiry is evident from his graduate school papers and from the numerous reviews he wrote for the *International Journal of Ethics* and other learned periodicals in his early years, reviews which touched often on the issues raised for religious faith by science, psychology, anthropology and sociology, as well as by philosophy and comparative religion.

Eliot judged a good deal of the liberal response to these challenges a mere attenuation of Christian truth, a method, as he said of Royce's efforts in this direction, of the last resuscitation of the dead. He was, however, by no means oblivious to or dismissive of modern tendencies in religion, and later his position in church politics and dogmatic disputes did not always place him on the conservative end of the spectrum. Contra Yeats, he did, of course, regard belief in such doctrines as the incarnation as touchstones of Christian faith, but he also wrestled again and again with the precise terms on which these doctrines could be affirmed in an intellectually responsible way. Similarly with a number of the issues which confronted and changed church life and even church policy in his times, he tried to be responsive both to the Catholic tradition and to the new forms of knowledge which required the shattering and refounding of that tradition from a more sophisticated point of view. Eliot's middle and later work reflects throughout this wrestle with words and meanings, as well as a tension between doctrinal formulations which demand assent or denial and those more diffuse and subtle, but by no means less powerful, appeals which require a transformation of emotion and will. Throughout, he attempted to hold skepticism not in abeyance but in solution, until it could be dissolved and recrystallized, again and again, into belief.

To some extent, this modern approach to religious certainty cohabits, not always smoothly, with Eliot's own devotional temperament and his deep assimilation of the inspirational and spiritual writing of other cultures and of the past. We can see him brooding over the resulting problems and contradictions in a small preface he wrote for an anthology of devotional writing by Tagore's son-in-law, N. Gangulee. Here Eliot wished to establish a certain hierarchy in ways of reading, whereby a devotional, as opposed to philosophical and aesthetic, response to a text is distinctly a higher enterprise, one in which differences of religious tradition and even discursive belief are transcended; though it is only in relation to these that the transcendence has meaning. Nevertheless, he did not want simply to ignore questions of doctrinal difference at the discursive level or pretend that these might simply be reduced to some lowest common denominator or perennial philosophy. Nor did he wish to ignore all the complex motivations for reading that psychology and to some extent sociology and history had taught him were implicated in the reception of any text. His summary of these problems has an Eliotic suavity and grace that conceal as well as reveal the profundity and wisdom of his own consideration of these issues. In devotional reading, he says:

> We have to abandon some of our usual motives for reading. We must surrender the love of Power—whether over others, or over ourselves, or over the material world. We must abandon even the love of Knowledge ... what these writers aim at, in their various idioms, in whatever language or in terms of whatever religion, is the Love of God. They gave their lives to this, and their destination is not one which we can reach any quicker than they did or without the same tireless activity and tireless passivity. (Gangulee x)

And yet, Eliot concludes, we must not, on the other hand, assume that doctrinal distinctions do not matter, for it was "only in relation to his own religion that the insights of any of these [devotional writers] had significance to him" at all (13).

We must note that the austerity and totality of response Eliot calls for in this preface reside in the activity of reading, rather than in any position affirmed within the text itself, and thus cannot be completely identified with the discursive content of the work considered independently of that response. Eliot thus establishes the force and validity of a way of reading which is open at once to the learned and the unlearned, and which depends on the attention and involvement of the whole self in the act of reading, not simply on the intellectual assent of the reasoning or logical part of the mind. This devotional attention does not finesse but surpasses the issues of doctrine and belief, making use of them as ladders, not as goals. It also insists on unmasking, through introspection and self-mastery, that will to power that lurks under the guise of the will to truth (and to doctrinal correctness) and even under the more apparently innocent aspect of the will to beauty.

Eliot's remarks on the question of the Christian relation to other faiths, particularly Eastern ones, spell out a kind of program for *Four Quartets*:

> Some readers, attracted by the occult, think only Asiatic literature has religious understanding. Others distrust mysticism and stay narrowly Christian. For both it is salutary to learn that the Truth is not occult, and that it is not wholly confined on the one hand to their own religious tradition, or on the other hand to an alien culture and religion which they regard with superstitious awe. (Gangulee 11)

The Dry Salvages may be read as a concerted effort to instill this salutary lesson by means of a poetic juxtaposition of Christian devotion as classically understood and the devotion of the *Bhagavad Gita*.

There is, however, a certain problem when this celebration of devotional reading is brought into relation with a modern sensibility, whether we think of the modern as an aesthetic or a religious category. In the first place, as Eliot clearly points out, the ultimate proof of a devotional text lies in its reading not its writing. This reception is, however, in the final analysis outside the writer's control. Issues of craft and technique in the text itself, issues so foregrounded in the modern tradition, will then have only a proximate relevance. Secondly, if the hallmark of devotion is simplicity and totality of response, the hallmark of modernity is complexity and qualification, and the two do not always easily coincide. How affirm a deep, nondiscursive truth requiring the full attention and assent of the whole reading self and at the same time insist that the reader bear in mind the relativism of its presentation, the presence around it of other, sometime opposing, traditions and points of view, the dangers of a will to power underlying its will to truth, the crucial dimension of historicity which conditions it, the ever-present possibility of unconscious psychological motivations which may subvert and even pervert its intended meaning, and the dependence of the whole effort on a highly sophisticated and continually changing tradition of interpretation? The two can only be brought together by a supreme effort, one which may well end less in a full yet multi-dimensional reading than in a kind of double-think or squint.

While there is perhaps no ultimate solution to this problem, at least part of the responsibility for the overcoming of which rests with the reader alone, it is still arguable that certain texts are better designed to evoke the kind of response that Eliot wanted for his work than others. As he matured, Eliot came to see the advantages in this respect of what he called *wisdom*, a term which implies both a stance toward experience and a way of writing. As a rhetorical mode, wisdom discourse has certain characteristics Eliot found appealing. First, it depends heavily not on discursive or doctrinal formulation, but on proverb or aphorism for its effect, thus making use of popular expressions, oral formulae, and communal tradition, and by-passing, often usefully, certain issues of dogma and rational belief. Secondly, it is often anonymous or pseudonymous, sometimes by attribution to some speaker with a ritual function, a Solomon, or a David, sometimes by association with a persona, Sophia, or the Shekinah, for example. Wisdom writing is thus "impersonal" in Eliot's sense, being divorced as much as possible from the accidents of particular characters or a particular ethos or political/social situation.

Finally, the wisdom tradition allows for wide, even, from a logical point of view, mutually exclusive stances toward experience and belief, ranging from the deepest and most logo centric affirmations—of, for instance, a transcendental Signifier, a God present in and above the entire universe and in language itself—to some of the most radical deconstructive gestures—as for instance the repeated insistence that notions such as God and direct linguistic revelation are worse, in their feebleness, than the silence in which skepticism and mystery are one. Hence, in the wisdom tradition of the Bible, such lines as "the fool has said in his heart, 'there is no God'" may be less contradicted than thrown into deeper relief by other, darker sayings such as "vanity of vanities, all is vanity saith the Preacher." In general, wisdom writing finds no need to reconcile, at least in discursive terms, such apparently divergent positions, allowing context, sensibility, and intuition to invoke them in ways that subvert, without ever entirely canceling, one another. To this end it tries to maintain a certain rhetoric of universality, which is not the same as a perennial philosophy or a reduction to a set of common propositions, though it is often weakly misread in that way.

The rhetoric and stance of the wisdom tradition often helped Eliot reconcile the conflicting demands of modernity and devotion. Of the advantages of this tradition for poetry he was himself entirely aware. In his late essay on Goethe, an essay he almost decided to call "A Discourse in Praise of Wisdom," Eliot explains that wisdom writing, for him, means writing that bases its appeal on something "deeper than ... logical propositions" and so does not always require assent or denial at the propositional level to be effective. "Of revealed religions, and of philosophical systems, we must believe that one is right and the others wrong," he maintains, "but wisdom is *logos xunos*, the same for all men everywhere" (OPP 264). It is at once simple, profound, and open in the ecumenical sense that the modern movement was to develop as it sought to come to grips with the respect and reverence due to other faiths.

In terms of Eliot's own work, the reference to *logos xunos*, common or open wisdom, takes us to Heraclitus and one of the epigraphs to *Burnt Norton*. This epigraph may be translated loosely—though Eliot does not translate it at all—as "wisdom is actually common property, but people treat it as if it were a special preserve." When it comes to the expression of this quality of wisdom, Eliot goes on in his Goethe essay, all language is inadequate but probably the language of poetry is least so. He concludes this essay, which itself makes a good gloss on several passages in *Four Quartets*, with an extended quotation from Ecclesiastes which pairs the Greek pre-Socratic philosopher with the Hebrew sage, and captures very well the self-evident, open, universalist simplicity of this poetic mode:

> Wisdom shall praise herself,
> And shall glory in the midst of her people.
> In the congregation of the Most High shall she open her mouth,
> And triumph before His power. (OPP 257)

These and similar models of wisdom and a wisdom mode of discourse informed, I think, much of Eliot's later verse, *Four Quartets* in particular, and helped him to write a relativized, self-conscious and complex kind of religious poetry, open to the existence of other faiths and experiences and "modern" in the sense I have tried to specify, and yet a poetry susceptible as well to devotional reading, and capable of evoking and supporting great simplicity as well as great complexity of response.

Eliot's use of the wisdom tradition to by-pass deliberately questions of dogmatic truth and doctrinal assent in *Four Quartets*, even when he himself had arrived at a provisional set of religious beliefs, is much in line not only with the modern movement in religion, but with the philosophical position he had worked out in *Knowledge and Experience*, his dissertation on F. H. Bradley for Harvard, many years before. In this work, skepticism and belief are not opposed to one another but represented as different points along a continuum of response, any absolute claims of either being subverted *a priori* by its dependence on the other. The question of belief in this case is not so much posed for a yes or no as relativized from the beginning. Such a mobile view of discursive truth is, needless to say, by no means a disadvantage when it comes to the writing of poetry. Indeed it allows and encourages that dialectic of "surrender and recovery," identification and detachment, Eliot himself understood the appropriation of poetic texts to entail. Hence "poetry" may be both distinguished from and inhabited by "belief" in very complex ways, with neither entirely privileged over the other.

This wisdom tradition, however, was not without its dangers for a poet like Eliot. To take only one facet of the problem, "simple wisdom" can very easily look more like platitude than insight, more like sentiment than feeling, more like the ridiculous than the sublime. A quarter turn from its lofty perspectives and one gets hot air rather than inspiration, Polonius rather than the Preacher, Goethe as didact rather than Goethe as sage. We need think only of Whitman at his worst to be reminded of the pitfalls here. Secondly, there is the danger of sentimentality, compromise and appeasement, what Eliot called the "false wisdom" of old age. Here the sharpness of the agonies of youth, the moment in the hyacinth garden or at the top of the stair, are not so much transcended as repressed, and desire is pacified rather than transformed by genuine purgation. Finally, there is the danger of conflation of opposing doctrines and positions, of what Eliot called the "luxury of confounding" as opposed to the "task of combining" different doctrines and points of view (rev. Wolf 426).

In *Four Quartets* Eliot seeks to avoid these pitfalls by insisting that the cost of wisdom is "not less than everything" (CPP 145). "Everything" here must, I think, be seen to include much doctrinal and pious certainty often associated with these poems. 'That old-time religion' is simply not celebrated here, not even in the service of "a further union, a deeper communion" (CPP 129). Among the certainties which, for Eliot, must be sacrificed are a naive and uncritical belief in the immortality of what we like to think of as the individual self or soul, an unqualified affirmation of Christian belief as superior to other beliefs in all respects, and an easy expectation that all pain and suffering will be taken care of either by a simple passage of time or by some system of rewards and punishments after death. These are excess baggage that Eliot's brief but intense sojourn in the mazes of Buddhism and later intense practice of Christian meditation further persuaded him must be jettisoned. That his call to a more rigorous faith has been so often misread and misunderstood is only one of the multiple ironies that have always attended the reception of his work.

We can see this more rigorous formulation of the tradition, a formulation at once modern and yet infused with the immediacy of an active devotional practice, at work throughout *Four Quartets*. These four linked poems, while accessible on the surface, are by no means as genial and instantly affirmative of traditional Christian truths and pieties as they might at first appear. If they do offer pious consolations, those consolations are of a peculiarly radical sort, and the cure may be worse than the disease. Consider, for instance, *East Coker*, the second of the quartets. This is the one first prompted, as A. D. Moody has pointed out, by the shock to Eliot's sometimes complacent neutralism in politics occasioned by the advance of the Second World War, and in particular by Chamberlain's placation of Hitler at Munich. Here Eliot writes of the first step toward wisdom, which is to be able to recognize its counterfeits. "What was to be the value," he asks, "of the long looked forward to, / Long hoped for calm, the autumnal serenity / And the wisdom of age? Had they deceived us / Or deceived themselves, the quiet-voiced elders, / Bequeathing us merely a receipt for deceit? / The serenity only a deliberate hebetude, / The wisdom only the knowledge of dead secrets / Useless in the darkness into which they peered / Or from which they turned their eyes" (CPP 125). A few lines later there follows one of those aphorisms with which Eliot tried repeatedly to capture the tone and function of the wisdom tradition, aphorisms so finely turned that they seem cited from long tradition already present in the language rather than composed: "We are only undeceived / Of that which, deceiving, could no longer harm."

This section of *East Coker* ends by insisting that the only real wisdom is the wisdom of humility, but the movement of the poem is off and away from this somewhat dead center, which is rather weak at this point, as if Eliot were telling, not showing, preaching, not evoking. Whatever may be premature about the wisdom of *East Coker*, however, is amply destabilized and thrown into question in the great third quartet, *The Dry Salvages*. Here begins a long engaged confrontation with all that makes wisdom seem at times so weak: the savagery of experience, including the experience of holiness, its roots in pain, and the multiple ironies of suffering generated by its extension over time. The problem of this quartet is to peer into that darkness from which the old men of Munich turned their eyes, but to do so without either bitterness or rhetoric or excess.

The techniques Eliot begins to develop here include again the aphorism, the use of a deceptively conversational, ruminative and apparently relaxed style for extremely frightening, catastrophic and subversive insights, the sudden shift from a voice of speculation, as if you were listening to some old friend muse, somewhat disjointedly, over a glass of brandy at the club, to a voice of absolute authority in which the sum of the starkest truths of the poem are delivered. Hence you have "It seems, as one becomes older ..." (CPP 132)—ah, yes, now we know exactly what to expect, the vapid reminiscences of a sweet old man. What, though, do we get? Well, some of this, to be sure, but as the passage unwinds, we "come to discover" that "the moments of agony ... are likewise permanent / With such permanence as time has" (CPP 133). Furthermore, since true wisdom is often corrosive as well as salutary, we are then reminded that we "appreciate this better" in the "agony of others" than in our own. This is surely not the wisdom of hebetude or senility or even conventional Christian piety; indeed it rises at times to a dry realism, a sharpness, which is redeemed from misanthropy only by accuracy of insight. One finds this kind of writing elsewhere only in the French tradition, in La Rochefoucauld or Montaigne. Or think about this one: "You cannot face it steadily, but this thing is sure, / That time is no healer: the patient is no longer there" (CPP 134). Easy notions of cheap redemption and ready personal immortality, the false wisdom of the 'long view' and the 'long run,' do not easily survive this quartet. They are part of that cost of "not less than everything" to which the last lines of *Little Gidding* refer, and for which they are an important preparation (CPP 145).

Little Gidding itself opens with a rather brilliant *tour de force* in Eliot's old metaphysical style. It sounds a bit like the opening of *The Waste Land*, a poem no one has accused of being too sunny. "Midwinter spring is its own season" answers neatly to "April is the cruelest month" (CPP 138, 37). Here we are back again at the beginning, where desire and death are reborn at one and the same moment, leading, it might seem, to the same sterile repetitions, the same hell of necessity without end. We almost expect to meet Tiresias again, that great waste land figure of partial wisdom at its most bleak and most impotent, unable either to break the deadlock of the past or to imagine a different future. In a way, in fact, we *do* meet Tiresias here again, or something like him, for this poem, like *The Waste Land*, like the first of Pound's cantos, begins with an invocation of the spirits of the dead as found in the Odyssey and in Virgil, an invocation out of which Tiresias' is, traditionally, the first voice that rises. It is possible to read the following three stanzas of part 2, the lyrics of death by air, earth, and fire, as placed, as it were, in the mouth of Tiresias, the great steady observer of inevitable human futility from Eliot's earlier work.

To continue in this vein, it is perfectly possible, as well, to add to the long list of compound features of the uncanny ghost or figure the speaker encounters in part 2 those of Tiresias, especially in his capacity as harbinger of what awaits us after death. The message isn't particularly pleasant. "Let me disclose," the ghostly double proposes, "the gifts reserved for age / To set a crown upon your lifetime's effort. / First, the cold friction of expiring sense / Without enchantment, offering no promise / But bitter tastelessness of shadow fruit . . . / Second, the conscious impotence of rage / At human folly, and the laceration / Of laughter at what ceases to amuse" (CPP 141, 142). And as if this were not enough, "last, the rending pain of reenactment / Of all that you have done and been; the shame / Of motives late revealed, and the awareness / Of things ill done and done to others' harm / Which once you took for exercise of virtue." Surely this is an echo of that walk "among the lowest of the dead" that showed an earlier version of Tiresias those automatons of empty sex and failed humanity, the "typist home at teatime" and the "young man carbuncular," who are also, as *The Waste Land* makes ineluctably clear, earlier versions of ourselves (CPP 44). Then indeed, to cut back to *Little Gidding* again, one might say with Eliot, that "fools' approval stings, and honor stains" (CPP 142). Humility here is less a rather pompous and pedantic virtue, as it can seem in *East Coker*, than a rigorous exercise in confrontation with the self, one in which no dark stone is left unturned.

If this is wisdom, some may prefer folly, or prefer at least *The Waste Land*'s passionate drive, right to the breaking point of the mind, to be free of this endless circle of self-interested, self-reflexive and self-deluded motivations. Here, however, given his commitment to what he calls *logos xunos*, open wisdom, Eliot cannot turn directly either to Sanskrit or Latin, Italian or Provençal, to find words which will convey both the simplicity of the solution to this problem and its absolute freshness and surprise. Nor can he rely automatically, in the way that many of even his best critics presume he does, on a simple last minute 'save' by tradition or history. If he is to draw on the resources of his culture, he must do so in a way that has authority and originality, as well as congruence with the past, and that changes the direction of his culture even as it summons up its strength. Otherwise, he will simply be rehearsing dead wisdom instead of rediscovering the wisdom of the dead.

His solution at the thematic level is to draw into the poem not the energy of his culture's great victories, but the profundity of its major losses. We do indeed hear the voice of that great sister of wisdom Julian of Norwich, but are reminded that her "all shall be well" emerged from a context of "incandescent terror" generated by extreme mental and physical pain. The reference to a "king at nightfall" (CPP 143) is likewise no exercise in partisanship or nostalgia for a time when one could be "classicist in letters, Anglican in religion and monarchist in politics" without sounding ridiculous, but a reminder of failure counter-balancing the equal and opposite failure of that king's political enemy, the poet who dies "blind and quiet" a few lines later. Likewise, there is no easy recourse to a notion of one's work or one's political struggle living after one by way of consolation. Action as well as contemplation here reach their end, where every gesture of transcendence is "a step to the block, to the fire, down the sea's throat / Or to an illegible stone" (CPP 144).

So what we have here, then, at the height of the war, precisely, in fact, as the battle of El Alemein is turning the tide in favor of the Allies and preserving the world for nuclear holocaust, is not a hymn to the glories of Western religion and culture but an epitaph for their end, at least as exclusive and self-evident goods. True wisdom lies, for Eliot, not in a false reaffirmation of traditional religious values but in a recognition of the essential conditioning of even the best of their representations by time and relativity. Paradoxically, however, only tradition can reveal its own ephemera; only history its own emptiness. As Gertrude Stein put it, "all that history teaches is—history teaches." Perhaps one's life had to have exactly the curve of Eliot's, coming of age when Western culture was first tearing itself to shreds and then coming to middle age as it did so again, to yield precisely this kind of bitter wisdom. "'Vanity of vanities, all is vanity,' saith the preacher."

The wisdom tradition, however, though based on just such paradoxes as these, ultimately requires celebration and simplicity, and comes to fruition only in these modes. But "[a]fter such knowledge, what forgiveness?" How was Eliot to find, to reaffirm, to induct into his poem these qualities of simplicity and joy? The answer, I would argue, lay in a renunciation not only of personal identity as conceived and cherished by the ego, but of the weight of a certain poetic and cultural capital as well. At the end of *Four Quartets* both tradition and the individual talent are sent to the block, down the sea's throat, to an illegible stone, are sent, that is, toward the vanishing point on the horizon of culture where many peoples, religions, value-systems are, in defiance of the wars that divide them, made one.

This renunciation, this vanishing point, cannot, however, for Eliot, be allowed to collapse into poetic or intellectual abdication, or into denial of that difference against which alone it has significance. There must be simplicity, but not oversimplification, ease but not laxity, repose but not a false peace. Eliot's solution to this problem in the last stanza of *Little Gidding* is a lesson in mastery of craft; it involves a highly studied combination of great levelness and decorum of diction, extreme syntactic and grammatical complexity, and a use of imagery as remarkable for its economy as for its power. The diction itself is telling, fulfilling the mandate announced earlier in the poem for a discourse where "every word is at home, / Taking its place to support the others, / The word neither diffident nor ostentatious" (CPP 144). The syntax, however, departs from this decorum, beginning with a phrase floating in white space:

With the drawing of this Love and the voice of this Calling
(CPP 145)

after which we almost hear a Poundian "so that": Then comes a straightforward sentence, or so it seems, but one which takes off again into an unfixed relative clause, "When the last of earth left to discover," and having in the end, if examined carefully, no established main subject or verb. These syntactic indeterminacies are suddenly interrupted by "quick now, here, now always" before flowing on again to their end in the final sentence. Even this sentence, however, takes its syntactical core and deep structure from a devotional text of the past, Julian of Norwich's "All shall be well and all manner of thing small be well," a core which Eliot carefully surrounds by his own conditional and qualifying clauses.

In that final sentence, the images which close the poem, the fire and the rose, are common to many traditions, occult and exoteric alike, from Buddhism's Fire Sermon to the gnostic traditions of the Rosicrucians or the Persian and later the Sufi celebrations of the traditional Middle Eastern flower of mystic love. There is, however, a sense here of these associations dropping away, along with a number of the doctrinal distinctions which cluster around them, so that the close becomes less a set of allusions than λόγος ξυνός, open wisdom. This wisdom is accessible indeed, but with an accessibility "costing not less than everything" (CPP 145). Part of that cost is the certainty of Christian pieties often taken for granted as part of the poem but actually asserted there, if at all, only as intensely modern, highly relativized and provisional truths. Having paid that price, moreover, the poem does not rest on its laurels, but asks for more: the sacrifice and purgation not only of idiosyncrasy and personality in Eliot's old sense, but also of pseudo-devotional sentimentality and unearned consolation as well. The "tireless passivity and tireless activity" required to give this poem the kind of reading it deserves are, then, not to be exhausted in one sitting, or even across a lifetime's renewed consideration, nor are they confined, as we are coming to learn, to one culture alone.

WORKS CITED

Costello, Harry T. *Josiah Royce's Seminar, 1913–1914: As Recorded in the Notebooks of Harry T. Costello*. Ed. Grover Smith. New Brunswick: Rutgers UP, 1963.

Eliot, T. S. Preface. *Thoughts for Meditation: A Way to Recovery from Within*. By N. Gangulee. London: Faber and Faber, 1951. 11–14.

———. Rev. of *The Philosophy of Nietzsche* by A. Wolf. *International Journal of Ethics* 26 (Apr. 1916) 426–27.

Moody, A. D. *Thomas Steams Eliot: Poet*. Cambridge: Cambridge UP, 1979.

JOHN PAUL RIQUELME

"Little Gidding" 3: Indifference and the Process of Reading Four Quartets

That Eliot's styles in *Four Quartets* are directed toward evoking something outside language, outside the bounds of ordinary consciousness, and alien to the self is implied in one way by some of the contrasts that, as in the second epigraph, turn out to be the same and, as in the first epigraph, turn out to be different from something else that can hardly be conceived or expressed. Through the simultaneous conjunction and disjunction that is the epigraphs' enigma inscribed in the poem's styles and structures, the reader can undertake an unusual, diverse mode of reading whose results are fundamentally unpredictable. One instance of the poem's structure of contrast and differentiation that can lead to a complex reading process occurs at the beginning of "Little Gidding" 3. The passage follows immediately on the departure of the "familiar compound ghost" at the end of the previous section:

> There are three conditions which often look alike
> Yet differ completely, flourish in the same hedgerow:
> Attachment to self and to things and to persons,
>   detachment
> From self and from things and from persons; and, growing
>   between them, indifference
> Which resembles the others as death resembles life,

From *Harmony of Dissonances: T. S. Eliot, Romanticism, and Imagination*, pp. 220–33. © 1991 by the Johns Hopkins University Press.

> Being between two lives—unflowering, between
> The live and the dead nettle.
>   (*CPP* 142; LG 3.150–56)

Stylistically, the passage is an odd mixture of apparently straightforward, logically declarative statements and figurative language that, when examined closely, transforms the determinate character of the distinctions being made.

As with many other passages in *Four Quartets*, the complexities of this one will not support the brief, confident glosses that critics sometimes provide. One critic, for instance, claims that "the point of this movement and the two following ones is that the flower of attachment and the flower of detachment (like rose and lotos) grow together and work in the poet's memory 'for liberation—not less of love but expanding / Of love beyond desire'" (Hay 186). As nettles, attachment and detachment may flower, but to call them flowers is to disregard the less attractive qualities of nettles. Since one is a live nettle and the other a dead one, even the attribution of flowering to both is unsupported.[15] The passage does mention growing, but not the growing and working together of flowers. Growing is attributed instead to indifference, which this critic goes on to associate with "Tennyson's lotos" of "forgetfulness" (Hay 187) as an unattractive contrast to the supposedly more positive flowers of attachment and detachment. The statement about "liberation," which is quoted as if it required no explanation, also poses some complexities in its context that need to be addressed.

It is unwarranted to portray indifference as simply negative and undesirable by contrast with attachment and detachment as simply positive and desirable. To do so is to overlook the transforming character of Eliot's poetry and to import into the poem perspectives that it calls up in order to alter. Whatever the words mean in other contexts, in Eliot's poem they take on new meaning by being embedded in various small and large structures that modify what they can suggest. Rather than something to be scorned, indifference is linked with death, and death plays a role in *Four Quartets* that cannot justifiably be disdained. In "Little Gidding" 1, the scene lies outside life, since "There is no earth smell / Or smell of living thing." In that part as well the importance of things dead is stressed, since "what the dead had no speech for, when living, / They can tell you, being dead: the communication / Of the dead is tongued with fire beyond the language of the living" (*CPP* 139; LG 11.51–53). In "Little Gidding" 2, when the dead speak, forgetting is recommended: "These things have served their purpose: let them be" (*CPP* 141; LG 2.113). Indifference may well be a name for part of the writing process, which these preceding sections evoke, a process in which something dead is put into words in a passage "Between two worlds become much like each other" (*CPP* 141; LG 2.122). When that passage occurs, indifference transforms mere attachment and detachment into something they could not otherwise be, for "We are born with the dead," who "return, and bring us with them" (*CPP* 144; LG 5.230–31) in poems that, as epitaphs, announce death. Indifference could be another "unfamiliar Name" for "Love," which, according to "Little Gidding" 3 wove the shirt of Nessus. That shirt bears a relation to the wearer's flesh that cannot be termed either attachment or detachment. The possibility of understanding indifference in this affirming way depends on taking a close look at the details of "Little Gidding" 3.

Attachment and detachment are semantically opposite, but the comparison with nettles in a hedgerow, suggesting former human habitation, aligns them, since they resemble "life," whereas the "indifference" "growing between them" resembles "death." The figurative contrast between organic and inorganic emphasizes the distinction between indifference and its two companions, yet the assertion of difference is itself called into question by the notion of indifference, understood as a state in which distinctions would disappear. And the character of the difference comes into question when attachment and detachment are themselves distinguished as live and dead.

Taking the complex relations among the words seriously can lead to setting aside their everyday meanings, which pertain to personalities. The passage encourages that setting aside by suggesting that the very difference between attachment and detachment, on the one hand, and indifference, on the other, is that indifference does not involve the self. Indifference would not be the self's orientation toward a situation but rather the disappearance of the self that is capable of orientations. In this context "indifference" seems to be outside the sphere of personal motivation and desire with all the dynamism and concern for self they imply, whereas "detachment" and "attachment" are both still within that sphere of "life" despite their apparent differences. "Detachment" could suggest a kind of clinical attitude that carefully calculates or stages its every movement. Even though this "detachment" is "From self," "indifference" goes beyond it into an arena so far removed from ordinary affairs and considerations as to be comparable to death. It occurs in the context of, or "between," the others, which are "two lives," but these two lives are also nettles, the one "live," the other "dead," though both are nettles nevertheless.

The relations are discernible later in the verse paragraph in the assertion that

> ... love of a country
> Begins as attachment to our own field of action

And comes to find that action of little importance
Though never indifferent.
   (*CPP* 142; LG 3.159–62)

The presence of the adjective "indifferent" complicates matters, since it carries another, more usual meaning than the state of indifference mentioned
earlier in the section. The detachment that eventually finds the action of
little importance is no more indifferent—in the sense of unconcerned—than
is the original attachment. The condition of indifference would be quite
another state, in which "The faces and places" "vanish," along "with the self
which, as it could, loved them" (*CPP* 142; LG 3.163–64).

Indifference provides an illustration of the manner in which *Four Quartets* works to evoke meanings that are counterintuitive. The poem enables a
rethinking of the meanings of words that we assume in advance we understand. The possibility for that rethinking involves a questioning of the principle of noncontradiction, which occurs because of peculiar alignments,
contrasts, figurations, and grammatical relations. In this case, the principle
is subverted when both attachment and detachment are set in contrast to an
indifference that emerges as itself a detachment from self that goes beyond
detachment because the self actually vanishes. The vanishing point, as in per-
spectival painting, has a status like zero, which is identical with nothing else
but also not with itself, since it is a form of nothing.[16] The odd condition of
vanishing, zero, and indifference, which is not approachable through language
that is not contradictory, resembles the condition of boredom as Martin Heidegger describes it in "What is Metaphysics"? In his brief discussion of that
state, Heidegger points to "a fundamental experience" that occurs independently of "the objections of the intellect" (*Writings* 101), that is, out of step
with "the commonly cited ground rule of all thinking, the proposition that
contradiction is to be avoided" (99). According to Heidegger, "profound boredom. . . . removes all things and men and oneself along with it into a remarkable indifference" (101). This state of indifference as a de-differentiation that
undermines the basis for logical discriminations is an emptying out that is
indistinguishable from a filling up. Like boredom in Heidegger's intransitive
sense, indifference occurs independently of particular objects of consciousness, which would be important only to a self. Outside the rational, logical
intellect, it pertains to an experience not of knowledge but of an ignorance
that puts conventional wisdom, common sense, scientific knowledge, and the
normal meanings of words in abeyance. To evoke such an experience, Eliot
uses contradictory perspectives resembling those of the epigraphs.

In one of many instances of mutual framing in *Four Quartets*, the epigraphs provide a pattern for arranging the contrasts and connections of

"Little Gidding" 3, which suggest in turn a way to read the epigraphs. In the epigraphs and the passage, opposites are identical, but the identity may be largely a matter of a difference from something whose character is not entirely specifiable. The live and the dead nettle are one and the same as ways of living, both being nettles, but indifference is as different from them as death is from life or the one is from the understanding of the many. Indifference resembles the nettles because, like them, it flourishes though perhaps for different reasons that make it "unflowering." The resemblance retrospectively interprets and extends the first epigraph by suggesting that the logos would be hard to identify if encountered among the many, despite its extraordinary character.

Indifference occupies the space "between," which in some of Eliot's earlier poems, such as "The Hollow Men," seems to be an uncanny space describable only in fragments of obscure language and by means of sharp contrasts. When Eliot presents this space in "Little Gidding" 3 as different from conventionally formulated determinate oppositions, such as the ostensible contrast between attachment and detachment, he implies that something exists that does not conform to our normal ways of thinking. It does not because it exists outside the law of noncontradiction. Although it is not contradiction or dissonance per se, both are symptoms of its existence. In this regard, the enigmatic condition of "indifference" resembles "beatitude" as Eliot discusses it in relation to Dante. This is not to say that "indifference" is to be understood precisely as "beatitude," whatever that may be, but each resists being understood within the frame of our usual categories. Eliot's discussion in "Dante" of "beatitude," including his comments on the closing cantos of the *Purgatorio* (*SE* 224–26), are, however, relevant for interpreting the opening lines of "Little Gidding" 3, both the ones already quoted and those that immediately follow them. The evocation of memory and the transforming of love in "Little Gidding" 3 recall Eliot's presentation of the combined resurgence and renunciation of feeling at the *Purgatorio*'s end. And the "indifference of . . . inequality, in blessedness, of the blessed" (*SE* 226) is an important element in the perplexing character of beatitude.

Like beatitude in "Dante," indifference in *Four Quartets* encourages a rethinking of accepted categories in the attempt to find a place for the anomaly. Eliot's use of a religious vocabulary occasionally in *Four Quartets*, words such as God, Incarnation, Word, and Annunciation, can have a similarly disturbing effect. Even a word such as "humility" (EC 2.98), which need not be taken in a religious sense, will tend to aggravate our culturally induced allergy to any language or behavior that does not reinforce the concept of an aggressive, competitive self. Like "indifference" when its odd implications are recognized, these words can generate resistance because they do not conform to modern skeptical, logical ways of thinking. In his use of them, Eliot challenges the conventional response even if doing so causes irritation and impatience among readers whose education has made skepticism about such words and their implications seem a natural, inevitable reaction.

The fragments and contrasts of *Four Quartets* give the space "between" a less terrifying shape than do their counterparts in "The Hollow Men," even though it remains the space of something like death by contrast with life. This is so largely because the passages evoking this peculiar condition are less opaque than those of the earlier poem, though, as in the one dealing with indifference, the implications can be labyrinthine and difficult to formulate. Even when formulated, they still require elucidation. The passage concerning "indifference" actually seems fairly straightforward rather than fragmented and uncanny, though the details are joined in contradictory and confusing ways that, once exposed, undermine the apparent simplicity. Unlike "The Hollow Men," however, *Four Quartets* offers readers more opportunities for putting the poem's language to work in pursuit of explanations. Those opportunities tend to temper the obscurities' potentially grating effects. Two aspects of the language combine to make Eliot's style and the reading process in *Four Quartets* more dynamic and self-transforming than is the case in his earlier poetry. We have seen both already in the encounter with the "familiar compound ghost." One is the apparent, but deceptive stylistic simplicity of conversational sounding language that includes complex, self-reflexive, even self-reversing formulations. The other is the style's allusive tendency, which sends us to other poems or to other parts of this poem for possible elucidation.

In its appearance of being readily understandable, the style achieves what Eliot calls near the end of "Little Gidding" "A condition of complete simplicity / (Costing not less than everything)" (LG 5.253–54). This would be a complete simplicity that is also its own opposite, a total complexity and perplexity, for it is the sign of everything having been paid out or given up. It is the sign of death and indifference rather than either attachment or detachment. The simplicity is complete rather than "partial" in the sense of biased in any personal way, because it is the simplicity and completion that comes with dissolution, with having achieved what Eliot refers to at the end of "East Coker" as a "temporal reversion" contributing to the "life of significant soil." It would be the opposite of the completely partial condition that Yeats mentions admiringly in the third section of "Under Ben Bulben." Yeats's complete partiality occurs within the context of action and life, whereas Eliot's "indifference" seems closer to the attitude that Yeats recommends in the epitaph at the end of "Under Ben Bulben":

Cast a cold eye
On life, on death.
Horseman, pass by!
   (Yeats 328)

Although Eliot's "indifference" may not be exactly the attitude invoked here, it is at least related to the response that Yeats requests to his own epitaph as verse, a response lying outside personal feelings as well as outside calculated thought. Indifference of this sort allows, even requires, a turning away from the past, especially the personal past, without regrets. The possibility for an elegiac attitude and elegiac poetry is resolutely rejected. Toward the end of "Little Gidding" 3, for instance, we learn explicitly that there is no chance of a return to the past:

We cannot revive old factions
We cannot restore old policies
Or follow an antique drum.
These men, and those who opposed them
And those whom they opposed
Accept the constitution of silence
And are folded in a single party.
Whatever we inherit from the fortunate
We have taken from the defeated
What they had to leave us—a symbol:
A symbol perfected in death.
   (*CPP* 143; LG 3.185–95)

All forms of action, including writing, are resolved eventually into a single condition, that of being past, whose constitution, both authorizing document and makeup, is a form of silence.

Writing has been evoked along with political action a few lines before this passage in the allusion to Milton, "one who died blind and quiet" (l. 179). The silent document would be, among other things, the literary text separated from the author's living voice or shorn of the illusion of personal speech, but the constitution of silence would also be the death of the body, its reaching silence. Like the word "constitution," "party" has a political meaning, but it can mean an individual as well. The conjoining of these two meanings reflects back on the meditation about writing presented in the previous section during the encounter with the ghost. All dead authors, whatever their factional commitments in life, are of one party in death. By becoming a party to the constitution of silence, which is death but also writing independent of voice, each one is folded, like the "familiar compound ghost," into a single, composite figure that is also a group, or party, as in that word's political sense. In the republic whose constitution is silence, all are equal, since the fortunate and the defeated are one. The possessors are also the dispossessed. We inherit what they owned, or "had," but this they were forced to, "had to," leave us. The ambiguous phrasing here recalls the end of the preceding section, when the ghost seems forced to leave upon "the blowing of the horn" and we hear that he left the living poet "with a kind of valediction." These words describe both how he left, signalling farewell, and what he left the poet, a kind of poem, in this case a valediction that, like Yeats's epitaph, forbids mourning. The poetry, or "symbol," that the past has to leave us is "perfected in death" when it is revealed to be what it always was, something historical. Once poetry reaches that status, it is purified of the motives for action that tied it to self, factions, and the desire to be among "the fortunate" in a particular, limited historical situation.

Eliot takes a related stance in the concluding section of "Little Gidding" when he claims that

> Every phrase and every sentence is an end and a beginning,
> Every poem an epitaph. And any action
> Is a step to the block, to the fire, down the sea's throat
> Or to an illegible stone: and that is where we start.
>   (*CPP* 144; LG 5.224–27)

Every poem is an epitaph by indicating the equivalent of the author's death, a condition of "indifference" in which the poem was produced or that it has reached in becoming language. It is the "end" for the author in at least two ways, both literally as the completion of a preceding composing process and figuratively as evidence that the process resembled death. It is the author's "beginning," as well, because every attempt to write is inadequate and yields to the next one; there is never an end to writing but instead always the Sisyphean necessity of starting over after the last defeat.

The poem as the author's end is also the reader's beginning, for the work of reading takes up and continues where writing left off, especially when the text opens up many perspectives. Reading and writing can even be one insofar as both involve indifference rather than either attachment to the conventions of ordinary life or a willed detachment from them. Both processes can include an experience of distance from those conventions that has not been willed. It is unwilled because it relies centrally on memory, not as personalized recollection, but as the experience of something unknown mentioned in "Burnt Norton" 1. This kind of memory does not involve desire in the personal sense and is not limited to a conception of time that emphasizes the actions of a self defined in material and social terms. It would be the sort of memory mentioned in "Little Gidding" 3 immediately after the sentence about the nettles:

> This is the use of memory:
> For liberation—not less of love but expanding
> Of love beyond desire, and so liberation
> From the future as well as the past.
>   (*CPP* 142; LG 3.156–59)

This passage, like many others in *Four Quartets*, poses interpretative problems, including grammatical ones.[17] How, for instance, do the words after the dash relate to what precedes the dash? The combination of the dash with "not" suggests that a distinction is being introduced to avoid misunderstanding. Negations or partial negations are used in this way elsewhere in the poem, in "Burnt Norton" 5, for instance: "Not the stillness of the violin, . . . , / Not that only" (*CPP* 121; BN 5.144–45). And in "East Coker" 5: "—but there is no competition" (*CPP* 128; EC 5.185). The clarification in this case seems to be linked to the word "liberation." We find out what the liberation is from, not just from the past but from the future. It is not entirely clear, however, what the phrase "not less of love but expanding / Of love beyond desire" might mean. Had Eliot written "only from" instead of "less of," the statement, while still elliptical, would make sense: the use of memory is for liberation, not only from love but to something also called love that would be different from desire. Read in this way, the lines help clarify the preceding statements about attachment, detachment, and indifference. Memory would enable the shift from love, or attachment, not to detachment but to another sort of love, which is not desire; that love would presumably also be "indifference."

But by writing "less of," Eliot suggests a possible parallel between "of love" and "of memory." Had he written "only of" instead of "less of," the parallelism would be stronger: the use not only of love but of memory, which involves an expanding of love beyond desire, is for liberation; in the case of memory, but perhaps not of love, the liberation is not just from the past but from the future. Yet another possibility would be to read the words after the dash as a description of what this particular liberation involves: the use of memory is to achieve a liberation that is not a loss but a gain in love, and therefore is a freeing from the future as well as the past. The fact that the lines suggest all three of these readings without providing a basis for limiting the meaning to any one of them indicates the character of the poem's style, which discourages anything but slow reading and rereading. The elements that compose the statement are clear enough. Memory can be used to achieve liberation; love can be expanded beyond desire; in some way because of that expansion, the liberation is from the future as well as the past. But the coordinating of those elements, which can be variously configured, is left to the reader.

The syntactic difficulty in the lines dealing with memory creates a permanent grammatical dissonance, one that will not disappear entirely, short of a rewriting of the passage. Combined with the conceptual dissonance of the assertion that memory can be used to achieve freedom from past and future, the grammatical disruption contributes to producing an effect that is one version of the "harmony of dissonances." It makes that contribution by inviting the reader to pause in order to consider carefully the implications of the lines. One possible result of the reader's doing so is the undertaking of shifting movements among scattered segments of the poem in an attempt to understand the lines. The difficulties help prevent the misunderstanding that a conventional, easily graspable meaning is being expressed. The statement that precedes the dash is, for example, subject to misunderstanding, since it can be readily understood independently of the poem. There are various ways in which memory might be used to achieve freedom in contexts that are not important in *Four Quartets*, for instance as a source of fantasies providing compensation for a self dissatisfied with present realities. Without the insistent difficulties, such a coherent, conventional reading of the statement might be sufficiently satisfying and distracting to prevent the assertion about the future at the end of the lines from being recognized.

Eliot claims in *The Use of Poetry* that meaning can be used in poetry to distract the reader in the way a burglar uses meat to distract a dog while the poem does its work in another way. In this passage, however, he tries to prevent a readily apprehended meaning from drawing attention away from the lines' implications. The grammatical and conceptual aspects work together to minimize the distraction. First, the grammatical dissonance makes it hard to overlook the conceptual dissonance in what is being asserted of memory. In the process of working on the grammatical problem, the reader will likely take a close look at the entire statement, which contains some surprises besides its grammatical ellipses. Secondly, the assertion at the end concerns not just memory's relation to the past, as we might expect, but its relation to the future. A statement about memory and the future is harder to pass over than one solely about memory and the past. The claim that memory frees us from the past is puzzling enough, but when it is linked to a claim about freeing us from the future the statement has a potentially more arresting effect.

In a different kind of poem the reader might have no place to go with the dissonances except on to the next lines. Arrest might be the primary effect produced, and the dissonances might remain simply that: points of disruption and discrepancy to be noted in passing but not worked with and possibly transformed. The reader of *Four Quartets*, however, has options other than accepting or ignoring the difficulties, both grammatical and conceptual: to take them as invitations to try comprehending the lines by reconsidering the attitudes the passage counters. The attempts to comprehend and reconsider involve the provisional construction of new conceptual connections from the elements that become clear and remain unclear after the passage's disruptions are taken into account. Using those elements, a reader motivated by the difficulties can move in various directions to reconfigure this passage and its elements with others in the poem. The reader has the opportunity to engage in a continuing process of construction, disruption, and deferral. Instead of presenting the reader with a textual situation in which confusion can be replaced with knowledge, the poem sets the reader into a motion that tends to perpetuate itself.

As in many other passages in *Four Quartets*, in "Little Gidding" 3 the interpretative difficulties encourage the reader to search for clarification elsewhere by relating the lines to various contexts: what precedes and follows; other third sections; other passages in which the same or similar elements appear; other texts, including in this case, "Dante." The process of deferral resembles the one Rudolf Arnheim mentions regarding perceptual responses to two-dimensional drawings that create optical illusions: "It is one of the functions of the third dimension to come to the rescue when things get uncomfortable in the second" (Arnheim 239). But each of the many directions of movement we can take in response to the interpretative discomfort generated by the poem has its own difficulties. It is not entirely clear, for instance, that memory and indifference are related, though the juxtaposing of the lines referring to them makes the connection possible. The linkage enables a reading of "Little Gidding" 3 as evoking something different from the self and indifferent to it. Memory would not be personal recollection that, by providing links to the past, supports the self's sense of continuity with the future, a sense of continuity that Eliot implies is a bondage. Rather than being a personalized tie to the past and to the desires of the self that are directed toward the future, memory as indifferent would disrupt the apparently continuous sequence of personal desires and a personal history. It could be the kind of experience that Eliot mentions in his description of "the auditory imagination." But, in light of "Little Gidding" 2, it could also involve the various effects of the cultural as well as the bodily past that persist and recur in consciousness even though their origin and their relation to either personal desire or individual actions is obscure.

The passage following the lines about the use of memory also provides a context for interpretation. They include the statement quoted earlier concerning the vanishing of "The faces and places, with the self which, as it could, loved them / To become renewed, transfigured, in another pattern" (LG 3.163–65). These lines suggest that the poem itself is the product of memory's use, a kind of linguistic embodiment of memory in the nonanthropomorphic sense in which the word *memory* is being employed in "Little Gidding" 3. "Faces and places" are, for instance, central to the poem considered as a text, as are "pattern" and figurations of all sorts, including what is "transfigured" and "disfigured" (*CPP* 142; LG 2.147 and 3.165). The process of writing as just represented in "Little Gidding" 2 involves faces, the faces of vanished writers that have been transformed and combined into a ghostly, "unidentifiable" "face still forming" that contributes to a doubling to be understood as the production of new figures.

"Places" are, among other things, the locations named in the titles of each of the poem's four named sections, locations that are absent but that have been renewed by being turned into *topoi* and *loci* through figuration. The complicated pattern of the poem, in which the figurations are arranged in networks of *loci*, opens the process of figuration and renewal to the reader who is willing to engage in the movements made possible by the pattern. Those movements, which involve the work of memory, are of the same use as memory. That is, by engaging in the movements of reading, through reconfiguring the poem's elements, the reader actualizes, as the writer has also done, the use of memory in obtaining freedom from the self, if only temporarily. In the case of this passage, the difficulty of understanding a word, such as *memory*, used in a peculiar way can encourage a shift from semantic interpretation to consideration of the reading process. In this poem that process becomes one primary referent not just for the words *form* and *pattern* but also for *memory*.

As a linguistically incarnated form of a nonpersonal memory, a poem is the author's epitaph inviting the indifferent, cold response that Yeats requests rather than the response of pausing to read the words as the writer's personal utterance coming from beyond the grave. Eliot's writing cannot persuasively be interpreted in relation to such an authorizing source. *Four Quartets* is in this regard a lengthy, culminating instance in Eliot's nondramatic verse of the defacement, the denial of prosopopoeia, that begins in such early poems as "Rhapsody on a Windy Night." For Eliot a poem encourages a cold response because the beginning and the end of writing are the same. The producing of poetry as your own epitaph "Is a step to . . . an illegible stone: and that is where we start." No voice at all, the poem as epitaph is silent, like "the tattered arras woven with a silent motto" mentioned in "East Coker" 1 (*CPP* 123; EC

1.13). From the start it is illegible, difficult to read, a kind of cacography that, like Eliot's poetry and Heraclitus's fragments, needs to be deciphered. Like all human action, its fate is eventually to become literally indecipherable, to decay to something more ruined and more silent than a tattered arras. In that condition, it stands in need of reconstruction and interpretation but not necessarily in terms that are either personal or rational. Eliot's supplementing statement, "and that is where we start," suggests in context that death and the illegible language of death and of the past make up the ultimately determining framework for all human enterprise. The setting for any human action is the unknowable experience outside of life and outside of language that we are reminded of by the past's alterity and illegibility and by other experiences of darkness and descent. The phrase points as well to the literal point "where we start" in *Four Quartets*, for Heraclitus's fragments are part of the past's illegibility that challenges us to decipher it and that has contributed in hardly knowable ways to making us what we are and this poem what it is.

Notes

15. Drawing on the correspondence between Eliot and John Hayward during the composition of *Four Quartets*, Helen Gardner explains that Hayward suggested a modification of the phrasing concerning the nettles. Eliot rejected the suggestion, saying that he was referring to two varieties of nettle, the "White Archangel" or "dead" nettle and the "stinging" or live nettle. Gardner further points out that Eliot was mistaken about the "White Archangel" and that the phrasing he finally chose still gives the impression of live nettles and dead ones rather than two varieties. Rather than take Eliot's oddly expressed intention in his prepublication materials as a substitute for the printed version, as some critics have done (e.g., Moody 254), I interpret the passage in the way that Gardner suggests a reader would.

16. Brian Rotman discusses the resemblance between the vanishing point and zero in *Signifying Nothing* (cited as Rotman).

17. John Porter Houston is one of the few critics to emphasize what he calls the "syntactic peculiarities" (Houston 147) of *Four Quartets*, which he discusses in relation to Eliot's combining of "antithesis, identification, paradox, dialectic, and enumeration" (154).

A.D. MOODY

T. S. Eliot: The American Strain

Eliot was an American, and a poet. But was he an *American* poet? In his origins and his upbringing he could hardly have been more American. His mother was descended from one of the original members of the Bay Colony, and his father was descended from an Eliot who settled there in 1667. His grandfather had been one of the founding fathers of St. Louis, and was especially noticed by Ralph Waldo Emerson when he visited the city in 1852: "This town interests me & I see kind adventurous people; Mr. Eliot, the Unitarian minister, is the Saint of the West, & has a sumptuous church, & crowds to hear his really good sermons. But," he added, in a comment to which time has lent its ironies, "I believe no thinking or even reading man is here in the 95000 souls. An abstractionist cannot live near the Mississippi River & the Iron Mountain."[1] We know that at least one "abstractionist" was born in St. Louis, on 26 September 1888, and did much of his growing up there. And then his northeastern roots carried him back to the Massachusetts coast, where the family spent their summers, and to Harvard University, with which they had strong connections. Given all this, how could Eliot not be an American poet?

Yet William Carlos Williams, with his commitment to creating a poetry from the local conditions of American life and from the speech of Americans, was quite sure Eliot was not with American poetry, but against it. In

From *The Placing of T. S. Eliot*, edited by Jewel Spears Brooker, pp. 77–89. © 1991 by the Curators of the University of Missouri.

"Prufrock" and in *The Waste Land*, he saw Eliot finding his inspiration in literature, and in foreign literature at that.

In 1987 Richard Poirier renewed Williams's attack on Eliot in his "Emersonian Reflections." The gist of his argument was that Eliot's tradition was not in the American tradition. In his view—and it is an old charge which Poirier hardly bothered to prove—Eliot had an excessive reverence for the literature of the past and supposed it to be "a storehouse of values and wisdom ... even more so when imagined as an alternative to some present day chaos." Poirier recommended Emerson as an exemplary American, citing his belief that "we are here not to read but to 'become' Dante," that is, to rediscover within ourselves the origins of such works as the *Vita Nuova* and the *Divine Comedy*, and to not let them be "obscured within the encrustations of acquired culture."[2]

Poirier's invocation of Emerson helpfully shifts the ground beyond the too simple implication that the authentic American poet must write about American life to the issue of originality versus derivativeness whatever the material. But I think both charges can be rebutted. I will argue that Eliot's American experience is the most vital strain in his poetry. And I will argue that his use of the literature of the past was original in exactly the way Emerson demanded. Moreover, these two things work together and constitute in their combination the peculiarly American character of his poetry.

My concern, then, is Eliot's American experience and his American way of handling it. It has to be said at once that his American experience is not the most obvious component of his poetry. There is "The Dry Salvages," of course. But otherwise only a few minor poems are conspicuously American. There are the early satirical vignettes—"The *Boston Evening Transcript*," "Aunt Helen," and "Cousin Nancy"—and the relatively late landscapes—"New Hampshire," "Cape Ann," and "Virginia." Eliot's only other Americana are the caricatures in "Mr. Apollinax," "Lune de Miel," "Burbank with a Baedeker," and possibly the Sweeney poems. With the sole exception of "The Dry Salvages," these are not the poems for which he is remembered. But even in the celebrated early poems, written when he was closest to his American origins, it is possible to find little or no trace of an American accent or of American life. It was long assumed, at least by English and other foreign readers, that "The Love Song of J. Alfred Prufrock" and "Portrait of a Lady" were set in London, not St. Louis or Boston. After all, when Prufrock listens for the mermaids' singing, he could well be on Arnold's Dover Beach, where the tide of Romantic faith is forever ebbing. And the yellow fog, which rubs its back upon the windowpanes, could well be taken for a London peasouper as seen by Dickens and Lewis Carroll.

But Eliot's St. Louis had its own fogs which were yellowed by its own factories. By his own account, his "urban imagery was that of St. Louis," though with descriptions of Paris and London superimposed. He spent his first sixteen years in St. Louis, "in a house at 2635 Locust street, since demolished."[3] Because his grandmother lived nearby, in a house built by his grandfather, his family preferred to live on in a "neighborhood which had become shabby to a degree approaching slumminess.... And in my childhood, before the days of motor cars, people who lived in town stayed in town. So it was, that for nine months of the year my scenery was almost exclusively urban, and a good deal of it seedily, drably urban at that."[4] Given that hint we can find definite indications of an American locale in the early urban poems.

The third section of "Preludes" is a particularly interesting case, since Eliot wrote it in Paris in 1911 and took much of its imagery from Charles-Louis Philippe's *Bubu de Montparnasse*, a novel which for Eliot "stood for Paris as some of Dickens's novels stand for London."[5] Still, Eliot's evocation of the morning vision when "the light crept up between the shutters" could just as well be an American scene, an Edward Hopper perhaps:

> You curled the papers from your hair,
> Or clasped the yellow soles of feet
> In the palms of both soiled hands.

When all four "Preludes" are considered together, they reveal quite specific American traces. Lot, as in "newspapers from vacant lots" (I), is one American usage, and *block*, as in "skies / That fade behind a city block" (IV), is another. *Shades*, in "One thinks of all the hands / That are raising dingy shades / In a thousand furnished rooms" (II), is used in the American way. In England, those shades would be called *blinds* (*shades* would be lampshades). But Eliot's blinds are on the outside: "The showers beat / On broken blinds and chimney-pots" (I). I have it from Cleanth Brooks that *blinds* is the Southern usage for what others call shutters. Such Americanisms disappear after Eliot's first collection, apart from a few deliberate effects. *Dooryard* occurs unselfconsciously in "Prufrock": "After the sunsets and the dooryards and the sprinkled streets." When it appears again, in "The Dry Salvages" ("the rank ailanthus of the April dooryard"), it is consciously associated with America and with Whitman.

But there is more to words than their variant meanings. Before meaning, there is sound; and there is the rhythm set up by a sequence of sounds. Eliot once said, with his mind on the problem of translating from one language to another, that it was in the rhythm of a language, in its natural speech patterns, that the vital national character was expressed.[6] The specific national character is not so easily detected when spelling conventions make the two languages appear nearly identical. In fact, British and American English can be pronounced very differently and can have quite distinct speech patterns. American English rhymes *potato* and *tomato*, and *hurricane* rhymes not with *American*, but with *Cain*. Such differences of accentuation are frequent, and they give American English a distinctive rhythm. The American tendency, to generalize, is to make more of the vowels by giving them more weight and duration; while the English tend to clip their vowels short with more defined consonants. As a consequence, the English of England has a more regular measure, falling more readily into the iambic beat. When Robert Frost writes to the measure of the English iambic pentameter, one can feel the tension between his natural speech rhythms and the more regular English speech. It is the vowels that are most affected, and in his recordings one can hear him clipping his vowels to keep the meter. That is just what Eliot did *not* do, except in his thoroughly English *Practical Cats*. Even in his latest recordings, made when he had long been resident in England, the weights and lengths of his vowels and the rhythm of his speech are not in the English measure. His versification was always a departure from the iambic pentameter, stretching and contracting the conventional line into another measure altogether, called *vers libre* for want of a better name. He did this, presumably, simply by following his own American speech rhythms. "Portrait of a Lady," for example, is written for an American voice, and sounds slightly "off" rhythmically when read by a standard English voice. A poet whose ear had been formed by English speech patterns would not have written in just that way. What had happened was a quiet takeover of the English verse line.

There is at least one other American quality in Eliot's work which should be recognized. This is his habit of skepticism, which surely has its roots in the American tradition. The "American Doubt" is set against the "American Dream," as in the concluding lines of part II of "Portrait of a Lady," where the street piano's "worn-out common song" and "the smell of hyacinths ... Recalling things that other people have desired" leave the narrator musing, "Are these ideas right or wrong?" This combination of romantic feeling with a skeptical questioning of it is the source and driving force of much of Eliot's poetry. The skepticism is more a questing than a questioning. If it begins as a questioning of his own youthful romanticism, it rapidly develops into a quest for something beyond what any experience can offer, a quest that carries his work from *The Waste Land* to "Little Gidding." Perhaps there is no accounting for this habit of skepticism. It is simply there, deeply ingrained in Eliot's temperament. Eliot himself observed it in Henry Adams and called it the "Boston Doubt."[7] His own family background gave him a connection with the "Boston Doubt," specifically through its Unitarianism. "Are these ideas right or wrong?" seems to catch its tone exactly. Eliot's temperament, then, as well as his rhythm, is more American than it first appears.

Yet the question remains, how can *The Waste Land*, with all its "encrustations of acquired culture," be an American poem? In the drafts there were two long passages, one dealing with Boston nightlife, the other with the fate of the crew of a Gloucester fishing boat, which would have connected it explicitly with America. But their cancellation meant that the setting of the poem, along with its great range of cultural reference, became exclusively English and European. The only authentically American detail left in the poem is the hermit thrush.

Critics from William Carlos Williams on have noticed all the non-American and "undemocratic" culture in the poem, but they have not adequately attended to what Eliot was doing with it. They have not noticed that he was dealing with it in his own speech rhythms, and from his own point of view; and that, above all, he was displaying it, subversively, as a heap of broken images, as stony rubbish that did not answer to his need. It has too often been said, as by Richard Poirier, that Eliot was setting up images of a glorious past to put down the sordid present. It is rather the case that he collapses the past and the present into each other in such a way as to suggest that they are much the same. Both are looked at from the viewpoint characterized as "Tiresias," the viewpoint of someone who has seen it all before. There may be a covert pun in its being a typist that he particularly regards, since for him everything is typical. His cynical, disillusioned view of human experience and history is of course an element in the European cultural tradition; if Eliot is to be charged with being too attached to that tradition, it should at least be on account of his disillusionment, and not on the false ground that he glorified the past. From his point of view, there has always been a desert at the heart of the romantic garden, and as in *The Waste Land*, passion always ends in desolation and despair:

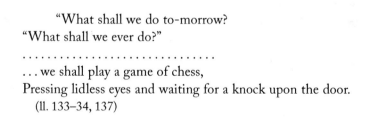

> "What shall we do to-morrow?
> "What shall we ever do?"
> ....
> ... we shall play a game of chess,
> Pressing lidless eyes and waiting for a knock upon the door.
> (ll. 133–34, 137)

In its search for a way out of that predicament—the permanent and universal predicament as the layers of cultural allusion imply—the poem offers intimations of a new life in what Eliot called the "water-dripping song." Eliot thought the thirty lines of "What the Thunder Said" which culminate in the hermit thrush's singing in the pine trees were the only *good* ones in *The Waste Land*: "the rest is ephemeral."[8] They are in fact not only the most vital lines in the poem, but also the most specifically American contribution to it.

I have argued elsewhere, in a paper on Eliot's formal inventiveness given at the Orono T. S. Eliot Centennial, that the "water-dripping song" completes the form of the poem by breaking out of the dramatic into the lyric mode, and that this was in effect a breaking out of a dead world represented there by the European past.[9] What I would add here is that it is the recourse to the American experience which effects the recovery. Eliot had heard the hermit thrush in Quebec Province, as his note indicates, and he would have been able to recognize and describe it because his mother had given him for his fourteenth birthday Chapman's *Handbook of Birds of Eastern North America*. But then it is likely that this personal experience would have been reinforced, possibly at a later date, by his reading of Whitman,[10] the Whitman who gave a vital function to American birdsong in "Out of the Cradle Endlessly Rocking" and "When Lilacs Last in the Dooryard Bloom'd." This is the Whitman that Eliot admired and deeply responded to:

> Then with the knowledge of death as walking one side of me,
> And the thought of death close-walking the other side of me,
> And I in the middle as with companions, and as holding the
>   hands of companions,
> I fled forth to the hiding receiving night that talks not,
> Down to the shores of the water, the path by the swamp in the
>   dimness,
> To the solemn shadowy cedars and ghostly pines so still.
> And the singer so shy to the rest receiv'd me,
> The gray-brown bird I know receiv'd us comrades three,
> And he sang the carol of death, and a verse for him I love.[11]

When Eliot introduced the same birdsong into *The Waste Land* (and followed it with what must be read as a further allusion to Whitman's poem: "Who is that third who walks always beside you?" [l. 360]), he placed himself quite firmly in the American tradition.

The importance of the "water-dripping song" for Eliot's further development as a poet can hardly be overstated. It is the point at which he detaches his poetry from the desert witnessed to by the "Mind of Europe" and enters upon the new life of *Ash-Wednesday* and "Marina," a new life rooted and founded in his New World experience. It is not that America gave Eliot the answer to the death of the Old World. For that answer, something more had to be added to his American experience, something which he found in Dante and Catholicism. There is another presence besides Whitman in the "water-dripping song," that of Dante and of Dante's Arnaut Daniel whose songs also are filled with birdsong.[12] One might say that the surface of *The Waste Land* is largely given by European culture. Beneath that surface there is another life, which finds expression in the American hermit thrush. But the full realization of that inner life will only come with the conscious explication of it.

Consider these lines from part VI of *Ash-Wednesday*, lines which are a distillation of the American strain in Eliot's poetry:

> though I do not wish to wish these things
> From the wide window towards the granite shore
> The white sails still fly seaward, seaward flying
> Unbroken wings
>
> And the lost heart stiffens and rejoices
> In the lost lilac and the lost sea voices
> And the weak spirit quickens to rebel
> For the bent golden-rod and the lost sea smell
> Quickens to recover
> The cry of quail and the whirling plover
> And the blind eye creates
> The empty forms between the ivory gates
> And smell renews the salt savour of the sandy earth

This is a time and place of tensions, as the next lines reveal. The white sails are flying seaward—toward the granite shore. The *lost* heart rejoices, in the *lost* lilac and the *lost* sea voices—the stress falls regularly upon "lost." And the heart, as it rejoices, *stiffens*. The *blind* eye creates *empty* forms, shades or phantoms; and smell renews the salt savor, not of the sea, but of the sandy earth. Thus, the images of sensual life have been patterned to insist upon mortality. Eliot's American experience is being shaped by a Catholic understanding. He is, in his own fashion, "becoming" Dante.

At the same time, the American experience remains the ground of the Dantescan understanding. "A writer's art," Eliot once wrote, "must be based on the accumulated sensations of the first twenty-one years." [13]

> There might be the experience of a child of ten, a small boy peering through sea-water in a rock-pool, and finding a sea-anemone for the first time: the simple experience (not so simple, for an exceptional child, as it looks) might lie dormant in his mind for twenty years, and re-appear transformed in some verse-context charged with great imaginative pressure. There is so much memory in imagination . . . [14]

We find such memories surfacing in "Rhapsody on a Windy Night." Eliot considered it his business as a poet to express and to interpret "the deeper, unnamed feelings which form the substratum of our being, to which we rarely penetrate," and he relied particularly on images laid down in his childhood to bring those mysterious feelings to consciousness. Eliot could say quite justly, therefore, that "in its sources, its emotional springs," his poetry "comes from America."[15]

But again there is the paradox, that the range of imagery drawn from his American experience is very limited. There is the urban imagery, which I have already noticed, and the Mississippi River "as it passes between St. Louis and East St. Louis in Illinois ... the most powerful force in Nature in that environment." There is what he called his "country landscape," "that of New England, of coastal New England, and New England from June to October." There, Eliot said, "I missed the long dark river, the ailanthus trees, the flaming cardinal birds, the high limestone bluffs where we searched for fossil shell-fish; in Missouri I missed the fir trees, the bay and goldenrod, the song-sparrows, the red granite and the blue sea of Massachusetts."[16] To complete the list we should add the memories of children in an orchard, playing and laughing in the foliage of an apple-tree, as in "New Hampshire" and *Four Quartets*. And that is about all. It is really only a small handful of childhood memories: certain birds and their songs, the children's voices, some trees and flowering shrubs, the Big River, the Massachusetts coast. And of course there is nothing in the way of an adult experience of American life and manners.

But having recognized how limited the range of his American material is, we must be all the more struck by how far he made it go and how vital it was in his poetic development. Out of such slender resources he fashioned a first version of his urban hell, a purgatorial sea, and a glimpse of paradise. From those few childhood memories, he fabricated the framework of his poetic universe.

Possibly the most purely American of Eliot's poems is "Marina." Its images are closely associated with the lines from *Ash-Wednesday* that I looked at earlier; in fact, "Marina" originated in the drafting of *Ash-Wednesday*. Significantly, and appropriately, the poem uses its New England coastal imagery to announce a new world and a new life, though not without an undertone of paradox. It begins:

> What seas what shores what grey rocks and what islands
> What water lapping the bow
> And scent of pine and the woodthrush singing through the fog

It ends wishing to resign the known life for the new life announced by the woodthrush calling through the fog upon granite islands, though there have been also "Whispers and small laughter between leaves."

The meaning of these images becomes explicit in "The Dry Salvages." This quartet begins with Eliot's big river, the only time he used the Mississippi in his poetry in spite of his saying that it had had such a powerful effect upon him. There are two remarkable features. Although Twain's treatment of the Mississippi in *Huckleberry Finn*, which Eliot deeply admired,[17] is referred to, most recognizably in "the river with its cargo of dead Negroes, cows and chicken coops," "the brown god" is not really Twain's river at all. And that is Eliot's point. The river has been bridged, controlled, "sivilised," as Huck would say, and Eliot evidently wants it to be destructive of the merely human order. The other odd thing, if this river is the Mississippi, is that it should appear to come out on the coast of Massachusetts. This is the geography of the imagination, in which local fact is dissolved in universal meaning.

The sea is the major image in "The Dry Salvages." Introduced in the closing lines of "East Coker," it effectively dismisses the Old World and its sense of history:

Here or there does not matter
We must be still and still moving
Into another intensity
For a further union, a deeper communion
Through the dark cold and the empty desolation,
The wave cry, the wind cry, the vast waters
Of the petrel and the porpoise.

This theme is taken up in "The Dry Salvages" after the opening river passage, and it is sustained and developed through to part IV ("Lady, whose shrine stands on the promontory"). The two quartets in effect form one continuous meditation, with the sea of the New World carrying us beyond the earth of the Old World, toward the "life of significant soil." Both the river and the sea are made to mean death, and then that meaning is altered so that death becomes the annunciation of another order of life. In this Eliot is shaping his American experience into a significant pattern, at one point by adapting the pattern of Arnaut Daniel's sestina, but more radically by following the inner form of Dante's Catholic sensibility. In "The Dry Salvages," the translation of the secular sea of Massachusetts into that of the "Lady, whose shrine stands on the promontory . . . Figlia del tuo figlio" (IV) is effected by the attempt to conceive the inconceivable in these lines from the third section:

At the moment which is not of action or inaction
You can receive this: 'on whatever sphere of being
The mind of a man may be intent

At the time of death'—that is the one action
(And the time of death is every moment)
Which shall fructify in the lives of others . . .

This passage is not only an annunciation of what the Incarnation might mean in the lives of individuals, but also an attempt to have the mind actually conceive the meaning.

"The Dry Salvages" might be called Eliot's *New World Quartet*, not only because it returns to his American sources, but because it discovers a new meaning in them, a meaning which goes back to the religious origins of New England. It goes back with a difference, because it seeks a world that is new in every moment. When Eliot goes on to speak of history in "Little Gidding," it is no more the history of America than of the Old World of "East Coker" that he has in mind. It is the history of the spirit which would find and create a new world, and which is defined in the tongues of fire and in other images of fire. It is intimated also in the hidden laughter of children in the foliage, children associated with birds and taking the place of the hermit thrush. The children's voices are heard in "Burnt Norton" (I) and again in the closing lines of "Little Gidding" ("At the source of the longest river / The voice of the hidden waterfall / And the children in the apple-tree") telling of a "condition of complete simplicity." That complex and mysterious condition is what Eliot has been seeking, and it is his American imagery that promises it and leads toward it. The coda of "Little Gidding" is deeply American, with just the significant addition of the tongues of flame and the crowned knot of fire. The rose, though it symbolizes several things, is at root the rose of memory, though its flowering in flame is metaphysical. It is in the end Dantescan, but in its source, it is American.

There are many ways of being American. *E pluribus unum*: the Union is made of many and diverse strains. In putting the word "strain" in the title of this paper, I was thinking of two of its meanings in particular. The first refers to the musical aspect, the melody, the lyric strain which is the vital principle of Eliot's poetry. The second is the genetic and genealogical aspect, the idea of an inherited quality. It is his American genes that make Eliot the kind of poet he is, and they show most markedly in the most vital parts of his work. His quest for a new life can surely be connected, through his family line and tradition, with the quest that brought his ancestors to New England in order to be, as Emerson was to put it, acquainted "at first hand with the Deity." One of the generic qualities of America, after all, is to seek the firsthand experience, to be original and independent. Emerson, the prophet, or at least the preacher of that spirit, might have been calling for Eliot as much as Whitman when he declared in the "Divinity School Address" that the "divine sentiment . . . cannot be received at second hand."[18]

Eliot's poetry is a practical application of Emerson's declaration of cultural independence: "The foregoing generations beheld God and nature face to face; we, through their eyes. Why should not we also enjoy an original relation to the universe? Why should not we have a poetry and philosophy of insight and not of tradition, and a religion by revelation to us, and not the history of theirs."[19] Eliot meditated more deeply and more darkly upon the word "original" than Emerson, and connected origins and ends in a more ultimate sense; but even that was going on *from* Emerson, not going against him. Furthermore, the language which Eliot found best served his vision was the one Emerson recommended when he said "Nature always wears the colors of the spirit" and provides a language to express our minds. That is, nature does this for the poet who "conforms things to his thoughts, [who] invests dust and stones with humanity, and makes them the words of the Reason."[20] In "Difficulties of a Statesman," the small creatures of Eliot's first world serve him in that way, and serve to measure the great world of public affairs:

Fireflies flare against the faint sheet lightning
What shall I cry?
. . . .
Mother
May we not be some time, almost now, together,
If the mactations, immolations, oblations, impetrations,
Are now observed
May we not be
O hidden
Hidden in the stillness of noon, in the silent croaking night.
Come with the sweep of the little bat's wing, with the small flare
of the
   firefly or lightning bug,
"Rising and falling, crowned with dust," the small creatures,
The small creatures chirp thinly through the dust, through the night.

With lines such as these, Eliot makes American nature a language of the spirit.

Eliot, clearly, is not an American poet in the sense that Whitman and Williams and Olson are. His poetry is as much English and European as it is American. It aspires to a vision and a wisdom not of any one nation or culture. But Eliot's is an English and European poetry that only an American could have written, and it is the American component that makes the difference.

Notes

1. *The Letters of Ralph Waldo Emerson*, ed. Ralph L. Rusk (New York: Columbia University Press, 1939), 4:338–39.

2. *The Renewal of Literature: Emersonian Reflections* (New York: Random House, 1987), 18, 45.

3. Quoted in "The Eliot Family and St. Louis," appendix to T. S. Eliot, *American Literature and the American Language: An Address Delivered at Washington University*. Washington University Studies, New Series, Language and Literature, no. 23 (St. Louis: Washington University Committee on Publications, 1953), 29.

4. T. S. Eliot, "The Influence of Landscape upon the Poet," *Daedalus, Journal of the American Academy of Arts and Sciences* 89 (Spring 1960): 421–22.

5. Eliot, Preface to *Bubu of Montparnasse*, by Charles-Louis Philippe, trans. Laurence Vail (Paris: Crosby Continental Editions, 1932), x–xi.

6. "A Commentary," *Criterion* 14 (July 1935): 611.

7. "A Sceptical Patrician," review of *The Education of Henry Adams: An Autobiography*, *Athenaeum* 4647 (23 May 1919): 362.

8. *The Waste Land: A Facsimile and Transcript of the Original Drafts Including the Annotations of Ezra Pound*, ed. Valerie Eliot (New York: Harcourt Brace Jovanovich, 1971), 129.

9. "Eliot's Formal Invention," in *T. S. Eliot: Man and Poet*, ed. Laura Cowan (Orono, Me.: National Poetry Foundation, 1990), 1:21–34.

10. See Eliot, "Whitman and Tennyson," review of *Whitman: An Interpretive Narrative*, by Emory Holloway, *Nation and Athenaeum* 40 (18 December 1917): 167.

11. "When Lilacs Last in the Dooryard Bloom'd," in *Leaves of Grass*, ed. Harold W. Blodgett and Sculley Bradley (New York: New York University Press, 1965), 334.

12. Dante's line for Arnaut Daniel's purgation—*"Poi s'ascose nel foco che gli affina"* ("Then he hid himself in the fire that purifies them")—will signal Eliot's next move: he reproduced the last line of Canto XXVI of the *Purgatorio* verbatim as line 428 of *The Waste Land*.

13. Review of *Turgenev*, by Edward Garnett, *Egoist* 4 (December 1917): 167.

14. *The Use of Poetry and the Use of Criticism: Studies in the Relation of Criticism to Poetry in England* (London: Faber, 1933), 78–79.

15. *The Use of Poetry*, 155; "The Art of Poetry I: T. S. Eliot," interview with Donald Hall, *Paris Review* 21 (Spring/Summer 1959): 70.

16. "The Influence of Landscape," 422; Preface to *This American World*, by Edgar Ansel Mowrer, quoted in "The Eliot Family and St. Louis," 28.

17. See Eliot, Introduction to *The Adventures of Huckleberry Finn*, by Mark Twain (London: Cresset Press, 1950); and Eliot, "American Literature and the American Language," in *To Criticize the Critic and Other Writings* (London: Faber, 1965), 54.

18. "An Address Delivered before the Senior Class in Divinity College, Cambridge, July 15, 1838," in *Nature/Addresses and Lectures* (Boston: Houghton Mifflin, 1903), 146, 127.

19. "Nature," in *Nature/Addresses and Lectures* (Boston: Houghton Mifflin, 1903), 3.

20. Ibid., 11, 53.

ANTHONY L. JOHNSON

T.S. *Eliot's* Gerontion *and* Journey of the Magi

I would like to compare and contrast some of the features of Eliot's *Geron-tion* (1919) and *Journey of the Magi* (1927), because they present a fascinating combination of similarities and differences.

In Eliot's mind *Gerontion* was at least partly integrated with *The Waste Land*, so that we read this exchange in the correspondence between Eliot and Pound:

> Eliot: 'Do you advise printing *Gerontion* as a prelude in book or pamphlet form?'
> Pound: 'I do *not* advise printing *Gerontion* as a preface. One don't miss it *at* all as the thing now stands'. (Eliot 1971: 127)

Despite Pound's view, Eliot's question is grounded in his knowledge of the close pertinence of *Gerontion* to *The Waste Land*, and the reverse. *Geron-tion* shares with *The Waste Land* the feature of a radical subordination of the syntagmatic by the paradigmatic axis (cf. Johnson 1985a). This appears in the challenging superabundance of rhetorical manipulation, allusion and bor-rowing in *Gerontion*, to a degree that surpasses nearly all, if not all, the most challenging passages of *The Waste Land*. We could say that, within Eliot's production, *Gerontion* stands as a peak or maximum of rhetorical challenge,

From *"The Spectre of a Rose": Intersections*, edited by Mario Domenichelli and Romana Zacchi, pp. 199–219. © 1991 by Bulzoni Editore.

61

innuendo and implication, whereas *Journey of the Magi* comes close to being a trough or minimum.

On the other hand there are stringent structural parallels and affinities between the two poems. In both cases the speaking voices represent more than a personal viewpoint. The poetic voice in *Gerontion* subsumes in its implicit terms of reference not just a lifetime but the whole span of Western civilisation from Classical Greece to the poem's present. Similarly, the speaking voice in *Journey of the Magi* is ostensibly looking back in old age to a successful quest for the discovery of Christ at birth—a quest that turns out to have been largely disappointing and unfulfilling for the speaker; but the adoption of a speaking voice rooted in a sermon by Lancelot Andrewes and proceeding in the guardedly formal but intellectually accessible speech patterns typical of cultured Anglicans makes it available, by extrapolation, as a projection of how a modern Anglican sensibility might have responded to such an experience. In both poems, however, the public or cultural facet presented by the poem leaves plenty of play for a private ideological orientation in which some of the sexual-sensual tensions that obsessed Eliot the man achieve a degree of poetic formulation.

Both poems begin by using other people's words, and I think that much can be learned about the differences between the poetic processes in the two texts by appreciating what Eliot has done. The simpler of the two is the *incipit*-quotation used for *Journey of the Magi*. Here Lancelot Andrewes is the source. He wrote:

> A cold coming they had of it at this time of the year, just the worst
> time of the year to make a journey, and specially a long journey in.
> The ways deep, the weather sharp, the days short, the sun farthest
> off, *in solstitio brumali*, "the very dead of winter"[1].

Sticking close to this text, Eliot replaced the "they" of Andrewes' text with the "we" of his *incipit*, cutting out a few other words and putting single inverted commas round this barely altered chunk of prose. This gave him the first five of his 43 lines, that is, in terms of lines, over 10% of his whole text[2]. The function of this quotation is eminently syntagmatic, since it is giving an initial contextualisation for all that is to follow, and the only paradigmatic question it raises is the adoption of a particular style of speech appropriate to a particular branch of Christianity as the rhetorical and discursive keynote of the poem. It is a syntagmatic cornerstone for a syntagmatic style of construction.

The *incipit* used for *Gerontion*—again a derivative one—is more complex. In the language of psychoanalysis, Eliot's opening gambit in *Journey of the Magi* is a substitution, since he is delegating his own power of speech on to a traditional spokesman for Anglican thought, Lancelot Andrewes, so excluding any mimetic attempt to divine the possible thought of one of the Magi in old age. By contrast, the *incipit* in *Gerontion* involves a condensation. One source is A.C. Benson's *Life of Edward FitzGerald*. Benson describes FitzGerald as sitting "*in a dry month, old* and blind, *being read to by a* country *boy*, long*ing for rain*"[3] (my italics emphasise elements used by Eliot). It is pertinent that FitzGerald was one of the few verbal sensualists of Victorian poetry and a man whose wide-ranging interests had led him to become the magnificent maverick translator of *The Rubáiyát of Omar Khayyám*. That source is made to intersect with words that Conrad, in *Heart of Darkness*, gives to Kurtz when Kurtz is close to death and speaking to Marlow: "I *am* lying here in the dark, *waiting* for death" (1946: 149, my italics). Kurtz, in a text that had immensely impressed Eliot, and which should, as Eliot had originally intended, have supplied the epigraph to *The Waste Land*, was a powerful literary symbol for a cultured idealist without restraint becoming a barbaric predator. As Mario Domenichelli has pointed out in his illuminating and wide-ranging paper on *Heart of Darkness*, "The 'Fair Harlequin' and the 'Black Lady': Conrad, Shakespeare and Oscar Wilde", Kurtz is "first of all, 'A voice!, a voice!'"[4] (1988: 267), but it is also highly significant that Conrad's hero-villain corresponds perfectly to the figure of 'the corruption of excellence' that appears in Book VI of Plato's *Republic*, 495. In this dialogue Plato makes Socrates expound his thought as follows:

> [...] the very qualities that make up the philosophical nature [...] become, when the environment and nurture are bad, in some sort the cause of its backsliding, and so do the so-called goods—riches and all such instrumentalities. [...] Such [...] is the destruction and corruption of the most excellent nature, which is rare enough in any case, as we affirm. And it is from men of this type that those spring who do the greatest harm to communities and individuals [...] but a small nature never does anything great to a man or a city. (1961: 731)[5]

Incidentally, to the best of my knowledge no one has noticed that the immediately preceding paragraph of the *Republic*, 494, contains a very probable source for Eliot's "Phlebas the Phoenician" (Part IV of *The Waste Land*, "Death by Water"). Phlebas was a man of good blood (as his name suggests: cf. Johnson 1976: 196, 349–52), came from a powerful region of city states ("Phoenician"), had known "the profit and loss" (which connotes the possession of wealth) and had been "handsome and tall". Plato's Socrates asks:

How, then do you think such a *youth* [i.e. possessing good qualities]
will behave in such conditions, especially if it happens that he
belongs to a great city and is rich and wellborn therein, and
thereto *handsome and tall*? (1961: 730, my italics emphasize words
appearing in Eliot's text)

To return now to our main topic, Eliot seems to have felt that a civilisation may undergo just as terrifying a corruption as a single person, if it had
once been endowed with a most excellent nature, and riches. And that, surely,
is a recurrent motif of Eliot's early work, appearing as early as *The Love Song
of J. Alfred Prufrock*, being developed by *Burbank with a Baedeker: Bleistein
with a Cigar*, and reaching its full flowering in *Gerontion* and *The Waste Land*.
It is also confirmed, with a nice Conrad–Marlow twist (corresponding to
Marlow's preference for Kurtz over all the colonial nonentities surrounding
him), when Eliot writes, in his essay on Baudelaire:

[...] the possibility of damnation is so immense a relief in a
world of electoral reform, plebiscites, sex reform and dress reform,
that damnation itself is an immediate form of salvation [...].
(1951: 427)

Now in the subtle condensation practised by Eliot in unifying words and
features derived from the figures of FitzGerald and Kurtz, it is FitzGerald as
cultured hedonist living his old age in a solitude of emotional withdrawal
who is the dominant element; this is true even on the plane of the contribu-
tions made to the signifier in lines 1 and 2. Consider too the self-satisfaction,
self-sufficiency, and emotional frigidity of FitzGerald in the second passage
used by Eliot for *Gerontion*, where Benson quotes a letter from FitzGerald to
Frederick Tennyson:

[...] I really do like to sit in this doleful place with a good fire, a
cat and a dog on the rug, and an old woman in the kitchen. This is
all my live-stock. (1905: 29; cf. Smith 1956: 63)

But the figure of Kurtz has its own importance. In the crucial passage
in *Heart of Darkness* that contains not only the source used in lines 1–2 of
Gerontion, but also the intended epigraph for *The Waste Land* and the epigraph of *The Hollow Men*, we read:

'One evening [...] I was startled to hear him say a little tremulously
"I am lying here in the dark waiting for death". [...]

'Anything approaching the change that come over his features I [. . .] hope never to see again. [. . .] I was fascinated.
It was as though a veil had been rent. I saw on that ivory face
the expression [. . .] of an intense and hopeless despair. Did he
live his life again in every detail of desire, temptation, and surrender during that supreme moment of complete knowledge?'
(Conrad 1946: 149)

In general, we could see the imprint left on *Gerontion* by Kurtz as its
implication of damnation for a predatory civilisation (outwardly Christian
but inwardly world-devouring) that had known excellence in its Greek origins and in its Elizabethan tragedy, but that has fallen ever deeper into corruption. We could call *Gerontion* a FitzGerald-type meditation synoptically
compressing the substance of a culturally Kurtzian doom, with its private
facet mainly facing FitzGerald and its public facet mainly facing Kurtz.

The condensation of FitzGerald and Kurtz also produces a concentration on the head and the brain, as opposed to the heart, the senses and spirituality. When first seen, Kurtz appears to Marlow as "an animated image of
death carved out of old ivory" (1946: 134), and his overall presentation is that
of a voice coming from a brain in an ivory head. Conrad writes: "A voice! a
voice! It rang deep to the very last. It survived his strength to hide in the magnificent folds of eloquence the barren darkness of his heart. [. . .] The wastes
of his weary brain were haunted by shadowy images" (147).

Thus the figure of Kurtz offered a prototype for *Gerontion*'s features of
a synoptic reliving of spiritual and emotional failure, and an eloquence of
a very special kind, which occurs nowhere else in Eliot in quite the same
form. This is an eloquence that knows no restraint, that tends to get out of
control and that is devoid of values—in Conrad's words, "hollow at the core"
(131). Very near the beginning of the draft of *The Waste Land*, above the title
of the first part, "The Burial of the Dead", Eliot had written (using capital
letters throughout) "He do the Police in different voices" (Eliot 1971: 4); to
some extent Eliot's *Gerontion* is 'doing Kurtz' (or a Kurtzian eloquence) in a
mosaic-like composite voice.

Besides this, the symbols that surround Kurtz's house are dead, drying
heads impaled on poles, and the last part of Kurtz left with an appearance
of life was his "ivory face" (149). Diachronically, Kurtz appears as a remarkable idealist who has shrunk to being an eloquent voice now coming from a
head obsessed by self-centred thoughts. This, combined with Benson's portrait of FitzGerald as an old man operating as a thinking head in solitude can
account for Eliot's synecdochically insistent concentration that first shrinks
Gerontion's self-presentation from "an old man" in line 1 to "A dull head" in

line 16, and then from "an old man" in line 72 to "a dry brain" in line 75. Both "dull head" and "dry brain" come close enough to Conrad's expression "wastes of his weary brain" (1946: 147).

Furthermore, just as there is an elaborate, beautifully contoured chiasmus situated at the centre of *The Waste Land*, at the start of the third part, centring on the contrast between the negative fishing for spiritual life in dull canal water and the positive memory of spiritual life in a death by sea water (Johnson 1976: 111), so too *Gerontion's* complex rhetorical structure of paradigmatic type, based on procedures of condensation and unification, employs a binding syntagmatic structure of chiasmic type[6]. It can be recognised as follows:

1 in line 1: "an old man in a dry month"
A2 in lines 15–16: "I an old man, / A dull head among windy spaces"
A2 in lines 31–32: "An old man in a draughty house / Under a windy knob"
B1 in line 33: "Think now" (ending the line)
B1 in line 33: "Think now" (again ending the line)
B2 in line 43: "Think" (ending the line)
B3 in line 48: "Think at last" (ending the line)
B3 in line 50: "Think at last" (again ending the line)
A2 in lines 72–73: "An old man driven by the Trades / Ta a sleepy corner"
AB1 in the last line, 75: "Thoughts of a dry brain in a dry season".

The global rhetorical pattern produced is A1, A2–A2, B1–B1, B2, B3–B3, A2, AB1. A1 and AB1 mirror each other through "dry month" against "dry season". In all three cases A2 associates the old man with what is for Eliot the positive element of WIND (cf. "The wind / Crosses the brown land, unheard" in *The Waste Land*, ll. 174–5); but lines 72–73 tell us that, instead of learning from the freedom of the wind, he has been driven by the "Trades"; this aligns him with Phlebas's attachment to "the profit and loss", and with the physical assimilation of Kurtz to the appearance of the merchandise he has been *trading* in—ivory.

In lines 33–53 the speaker's male polarity is concentrated on the function "Think", while female polarity appears in the complex modulations of a female "History" that "gives" (with six occurrences of that lexeme in lines 37–41), but always in deceptive ways. If the Elizabethans, including Shakespeare, tended to allegorise Fortune as a dangerous wheel or a shameless whore[7], Eliot reworks this by symbolising history as a kind of subtle vamp who saps the energy of implicitly male partners. In lines 54–60, despite having once had a full or attached heart ("$_{55}$ I that was near your heart"), the speaker now, like Kurtz, has a barren heart, and records a triple loss, of "$_{56}$ beauty", "$_{57}$ passion" and the senses (lines 59, 63). Because he himself has been unable to truly give, Gerontion has had his wholeness taken from him. He is a fragmentary self, "a dull head" or "a dry brain", who has been unable to draw life from the wind, and so will be symbolically killed by the wind, as suggested by lines 69–73. This runs parallel to the innuendo in lines 20–29 and 48 that, since 'we' have been unable to truly partake of Christ, simply devouring him, he will devour "us".

As to the significance of "dry", if we superimpose Benson's words "in a dry month, old and blind, being read to by a country boy, *longing for rain*" on Conrad's "I am lying here in the dark, *waiting for death*"—which Eliot has hybridised to yield "*waiting for rain*"—we find a suggestive equivalence between a 'desire for rain' and "death". Just as the 'waiting for rain' in *The Waste Land* is a false waiting for what in reality is spiritual death[8], so its opposite, the DRYNESS of the old man, corresponds to the male sublimation principle, and is perfectly in line with the phenomenal rhetorical vigour of this text. In this sense the *énonciation* bears out and fulfils the speaking voice's *énoncé*. Verbally, at least, the voice retains the vitalistic sensuality which it goes on to deny itself physically in lines 57–60:

> I have lost my passion: why should I need to keep it
> Since what is kept must be adulterated?
> I have lost my sight, smell, hearing, taste and touch:
> How should I use them for your closer contact?

These lines offer a startling bifurcation of sense between *énonciation* and *énoncé* (conveying vigour vs. dull exhaustion, exuberant eloquence vs. autistic withdrawal, respectively). The result is the setting up of creepy, elusive sense-effects, and this explains the apparent crumbliness the text offers to a critical appraisal, and the consequent puzzlement of many critics[9].

On either side of the central occurrence of "Think" in line 43, we find firstly "$_{38-39}$ gives with such subtle confusions / That the giving famishes the craving", which, with its many sexual overtones and its reversal of Enobarbus's praise for Cleopatra (in *Antony and Cleopatra* 2.2.241–3) displays male dissatisfaction with female sexuality, and secondly "$_{44-45}$ Unnatural vices / Are fathered by our heroism", which corresponds to a rejection of homosexual libido. This combination models a surreptitiously entrained sexual impasse which, in lines 54–60, leads into an implied paratonic flight from all sexuality[10].

Critics such as Grover Smith have pointed to the immense allusive wealth of *Gerontion*. Its complex reworkings of many sources, prevalently located in Elizabethan drama, help to enhance an acute sense of paradigmatic awareness elicited by the poem's sophisticated modernism. But, structurally, the most significant global figure is what could be termed its concentric shell structure of chiasmic type: this is not perfectly chiasmic because the last line blends the 'think' sequence with the 'old man—dull head/dry brain' sequence. Eliot uses a technique of allusive and rhetorical condensation and of symbolic metaphor so compellingly that a zero-degree of discourse is almost irretrievable. One result has been that critics fond of the paraphrastic mode have wisely tended to steer clear of this poem. Everything said works to 'metaphorise' everything else. In Richards's parlance, the vehicle overwhelms the tenor.

Thus *Gerontion* records an ambitious mental quest that has led to aesthetic emotion and spiritual loss and failure; this loss appears on the level of the *énoncé*, but not, or only marginally, on that of the poem's *énonciation* or its rhetoric. These have a scintillating, though often furtive, tone.

Turning now to *Journey of the Magi* (1927), the biographical datum of Eliot's gradually achieved conversion to Anglicanism, his admiration for Anglicans such as Lancelot Andrewes, and the traditional Christian unanimity in believing that the Magi's quest was fully successful, would lead a new reader of the poem to expect a sense of attainment, spiritual satisfaction and discovery in a poem entitled *Journey of the Magi* written at this point in his life. Instead of which we find a sense of loss and frustration both on the planes of the *énoncé* and of the *énonciation*. If *Gerontion* is generated according to a principle of condensation and unification, with paradigmatic linkage underpinning syntagmatic fragmentation and unannounced switching of semantic topics and frameworks, *Journey of the Magi* is built up on a prevalently syntagmatic basis. In it we find a clear subordination of paradigmatic units to a stronger syntagmatic process involving a toning down or substitution of the events alluded to by the title, especially the birth of Christ as a physical and sensory reality.

In some ways Eliot's poem appears to be telling a story, but, paradoxically, that story fails to materialise. The text skitters over the surface of an imagined journey, which is resolved first into depersonalised factors or features which at some points sound like a list (e.g. "the camels galled, sore-footed, refractory", "the villages dirty and charging high prices"), and then into a perverse familiarisation or levelling down of Christ's birth into an abstraction ("Birth [...] like Death") by which it is first likened to "Death" in general, and then to the "death" of the Magi, in particular. It is also significant that—with the single exception of lines 19–20[11]—the sense of measured worldliness and impersonality is so strong that this riffling through of unfavourable features supposedly retrieved from memory leaves no room for subjective or personal response, so much so that the poem's switches between the use of "we", "us" and "our" (for the Magi) and "I" (for the single speaker) seem to mean very little. The speaker emerges as a 'type' rather than a person, and in line 31, ending "it was (you may say) satisfactory", the text reaches a first disconcerting anti-climax (that is, prior to the equating of Christ's "Birth" with "Death") in a tone of almost bureaucratic pomposity.

Both the speech tone and the lexical choices (apart from the poem's sensual enclave in lines 9–10) register as being linguistically 'dry', and the rhythms too help to promote a pervasive sense of loss in the *énonciation* as well as the *énoncé*.

A clue to what is happening may be gathered by looking at the implementation of verbal functions. Setting aside the one gerund ("₁ A cold *coming*") and many participles (mainly present participles), we find relatively few true verbs, which are mostly common or very common ones. There are only 24 altogether in 43 lines: "had, regretted, had, preferred, came, galloped, came, was, continued, arrived, was, was, remember, would do, set down, set down, were, was, had, had seen, had thought, was, returned, would be". A scan of conjunctions and other connectives shows up the insistence on paratactic development, with as many as 23 instances of "and", 4 of "but", 3 of "then" and one each of "so", "no longer" and "at the end", while the overall effect is that of an inexorable going over of reasons for failure. Eliot's steady, rather monotonous build-up of these reasons is largely achieved through present participles, whose incidence is particularly high in lines 20–28. The poem contains 20 of these in all, against just one gerund. Instead of the sophisticated palimpsests and allusive mosaics of *Gerontion*, with its semantic switches and its many abrupt fractures in the flow of thought endangering coherence, here we find a very subdued paradigmatic presence, and a dilution of semantic strength through the accumulation of similar items. The best example of this occurs in lines 11–15:

11 Then the camel men cursing and grumbling
12 And running away, and wanting their liquor and women,
13 And the night-fires going out, and the lack of shelters,
14 And the cities hostile and the towns unfriendly
15 And the villages dirty and charging high prices:

These five lines yield a total of 10 instances of "and", six present participles following a noun, and no true verbs. Using the distinction adopted by Lukács in his *Aesthetics*, Eliot could be said to have opted for a descriptive rather than a narrative mode.

In the second verse paragraph (lines 21–31) some paradigmatic reso-
nance is achieved by the allusive presentation of features that foreshadow
events that were to occur in, or just after, Christ's life (e.g. "three trees", "dic-
ing for pieces of silver"), but the overall effect is one of syntagmatic domi-
nance taking shape in slack, rather repetitive rhythms. These effects peak in
lines 29–31:

29 But there was no information, and so we continued
30 And arrived at evening, not a moment too soon
31 Finding the place; it was (you may say) satisfactory.

Conceptually and lexically this amounts to an Eliotan desacralising or
quotidianising of a divine locus and of a supernatural topos. 'Unchristian'
Yeats[12] found "The uncontrollable mystery on the bestial floor" in his poem
The Magi (1913), so probing cooperative extremes of divine and bestial[13],
whereas Eliot confines everything in *Journey of the Magi* within a measured
middle ground through an emotional and rhythmic register of placid resignation, lexical norms located between the language of a contemporary quality newspaper and that of an Anglican sermon, and a frugal use of rhetorical
figures. His lines display a marked *Dämpfung* ('damping' effect).

By Eliot's pre–*Hollow Men* standards, the poem is paradigmatically
underpowered ('anemic') whereas it is fussily cluttered with syntagmatic
detail. The most prominent pair of paradigms is BIRTH and DEATH, which
appear especially in the last verse paragraph. Considering that the poem's
speaking voice bears the signs of authorial endorsement, it is surprising that a
text that presents—in the view of the religion Eliot had just chosen—a successful quest for the discovery of that religion's divine birth, should show a
predominance of DEATH over LIFE. We find:

Line 5 "The very *dead* of winter"
Lines 35–36: "[. . .] were we led all that way for / *Birth* or *Death?*
There was a *Birth* [. . .]"
Lines 37–39: "[. . .] I had seen *birth* and *death*, / But had thought
they were different; this *Birth* was / Hard and bitter agony for us,
like *Death*, our *death*".
Line 43 (last line): "I should be glad of another *death*".

Thus there are six implementations of DEATH and only four of BIRTH,
and the poem's reflective conclusion is, simply, a desire for death.

This poem, then, fails to convey any sense of cultural, spiritual or religious life at the spatio-temporal origin of the Christian era. The reader's

expectation of an expression of spiritual eros (adoration or love of the divine child) is brought up against the reality of an artistic resolution consisting of the spiritual thanatos felt by the poetic 'I': "I should be glad of another death". This gives a weird echo of the death-wish attributed to the Cumaean Sibyl—"'αποθανενὶ θέλω'": 'I want to die'. If Eliot's poem *Mr. Eliot's Sunday Morning Service* implicitly conveys the belief of a disbeliever, in an ethos of rebellion against the Church's desacralisation of the gospel message, this poem comes close to giving us the disbelief of a believer, through its virtual desacralisation of a divine epiphany.

In comparing *Journey of the Magi* with *Gerontion*, we certainly do find a few shared features in the *énoncé*, such as loss, sense of failure, dissatisfaction and regret, but there are very few in the *énonciation*. If lack of restraint in the modelling of *Gerontion* produces a sense of rhetorical excess, and impending semantic breakdown, the plane of expression is, nevertheless, intensely alive and dense with meaning, whereas *Journey of the Magi* suffers from a degree of sense-deficiency, and a withdrawal from involvement which debilitates not only the plane of thought but also that of expression. We encounter a kind of rhetorical atrophy or renunciation never found up to the end of *The Waste Land*.

Another striking change is that in the earlier stages of Eliot's work the terms of his paradigmatic oppositions were sharply differentiated, and rich in imaginative distinctiveness. For instance, a great deal of phanopoeic and emotional tension spanned and connected the rat and the bones, or vegetation and the desert (in *The Waste Land*), or money and culture (in *Burbank with a Baedeker: Bleistein with a Cigar*). In *Journey of the Magi* the lexical and paradigmatic thrust of "Birth" is cancelled by degrees in lines 36–39, by Eliot's assimilation of BIRTH to DEATH. The text says "I had seen birth and death, / But *had thought* they were different" (my italics); by implication, they weren't; and this elision of differences amounts to a radical elision of sense—the setting up of a semantic limbo. Eliot had never done that before—never cancelled the difference between paradigmatic opposites.

Admittedly, the poetic I's conclusion that "I should be glad of another death" tallies with the epigraph to *The Waste Land* quoted above, and with a reading of the first part of *The Waste Land* ("The Burial of the Dead") that views it as a reversal of the fertility cults (Johnson 1976: 66–68). But in Eliot's pre–*Hollow Men* poetry, the positive, Death-side of his paradigmatic system was not only held in strong tension against the negative, LIFE-side, it was also subtly enriched by the (sublimation-oriented) development of the DEATH paradigm in the direction of a LIFE-IN-DEATH configuration which *reverses* physical death by transforming it into LIFE at a spiritual level. Examples include the consciousness of the dead implied by "Winter kept us warm" (that is, by covering the dead "under forgetful snow"), and then the

'life' of "roots that clutch" and "branches" that "grow / Out of this stony rubbish" (*The Waste Land*, ll. 5–6, 19–20). More strikingly still, we find an implicitly positive metaphysical consciousness in Phlebas, after his death and as his
flesh is "Picked" from "his bones"; he is seen 'forgetting' "the profit and loss"
and 'passing' "the stages of his age and youth" when he has already been "a
fortnight dead" (ll. 312–8)[14]. Here in *Journey of the Magi*, by contrast, far from
there being a reversal of physical death into spiritual life, there is a disconcerting coincidence of, or *indifference between* the more paradigmatic, upper-case
"Death" and the more syntagmatic, lower-case "death". There is an overall
slippage or elision of sense that locks three terms together in an act of paradigmatic neutralisation, when we read "this *Birth* was / [. . .] like *Death*, our
death". Here the paradigms come together and lose their separate identities
by fusing. This unprecedented phenomenon in Eliot's work was symptomatic
of an underlying loss of tension in the deep structures subtending his work.

To use a metaphor, if there is no voltage difference between the poles of
thought (conceptual electrodes), no current of sense can flow between them. It
is as if, to a limited extent, Eliot were gently imprinting on *Journey of the Magi*
a line of research that was later developed—with full artistic consciousness—
by Samuel Beckett. If *Gerontion* offers us a syncretistic reliving of classical
and Elizabethan verbal splendour, *Journey of the Magi* gives us an *un*living or
a substitution of an encounter with a divine origin in terms of circumstantial
sequentiality, with a sense of a pre-Beckettian dismantling of verbal and conceptual power. It could be objected that this phenomenon is restricted to the
poetic voice, but there are no signs of authorial abdication of the text's sense-
vector—no ironic detachment from a voice that, anyway, speaks throughout,
after the keynote words of the admired Lancelot Andrewes.

So this poem is grudging towards linguistic capability and sense-
formation. Its reticent texture is—in a sense quite different from Eliot's
concept of "a continual extinction of personality" (Eliot 1951: 17)—tilted
towards impersonality. It has a semi-public, semi-private tone, a one-third
sensual, two-thirds ascetic voice; it stands as a self-controlling artefact. By
its throwing into reverse of the poetic unrestrainedness of *Gerontion* and *The
Waste Land*, it brings to mind Thomas MacGreevy's recollection of Yeats's
comment on Eliot's prose: "Eliot is dancing among eggs" (Mikhail 1977:
414); he was no longer 'disturbing the universe'. Whereas *The Waste Land* and
Gerontion offer a gigantic release of paradigmatic energy, this poem adopts
a damped-down *koiné*—the common language of an adopted cultural and
religious establishment—a cramped ventriloquism indifferent to the specifics
of historical and cultural identity.

If negative theology proposes a belief that none of the divine features
are expressible in words, then it is also true that Eliot's *Journey of the Magi*

proposes a sense-effect of double withdrawal—from the commitments of choice, and the commitments of full verbal expression. The 'dangers' of "the silken girls bringing sherbet" are ascetically refused, but the spiritual dangers of the divine "Birth" are positivistically refused, too: "We had evidence and no doubt" but "it was / Hard and bitter agony for us". More decisively, the divine object of discourse is left unexpressed in a state of ellipsis, as if 'too painful to speak of'. We infer Eliot's reluctance to give verbal form to religious belief, at least with reference to the figure of Christ. If in *The Waste Land* the "$_{60}$ Unreal City" is damned (with involvement), there is resignation (with a suggestion of experience), but no denunciation, in *Burnt Norton*'s "$_{44-45}$ human kind / Cannot bear very much reality". *Journey of the Magi* marks one stage in Eliot's movement towards detachment, his refusal to be too deeply involved.

In *Gerontion* a single voice splits up and fans out into different styles, different rhetorical fragments, so yielding an internal polyphony, whereas in *Journey of the Magi* it is as if the voices of the three Magi, plus that of Lancelot Andrewes, plus personal reminiscences of Eliot and the hints at the circumstances of Christ's death are amalgamated and flattened into a single voice or monophony. This monophony, unlike *Gerontion*'s bias towards orality and staginess, shows an opposite bias towards public documentation and writing-style, not only through the diffuse stylistic effects we register in reading the poem, but, more specifically, in the equivocal founding of the poem on the five lines hived off almost unchanged from Andrewes, and in lines 33–35: "set down / This set down / This".

This peculiar kind of poetic stammer corresponds to a lack of poetic conviction, a falling back or failure of the 'speaking out' of poetic *eloquentia*, a breakdown of monophony into aphony. It also gives a 'phatic confirmation' of the poetic I's need to confide speech to paper—itself a distancing from the life-process. This (again, unprecedented) internal validation of the non-orality of a speaking voice is, coherently, located within what is—for a poet of Eliot's major stature—a disappointingly positivistic reportage.

Even if *Gerontion*'s title makes it, ostentatiously, an *old man*'s talking, it can still be read as a 'bringing to life', or 'acting out' of the axiological necrosis of Western culture, by the sheer *vis* of its eloquence. By contrast, *Journey of the Magi* is a 'bringing to death' of a key point in that culture's genesis. Instead of giving a direct response to the divine birth (the poem's presumed source of values) Eliot makes the poem into a 'making old' by entrusting it to a positivised Magus at the end of his life using a distant, "alien" style that maximises its detachment from the event. It converts a successful religious quest for birth into the discovery of a paradigmatic and syntagmatic death, in which, anyway, both 'Birth-birth' and 'Death-death' have been rolled up into a single monadic nullifying of sense, in discourse which has even taken on the autistic bias of a 'letter to no one', a credo of disbelief. The poem is a voice of death, but also a dying voice.

To sum up, it may be useful to draw up a two-column contrast between some of the main characteristics of the two poems. Giving the features of *Gerontion* first in each case, and those of *Journey of the Magi* second, we discover:

GERONTION
Poetic overdetermination
Paradigmatic supremacy, with rhetorical excess
Kaleidoscopic effect heightened by allusion and breaks in cohesion and coherence
Polyphony in one voice (with different I's compressed into one 'I')
Epigrammatic compression, with few connectives
Metaphoric procedures without a clearly indicated referential frame
Condensation and unification
Concentric rhetorical structures
Heightening of personal eloquence
Difficulty of semantic decodification
Heightening of the signifying process, through interruption of discursive development
'Bringing to life' of cultural necrosis

JOURNEY OF THE MAGI
Poetic underdetermination
Syntagmatic supremacy, with rhetorical restraint
Linear monologic effects heightened by full cohesion and coherence
Monophony of plural experience (with 'we' equivalent to 'I')
Prosaically full syntax relying on parataxis (much use of "and")
Metonymic proliferation building a referential frame that tends to paradigmatic emptiness
Substitution
Sequential rhetorical structures
Damping of eloquence: reticent, impersonal sobriety
Ease of semantic decodification
Laxity of signification, with generally uninterrupted discursive development
'Bringing to death' of cultural genesis

NOTES

1. The passage appears in Lancelot Andrewes, *Works* (1841–54), I, 257 and *Selected Essays* 297; it is also discussed by Grover Smith (1956: 123).

2. With the special exception of the list appearing in "Triumphal March" (Part I of *Coriolan*, lines 14–24), which, as Smith points out, "was purloined almost verbatim from Ludendorff's *The Coming War* (1931)" (Smith 1956: 162), this seems to be the longest quotation from any source in Eliot's poetry, certainly for an *incipit*. Its very length increases its syntagmatic importance, and its excision would leave the poem in a radically incomplete from.

3. The source is A.C. Benson's biography *Edward FitzGerald* (New York and London, 1905: 142). In discussing this borrowing, Matthiessen quotes the view of Morton Zabel (private communication) that Benson's "whole book, with its picture of Fitzgerald [*sic*] in his pathetic, charming, and impotent old age, pondering on the pessimism of Omar, and beating out the futility of his final years, may have crystallized in Eliot's mind the situation [. . .] of *Gerontion*" (1958: 74).

4. Domenichelli sees the Harlequin figure as a *puer* who is "pure action without knowledge", and Kurtz as a *senex* who is "knowledge and the impossibility of action" (268). On Kurtz's valency as a 'poet', see Giuseppe Sertoli's introduction to *Cuore di Tenebra*, Einaudi, Turin, 1984.

5. Further evidence of the extent to which Eliot was thinking of Plato's *Republic* is provided by the Drafts of *The Waste Land*, where Eliot, before one of Ezra Pound's cuts had removed it, had the line "Not here, O. [Ademantus] Glaucon, but in another world". The exchange between Glaucon (not Adeimantus: both were brothers of Plato) and Socrates occurs in *Republic*, Book IX, 592 A–B). It hinges on the concept of "the city whose home is in the ideal", as Glaucon says; Socrates replies that "perhaps there is a pattern of it laid up in heaven for him who wishes to contemplate it and [. . .] constitute himself its citizen" (Plato 1961: 819; Eliot 1961: 127–8). This source provides an added dimension to Eliot's "60 Unreal City" (the 'real' City being the Platonic, ideal one) over and above the sense of all-pervasive unreality experienced by Marlow in the presence of the other Europeans at the station: "'I've never seen anything so unreal in my life'" (Conrad 1946: 76 cf. 78).

6. The most intensely paradigmatic moments in both Eliot and Yeats (otherwise very different verbal artists) have this striking feature in common—a recourse to chiasmus as displaying a 'paradigmatic bias' within and despite its inevitably syntagmatic (because *in presentia*) grounding in a text. If we see the paradigmatics of a text as a pattern of suggestive recurrences, its syntagmatics can usually be read as a pattern of exploratory development—of progressive newness. Since a chiasmus 'palindromically' curls back on itself (ABC . . . CBA) to transgressively return to what has gone before, instead of advancing, a chiasmus—especially if *lexically* repetitive—represents the surfacing of a paradigmatic principle outside its own (*in absentia*) domain. To the extent that a poet arranges paradigmatic prevalence over syntagmaticity in his or her own work, the chiasmus can be seen as a more or less intense enactment of the paradigmatic principle on the plane of rhetoric. And when, as here, a chiasmus uses identity on near-identity in its *syntagmas* to compose its pattern (rather than being marked by lexically varied enactments of repeated paradigms), then it can be viewed as an intensive paradigmatic presence—an enclave or series of enclaves within the precinct of syntagmatics.

7. See, for instance, *Macbeth* 1.1.14–15: "And Fortune, on his [Macdonwald's] damned quarrel smiling, / Showd like a rebel's whore" (Arden edition, Methuen, London, 1972: 6).

8. Cf. Alessandro Serpieri, who perceptively notes that in *Gerontion* and *The Waste Land* "the wait for rain, in a dry brain [. . .] or in a land laid waste by drought, will raise up the deceptive positive hope of a purification-rebirth in water" (1973: 122, my translation).

9. One resourceful critic who is puzzled is Grover Smith. He writes that "The ambiguity [of a female 'History' whose presentation leads into a refusal of passion], referring as much to belief as to potency or love, tends to be puzzling when one reads the next section, in which, after the mention of the tiger, there is no longer any visible connection with the idea of secularism" (1956: 64). Smith does not seem to appreciate the distinction between the poetic I's mental and verbal passion, and his withdrawal from spiritual and sensual passion. He also fails to detect Eliot's strategy of Kurtzian—a "remarkable" (1946: 69, 138, 151, 158, to use Conrad's term)—combination of "magnificent eloquence" with a value system that Eliot projects through the speaking voice as being "hollow at the core" (Conrad 1946: 147, 131).

10. The situation of a total barrier to sexual commitment is a recurrent topos in Eliot. It is found in *The Love Song of J. Alfred Prufrock* (lines 90–98, 120–131), *The Waste Land* (especially lines 35–42, 418–422), *The Death of St. Narcissus* (*passim*, see especially the second draft in Eliot 1971: 94–97).

11. "With the voices singing in our ears, saying / That this was all folly".

12. Cf. *Vacillation*, Part VIII (with its implication of authorial endorsement): "I—though heart might find relief / Did I become a Christian man and choose for my belief / What seems most welcome in the tomb—play a predestined part. / Homer is my example and his unchristened heart" (Yeats 1957: 503; these lines were written in 1932).

13. In line with Blake's dictum "Without Contraries is no progression" (1979: 149), Yeats's opposites do not statically stay apart, but react dialectically and can even converge to form 'unities of opposites' (Johnson 1985b).

14. Two more intriguing examples can be cited from the drafts of *The Waste Land*. In the first draft of *Dirge* there is the implication that, as the dead man there is freed of his flesh by marine animals, his still living consciousness (after physical death) becomes "Still and quiet" (Eliot 1971: 123). Similarly, in *The Death of St. Narcissus*, there is a revealing simultaneity between spiritually ecstatic acceptance of physical death and a fleshly consciousness of "the penetrant arrows". This takes shape as a deathly (but self-conscious, literally 'Narcissistic') climax of pleasurable pain ("his white skin surrendered itself to the redness of blood, and satisfied him"). Here too a sublimation-oriented male figure ("he became a dancer to God") survives into LIFE-IN-DEATH: "Now he is green, dry and stained / With the shadow in his mouth" (1971: 97). Infertility in terms of human reproduction is reversed into the metaphysical fertility of a 'full word', and a "dry" form of life after death. Cf. also the words "the bones sang" in *Ash-Wednesday* (Part II) after those bones have been freed of flesh by the "three white leopards". This poem too specifies that the bones "were already *dry*" (my italics).

References

Blake, W. 1979. *Complete Writings*, edited by Geoffrey Keynes (Oxford: Oxford University Press).

Conrad, J. 1946. *Youth—Heart of Darkness—The End of the Tether* (London: Dent).

Domenichelli, M. 1988. "The 'Fair Harlequin' and the 'Black Lady': Conrad, Shakespeare and Oscar Wilde", in *The Ugo Mursia Memorial Lectures*, edited by Mario Curreli (Milan: Mursia International).

Eliot, T.S. 1936. *Collected Poems 1909–1935* (London: Faber and Faber).

———. 1944. *Four Quartets* (London: Faber and Faber).

———. 1951. *Selected Essays* (London: Faber and Faber).

———. 1971. *The Waste Land: A Facsimile and Transcript of the Original. Drafts Including the Annotations of Ezra Pound*, edited by Valerie Eliot (London: Faber and Faber).

Johnson, A.L. 1976. *Sign and Structure in the Poetry of T.S. Eliot* (ETS: Pisa).

———. 1985a. "Broken Images": Discursive Fragmentation and Paradigmatic Integrity in the Poetry of T.S. Eliot", *Poetics Today* 6:3, 399–415.

———. 1985b. "W.B. Yeats' 'The Magi'", *Analysis: Quaderni di Anglistica*, 3:5–22.

Matthiessen, F.O. 1958. *The Achievement of T.S. Eliot* (London: Oxford University Press).

Mikhail, E.H. 1977. *W.B. Yeats: Interviews and Recollections* (London and Basingstoke: Macmillan).

Plato. 1961. *The Collected Dialogues*, edited by Edith Hamilton and Huntington Cairns (Princeton: Princeton University Press).

Serpieri, A. 1973. *T.S. Eliot: Le strutture profonde* (Bologna: Il Mulino).

Smith, G. 1956. *T.S. Eliot's Poetry and Plays* (Chicago and London: University of Chicago Press).

Yeats, W.B. 1957. *The Variorum Edition of the Poems of W.B. Yeats*, edited by Peter Allt and Russel K. Alspach (New York: Macmillan).

LEE OSER

Prufrock's Guilty Pleasures

Eliot descended from the original Puritan settlers of the Massachusetts
Bay Colony, who believed that the Bible alone held the means of organizing a
successful polity.[1] His mother's ancestor Isaac Stearns arrived from England
in 1630 and helped found the city of Salem. Eliot's first patrilineal ancestor
in New England, Andrew Eliot, emigrated from East Coker, Somerset, to
the Bay Colony in about 1667. A "cordwainer" or shoemaker by profession,
Andrew was several times chosen selectman of Salem and finally became
town clerk. In 1692, he sat in judgment of the Salem witches; later in life he
is said to have suffered great agony over his part in the hangings.[2]

As a member of the Bay Colony, Andrew Eliot hewed to an idea that
was the foundation both of church government and of social unity, namely,
the public covenant between God and his people.[3] Distinct from the covenant of grace, which signaled a private compact between God and the sainted
individual, the public covenant established the Bay Colony's relations with
Jehovah on the basis of its pledge to build a city of God: if the colonists sank
into the mire of worldliness and corruption, the covenant would be revoked.
Formally outlined by John Winthrop in 1630, in his lay sermon "A Modell
of Christian Charity," the covenant represented a unique "bond of marriage"
between God and New England, and it engendered responsibilities that fell

From *T. S. Eliot and American Poetry*, pp. 26–41. © 1998 by the Curators of the University
of Missouri.

heavily on every individual, rich and poor alike. It especially succeeded in ensuring dedication to communal decisions, such as declarations of war.

The public covenant inspired the invention of an American sermonical form, which Perry Miller called "the jeremiad," and which he described as having crystallized in a series of sermons delivered by second- and third-generation New England Puritans. In weighing the connotations of Samuel Danforth's "Errand into the Wilderness," Miller perceived in Danforth's words a sundering of the colonists from their original mission, and of their rhetoric from their emerging history. According to Miller, Danforth's 1670 sermon functioned as a ritual admission of guilt and loss of moral purpose during a mercantile "process of Americanization."[4] The term "jeremiad" referred to the clergy's formulaic tongue-lashings of their flock, whose members were endangering the covenant by developing a commercial society.

In *The American Jeremiad*, Sacvan Bercovitch acknowledged the permanence of Miller's work but argued that Miller had failed to recognize how the preachers adopted the jeremiad—as America expanded in unlooked-for ways—in the service of reinforcing community. Bercovitch defined the American jeremiad as "a ritual designed to join social criticism to spiritual renewal, public to private identity, the shifting 'signs of the times' to certain traditional metaphors, themes, and symbols."[5] Where Miller regarded the jeremiad in terms of the heavy sense of dereliction that haunted the children and grandchildren of the visionary first settlers, Bercovitch saw an effort to recoup a feeling of collective identity and purpose. I will be building on Bercovitch's thesis that, from Danforth on, the call to unite private and public identities on behalf of an American ideal is a key element of the American Puritan sermonical tradition. Yet, with an eye toward the later Eliot, I want to preserve the integrity and personal significance of the covenant of grace, which exists apart from structural effects that Bercovitch isolates.

One is struck by the number of ministers that descend from Andrew Eliot: a later Andrew Eliot, Congregationalist pastor at Boston's New North Church during the revolutionary period and T. S. Eliot's great-great-great-grandfather; the poet's grandfather, William Greenleaf Eliot, who moved west in 1834 to establish a Unitarian church in St. Louis; his uncle, Thomas Lamb Eliot, who founded the Unitarian ministry in Portland, Oregon; his first cousin, Thomas Lamb Eliot Jr.; and another first cousin, Frederick May Eliot, who attended Harvard with T. S. Eliot and became the premier American Unitarian spokesman of the twentieth century. With similar ties on her side of the family, Charlotte Champe Stearns Eliot, the poet's mother, extended this clerical heritage in her poetry and in a biography of her father-in-law, *William Greenleaf Eliot*, which is dedicated to her children, "lest they forget." If Margaret Fuller never saw much in William Eliot, Emerson, visiting St.

Louis in the 1840s, praised his sermons.[6] T. S. Eliot's own remarks about his grandfather are often quoted, but they will bear repetition:

> I never knew my grandfather: he died a year before my birth. But I was brought up to be very much aware of him: so much so, that as a child I thought of him as still the head of the family—a ruler for whom *in absentia* my grandmother stood as vicegerent. The standard of conduct was that which my grandfather had set; our moral judgments, our decisions between duty and self-indulgence, were taken as if, like Moses, he had brought down the tables of the Law, any deviation from which would be sinful. Not the least of these laws . . . was the law of Public Service. . . . (*TCTC* 44)

Echoing the typological language of American Puritan chroniclers like William Bradford and Cotton Mather, Eliot describes his grandfather as a Moses bringing the Law of God to the wilderness—and St. Louis practically was the wilderness in 1834. A tinge of irony does not belie the speaker's seriousness; rather, it reflects his complex sense of history. For T. S. Eliot, William Eliot personified the Puritan errand, an errand that had achieved very mixed results.

T. S. Eliot entered Harvard College in 1906 at the age of seventeen; he was five years away from "The Love Song of J. Alfred Prufrock." In 1908, he reviewed Van Wyck Brooks's lyrical but penetrating account of a sinking culture, *The Wine of the Puritans*. Brooks had himself attended Harvard, where he and Eliot were on friendly terms, and his book provides a record both of the social shifts that awaited the new generation, and of the consequent debates. For Brooks, the Puritan legacy in the twentieth century was not even in crisis—it was merely superannuated: "The New England idea, adequate for a small province, naturally became inadequate for the expression of a great nation. Adapted as this idea was to the needs of a frugal, intellectual people whose development was strictly intensive rather than extensive, it was unable to meet the needs of great prosperity, imperialism and cosmopolitanism."[7] The young Brooks—prior to his nervous breakdown and ensuing change of values—regarded old New England with the poise of an anthropologist. Identifying with Brooks's cultural assessment, Eliot remarked:

> This is a book which probably will chiefly interest one class of Americans (a class, however, of some importance): the Americans retained to their native country by business relations or socialities or by a sense of duty—the last reason implying a real sacrifice— while their hearts are always in Europe. To these, double-dealers

with themselves, people of divided allegiance except in times of emotional crisis, Mr. Brooks' treatise will come as a definition of their discontent. But he should find a larger audience than this class alone. The reasons for the failure of American life (at present)—social, political, in education and in art, are surgically exposed; with an unusual acuteness of distinction and refinement of taste; and the more sensitive of us may find ourselves shivering under the operation. For the book is a confession of national weaknesses; if one take it rightly, a wholesome revelation.[8]

The review mingles two types of expression, an elegant aestheticism characterized by the words "unusual distinction and refinement of taste," and a Calvinistic concern with atonement and sanctification that underlies such metaphors as "surgically exposed," "shivering under the operation," and the homiletic "wholesome revelation." In the first register, Eliot wears the connoisseur's sensibility that became one major response of patrician sons to their political disenfranchisement; in the second register, that of the American Puritan sermonical tradition, he activates the pastoral conscience that undergirded his family's power and importance in the eighteenth and nineteenth centuries. Like a Puritan preacher, Eliot admonishes his own people: his stinging remark about education aims at Harvard University and its president, Charles William Eliot, his third cousin twice removed and yet another descendent of the original Andrew.[9] Especially significant for the author of "Prufrock," however, is the review's dramatic sense of "divided allegiance," between "duty," on one side of the Atlantic Ocean, and Europe, with its associations of poetry and art, on the other.

My purpose in this chapter is to connect "The Love Song of J. Alfred Prufrock" to the tradition surveyed by Miller and Bercovitch, a tradition that endured for centuries in the homes of clergymen, and that furnishes a common bond between Eliot and Emerson. It might seem more appropriate to link Eliot to English preachers: one thinks of his interest in Donne, Hugh Latimer, and Lancelot Andrewes. Here, however, as is very often the case with Eliot, American subtexts accompany English topics. In a 1919 review, he drew attention to the sermon as "a form of literary art," and by way of Donne pondered the supreme difficulties posed by the sermon for the artistic ego;[10] the same year, he asked his mother for sermons by Andrew Eliot and Theodore Parker (LTSE, 274). Though satirical, "Mr. Eliot's Sunday Morning Service," written in 1918, reveals a concern with sermonizing, while the ambiguity of "Mr. Eliot" suggests an encounter with ancestral preachers.[11] And with "Gerontion" and The Waste Land, published in 1920 and 1922, respectively, Eliot turned visibly to his roots in the sermon: the theme of errand, the jeremiad, the Augustinian covenant of grace.[12]

In "Prufrock" he rebels against the family pulpit. I will discuss how Eliot confronts his clerical inheritance, both through his irreverent use of sermonical language in the poem, and through a *bellum intestinum* that marks his coming of age as a poet: his resistance to the sermonical writings of his mother. For whatever reasons—canonical tastes, international biases, or perhaps old-fashioned snobbery—modernist critics have tended to ignore Charlotte Eliot. As if to compensate for this critical neglect, several of T. S. Eliot's biographers have claimed a literary significance for the Eliots' remarkable mother–son relationship.[13] Well-educated by nineteenth-century standards, devoutly Unitarian, liberally Republican, and a versifier who occasionally verged on poetry, Charlotte Eliot has emerged as a considerable influence on her son's artistic development.

The composition of "Prufrock" dates from 1910, when Eliot was pursuing his master's degree at Harvard. He finished the poem the next year in Europe. Among other themes, a debate between duty and love of European culture, much like the conflict expounded in the review of Brooks, reverberates in the poem's opening lines:

> Let us go then, you and I,
> . . . .
> Let us go, through certain half-deserted streets,
> The muttering retreats
> Of restless nights in one-night cheap hotels
> And sawdust restaurants with oyster-shells:
> Streets that follow like a tedious argument
> Of insidious intent
> To lead you to an overwhelming question . . .
> ("Prufrock" 1, 4–10)

This opening invites comparison with a work by Charlotte Eliot, a poem in three sections totaling almost two hundred lines, called "The Wednesday Club." Her son was about twelve when Charlotte wrote "The Wednesday Club," and its progressivist message resembles that of his Smith Academy graduation poem, written when he was sixteen.[14] I have no proof that T. S. Eliot knew the poem, but it is likely that Charlotte would have shown this ambitious work to her son, whom she treated as an intellectual peer, and whose literary inclinations were obvious to the family from an early age. The Wednesday Club was a women's organization and an instrument of reform:

> Though culture may be our corner stone,
> We cannot exist for culture alone
> In scholarly retreat.
>
> For lo! grave problems press.
> The pleadings of distress
> Will follow the mind's sublimest flight,
> A voice from the depths disturb the height,
> When wrongs demand redress.
> The Wednesday Club in its action leads,
> Crowning progressive thought with deeds,
> It works for righteousness.[15]

Charlotte Eliot beats the drum of "progressive thought": the enemy in her poem is "retreat," the antithesis of progress. For T. S. Eliot in 1910, his mother's progressivism runs counter to poetry and contrary to wisdom and truth. The "muttering retreats" that allure him connote a domain of poetic intensity, an embrace of "culture alone" where culture is high and European. I associate "retreats" with poetry because the urban setting of "Prufrock" evokes Eliot's study of French models. As he would recall: "I think that from Baudelaire I learned first . . . the poetical possibilities . . . of the more sordid aspects of the modern metropolis, of the possibility of fusion between the sordidly realistic and the phantasmagoric. . . . I learned that the sort of material that I had, . . . in an industrial city in America, could be material for poetry" (*TCTC*, 126). In assimilating the urbanism of Baudelaire and Laforgue, Eliot developed a European style and abandoned his mother's American social consciousness. "The Love Song of J. Alfred Prufrock" records his altered social and emotional responses to his native surroundings, as well as an accompanying shift from moral to aesthetic concerns.[16]

Where in "Prufrock" "streets" "follow [you] like a tedious argument," in "The Wednesday Club" "pleadings" of conscience "follow the mind's sublimest flight." Charlotte's "pleadings" constitute a call for self-sacrifice that rings throughout the religious, literary, and political writings of late-Puritan America—a call vigorously seconded by "The Wednesday Club."[17] Speaking of "we," she assumes that the solitary mind in its "sublimest flight" will respond to duty's command. By contrast, the fact that Prufrock addresses "you and I" reflects authorial self-division. Like a guilty conscience, the "argument of insidious intent" has the effect of dividing the speaker, of separating "us" into "you" and "I."

Eliot's description of Laforguian irony as "a *dédoublement* of the personality" is often cited by critics of "Prufrock" to explain the poem's motif of self-division.[18] In his 1926 Clark Lectures, Eliot made some clarifying remarks about the French poet in whom he recognized "a temperament akin to" his own (*TCTC*, 126): "For Laforgue, life was *consciously* divided into thought and feeling.... They did not fit. Hence the metaphysicality of Laforgue reaches in two directions: the intellectualising of the feeling and the emotionalising of the idea. Where they meet, they come into conflict, and Laforgue's irony, an irony always employed against himself, ensues" (*VMP*, 212–13, Eliot's emphasis). Like Laforgue, the Eliot of "Prufrock" encountered a resounding clash between his thought and his feeling. The failure of inherited systems of thought, especially in the areas of morality and religion, to arouse the required emotions in him, compounded the lack of accommodation in those inherited systems for the emotions and feelings that he did experience, no doubt intensely. The result was Eliot's early interest in Laforguian *dédoublement*. Self-division became his subject.

Resuming the comparison of "Prufrock" and "The Wednesday Club," I would note that, after the parallels "retreat"/"retreats" and "follow"/"follow," there is another close likeness between the poems in the words "leads" and "lead." Where the Wednesday Club "leads" in its "action," the "argument" of "Prufrock" is said to "lead" to an unspecified "overwhelming question." Though Prufrock's "argument" and his "question" remain as vague as their setting, a clue for tracking his movement of thought is provided by the systematically inverse parallels with "The Wednesday Club." Charlotte Eliot in effect admonishes: "Do not retreat, follow your conscience, we shall lead together in our action." Prufrock may be said to mutter: "Let us retreat, a tedious argument will follow automatically, and it will lead to self-division."

An early Eliot manuscript throws considerable light on "the overwhelming question" and the origins of "The Love Song of J. Alfred Prufrock." It is an untitled fragment of twenty-two lines beginning "Of those ideas in his head," which survives on a small sheet of white stationery inserted into Eliot's Gloucester notebook, between leaf 51, "Morning at the Window," and leaf 52, "The Little Passion From 'An Agony in the Garret.'"[19] The narrator of this curious poem describes the ordeal of a deranged *flâneur* who hallucinates his way through the streets of an unnamed city. Though the narrator is skeptical about "those ideas" in the other man's head, he is implicated in the other's urban wanderings; the two share in the febrile experience that the poem depicts.

The handwriting of the manuscript is the elongated and spiky "Paris hand" of 1910–1911 (Eliot changed his handwriting dramatically during his year abroad),[20] whereas "The Little Passion From 'An Agony in the Garret,'" like "Morning at the Window" (composed in England in 1914), is drafted in the rounded, more fluid, post-Paris hand. Citing as support the datable handwriting, I want to propose that "Of those ideas in his head" belongs to the early draft material of "The Love Song of J. Alfred Prufrock." It is likely that the parallels between Eliot's and his mother's uses of "retreat," "follow," and "lead" first occurred here: the words are closely arranged and, with one repetition, in the same order as in "The Wednesday Club" and "The Love Song of J. Alfred Prufrock." Yet my main interest in this draft stems from a point of difference: in it the city wanderings lead to an "inevitable cross/ Whereon our souls are spread, and bleed" (*IMH*, 57), and not an "overwhelming question." I interpret this "cross" as evidence that, consciously or unconsciously, Eliot in "Prufrock" was responding to his mother's argument for self-sacrifice, an argument for surrendering one's private desires on behalf of a great Christian ideal. Of course, an argument for self-sacrifice need not be understood in terms of crucifixion, but, like his mother, Eliot makes prominent use of the sacrificial themes of crucifixion and martyrdom in his writing.

The "overwhelming question" belongs to a work that is everywhere porous to ambiguity. Arising twice (lines 10 and 93), it accrues an aura of sublime mystery, despite Prufrock's inconsequence. Comparison of the poem with "Of those ideas in his head" and "The Wednesday Club" tells us something of what Eliot meant by his "question," however, and thus gives entry to the American background of the poem. Whatever its larger import, the "overwhelming question" subsumes a crisis of conscience and identity. It may be said to signify the pivotal debate on which the poem's opening hinges. When he wrote "Prufrock," the poet T. S. Eliot, in some sense the Prufrockian "I," registered his resistance to the sacrifice of European poetry and culture on which his identity as an American Eliot, conversely the Prufrockian "you," was contingent. Put another way, he turned his back on a family obligation, voiced by "The Wednesday Club," to unite his private and public identities.

A prophetic sense of American history, a national mission, imbues American Puritanism. Clergymen's households have been especially receptive to this missionary heritage and, as I have been arguing, T. S. Eliot's family was no exception. Rebelling against his heritage, Eliot takes wry aim at all things churchly in "The Love Song of J. Alfred Prufrock." The allusion to John the Baptist, set within a sequence of comic rhymes, illustrates the poet's irreverent approach to this category of symbols and idioms:

> Should I, after tea and cakes and ices,
> Have the strength to force the moment to its crisis?
> But though I have wept and fasted, wept and prayed,
> Though I have seen my head (grown slightly bald) brought in
> upon a platter,
> I am no prophet—and here's no great matter;

I have seen the moment of my greatness flicker,
And I have seen the eternal Footman hold my coat, and snicker,
And in short, I was afraid.
  ("Prufrock" 79–86)

Commentators have cited Laforgue's *Salomé*, from the *Moralités légen-daires*, as a source for Prufrock's "head . . . brought in upon a platter." In his elaborate portrayal of Salome, Laforgue burlesques the femme fatale of nineteenth-century European painting and literature, including other depictions of Salome herself.[21] Iaokanann, an updated John the Baptist, takes her virginity and must pay with his head. Besides the traditional motif of decapitation, Eliot seems to have adopted Laforgue's idea of a modernized treatment of the biblical tale.

The religious and literary culture of New England provides a context for Prufrock's allusion to John the Baptist that has not been considered by critics. According to Bercovitch, the "figural use of John the Baptist is a character-istic of the New England pulpit, and part of the Puritan legacy to Ameri-can rhetoric." Bercovitch cites Danforth, Thomas Hooker, Edward Johnson, Increase Mather, and Jonathan Edwards as examples of Puritan writers who interpreted John as a typological forerunner of their own mission to prepare the way for Christ in the American wilderness. By the nineteenth century, the figure of John the Baptist prophesying to Americans had become a famil-iar sight to readers in New England. Nationalized versions of the prophet appeared in the prose of Emerson and Horace Bushnell.[22] Additional research shows that poets William Cullen Bryant, John Greenleaf Whittier, and James Russell Lowell treated John as a symbol of either national or Puritan mission in "The Prairies," "The Preacher," and "An Interview with Miles Standish" respectively.

Charlotte Eliot also wrote in this tradition. Among the miscellaneous poems that survive in a scrapbook in Harvard's Eliot Collection is one enti-tled "God's Kingdom Is at Hand. Repent!" Published in the *Christian Regis-ter*, a Unitarian weekly, the poem says a good deal about the clerical ethos of the Eliot family:

His voice was heard in wild Judaea,—
  A voice of gladness and lament.
He cried in accents strong and clear:
  "God's kingdom is at hand. Repent!"

That voice still echoing remains.
  We listen, startled and attent;

We grasp our treasures, count our gains:
"God's kingdom is at hand. Repent!"[23]

Charlotte's poem helps confirm the ubiquity of John the Baptist as a symbol of the prophetic and missionary ideals of late-Puritan culture; Eliot's background was such that he would have known this symbol.

From Eliot's perspective the figure of John the Baptist prophesying was very probably a cliché, a tenuous link to Puritan traditions that were becoming part of the dead past. George Santayana, who taught Eliot at Harvard, had enjoyed a sally at the expense of Puritan cultural and literary traditions by having a fictional undergraduate describe Whitman as "the voice of nature crying in the wilderness of convention" (cf. Matt. 3:3).[24] Applying Laforgue's example, Eliot outdid his teacher in the sheer force of his iconoclasm: the *Moralités légendaires* had presented the Baptist in an aspect ripe with expressive possibilities for a disaffected late-Puritan writer circa 1910. In "The Love Song of J. Alfred Prufrock" the prophet no longer prophesies in the American wilderness; instead he is silenced and somewhat comically disfigured. With the image of Prufrock's "head ... brought in upon a platter," Eliot disrupted a long tradition of American Puritan iconography, and implicitly repudiated a legacy of mission and prophetic calling that survived within his immediate family.

A second element in the passage, which immediately precedes the reference to John the Baptist, elucidates the depth of the poem's engagement with American Puritanism. Prufrock's self-portrait of weeping, prayer, and fasting (line 81) recalls the ritual day of humiliation that Puritan New England had formerly observed in response to social disaster. The Fast Day, the last vestige of the day of humiliation, was not officially abolished in Massachusetts until 1894. A book published in Boston in 1895, W. Love's *The Fast and Thanksgiving Days of New England*, underscores Eliot's connection to the Puritan tradition of fasts by citing the Reverend Andrew Eliot's "A Sermon Preached on the Publick Fast."[25] Like the allusion to John the Baptist, Prufrock's fasting bespeaks an intimate knowledge of the sermonical traditions of New England, and registers the breakdown of those traditions.

Much of the poem's skewed sermonizing is directed by the author at his own heritage. In the following passage, Prufrock's parody of the biblical "Preacher" in Ecclesiastes[26] evokes both a missing narrative of history and its homiletic expression, an attempt to reclaim a sense of "purpose under heaven" (Eccles. 3:1). Freed from history, wholly subjective, time has no end for a man with no mission:

And indeed there will be time
For the yellow smoke that slides along the street

Rubbing its back upon the window-panes;
There will be time, there will be time
To prepare a face to meet the faces that you meet;
There will be time to murder and create,
And time for all the works and days of hands
That lift and drop a question on your plate;
Time for you and time for me,
And time yet for a hundred indecisions,
And for a hundred visions and revisions,
Before the taking of a toast and tea.
    ("Prufrock" 23–34)

A mock preacher celebrating a Eucharist of "toast and tea,"[27] Prufrock lampoons the biblical idiom with sonorous but empty phrases of murder and creation. Eliot is suggesting that the American Puritan errand, the legacy of theocratic preachers, has failed to find present-day continuators: "all the works and days of hands / That lift and drop a question on your plate" implies a momentous inheritance of others' time and labor that, in the trivial setting of genteel society, can no longer inspire a spirit of self-sacrifice. The situation has its devilish side for the poet, who found his epigraph in Dante's *Inferno*. In the persona of Prufrock, Eliot cannot in good conscience accept the solace of aesthetic pleasure: to escape, self-indulgently, into the subjective time of the poem, the vehicle of his wordplay and imagery, is to insinuate the loss of a redemptive history that it is his duty to fulfill.

A brief comparison with some English poets helps set off Prufrock's connection to New England. It may surely be said that Tennyson admitted guilt, that he felt uneasy about the isolation of the poet from his community and about his absorption in aesthetics, but "all the works of days and hands / That lift and drop a question on your plate" expresses (leaving matters of imagery aside) something distinctly un-Tennysonian: it collapses private into public identity through a ritualized act of ingestion—the figure of the Eucharist persisting in the background. In Tennyson, as is the case with Browning, Arnold, and Swinburne, the poet may laud or criticize his country, but his perspective and England's are not identical. In "The Love Song of J. Alfred Prufrock" (and throughout Eliot's oeuvre), there is a pressure, sermonical in origin, to unify private identity and public history. By inventing a persona, Eliot dramatizes this relation of private and public, and ensures that Prufrock confront the structures of thought and feeling prescribed by the national mission.

A key difference between English and American poetry emerges in the Divinity School Address, where Emerson remarks: "None assayeth the stern ambition to be the Self of the nation, and of nature, but each would be an easy secondary to some Christian scheme, or sectarian connection, or some eminent man" (*Works*, 1:145). On the union of nature and humanity, Coleridge had written, "[Nature] is not only coherent but identical, and one and the same with our own self-consciousness." On the subject of originality, Wordsworth, crowning the eighteenth-century reception of Longinus, had argued, "Every author, as far as he is great and at the same time *original*, has the task of *creating* the taste by which he is to be enjoyed...."[28] Emerson built on Coleridge in extending the union of self and nature to include the nation, and resembled Wordsworth in arguing the greatness and originality of his cause.

Emerson told his audience at Harvard that the self should strive to become the embodiment of a nation where humanity would realize the full potential of nature. He had found a way of reclaiming the old American Puritan sense of duty in terms that were consonant with the age of Wordsworth and Coleridge. The point becomes clearer when we observe the resemblance of Emerson's threefold union to Trinitarianism, with nature as a version of God, the self as Divine Son, and the nation as Holy Spirit. The Harvard address invites this comparison, with Emerson urging his hearers: "Yourself a new-born bard of the Holy Ghost,—cast behind you all conformity, and acquaint men at first hand with Deity" (*Works*, 1:146). The means of contact between self and community, as between prophet and nation, would be spirit.

Though Emerson was in fact ringing the death knell of Puritanism in America, he was also seeking to transform, so as to renew, the spiritual intensity of his Puritan ancestors.[29] Governor Winthrop's vision of a "city upon a hill" survives in the Divinity School Address as a spiritual inheritance. Whether or not we read Emerson as a social progressive, his impulse to unite the self with an idealized America is quite strong. However mechanically, however pathetically, this impulse survives in the Eliot of "Prufrock," and connects him to Emerson and the American Puritan sermonical tradition.

Neither Tennyson nor Browning respond to this kind of social pressure in their uses of the dramatic monologue. To be sure, they are often preoccupied with conflicts between the aesthetic and the ethical; but they perfect their art in better conscience. Eliot, to use a Prufrockian word, "malingers" with the aesthetic. Tennyson gives us song after song in *Maud*, form after form. English history waits patiently before entering at the end of his poem. Prufrock's litany of time is an expression of nervousness that betrays anxiety and guilt about the elision of redemptive history. In large measure, Prufrock is Eliot trying to abandon the mission of his ancestors. His "plate," like the "platter" on which his head appears, was fired in Boston.

In a letter written in 1914 to his cousin Eleanor Hinkley, Eliot returns to the theme of his family's missionary heritage. Scripting various "brilliants" for his cousin's amusement, he describes a "Thanksgiving Day sermon": "'And what are we, the young men of America, doing to help build the city of God?' ... (Silence, followed by heavy breathing)" (*LTSE*, 73). The sense of bathos, of an overwhelming task that dwarfs the would-be heroes, recalls the terminal inadequacy of Prufrock. Like the letter to Eleanor Hinkley, "The Love Song of J. Alfred Prufrock" represents Eliot's reaction against a legacy at once too demanding and too futile to be renewed.

When one considers the depth of Eliot's rebellion against his familial inheritance, it is unsurprising that he felt stymied as a poet during the years immediately following "Prufrock": he had little idea how to develop because he had so utterly rejected his history and its resources. After a number of false starts, his career as a poet would resume in a more rigorous and thorough renunciation of New England and America. He would proceed from reaction to reaction.

NOTES

1. Not that their leaders were narrow in their learning: they brought to New England a rich tradition, in theology, psychology, logic, and rhetoric, which, according to Perry Miller, "incorporated the learning of Humanism and the erudition of Renaissance Protestantism" (Perry Miller, *The New England Mind: From Colony to Province*, 14).

2. My source is Matthiessen, *Achievement*, xix.

3. Miller, *New England Mind*, 21–22.

4. Perry Miller, *Errand into the Wilderness*, 8–9.

5. Sacvan Bercovitch, *The American Jeremiad*, xi.

6. Charlotte Eliot, *William Greenleaf Eliot*, v (in return, T. S. Eliot would dedicate *For Lancelot Andrewes* to her). William Deiss, "William Greenleaf Eliot: The Formative Years (1811–1834)," 15. Ralph Waldo Emerson, *The Letters of Ralph Waldo Emerson*, 4:338.

7. See Eliot's letter to Brooks (August 9, 1920), in *LTSE*, 397. Van Wyck Brooks, *The Wine of the Puritans*, 5.

8. Eliot, review of *The Wine of the Puritans*, 80; quoted in Eric Sigg, *The American T. S. Eliot: A Study of the Early Writings*, 149.

9. For T. S. Eliot's critique of the educational policies and liberal reforms of Charles William Eliot, see Herbert Howarth's invaluable *Notes on Some Figures behind T. S. Eliot*, 86–89.

10. T. S. Eliot, "The Preacher as Artist."

11. I am indebted to Sigg, *American T. S. Eliot*, 252 n.

12. Miller described *The Waste Land* as "pos[ing] all the religious questions anew ... in [a] tremendous revival sermon" (Perry Miller, *Nature's Nation*, 282). In a thoughtful article, Robert Abboud distinguishes between the American and the English jeremiad, and defines "Gerontion" and *The Waste Land* as returning "to a more traditional, European-type jeremiad," although Eliot is responding to "a long tradition of American jeremiads" (Robert Abboud, "Jeremiah's Mad Again").

13. See Ackroyd, *T. S. Eliot*, 19–20; Lyndall Gordon, *Eliot's Early Years*, 4–6; and Herbert Howarth, *Notes*, 22–35, and "Charlotte Champe Stearns Eliot."

14. The graduation poem is untitled. In the thirteenth section Eliot apostrophizes Smith Academy: "And let thy motto be, proud and serene, / Still as the years pass by, the word 'Progress!'" ("[At Graduation 1905]," *PWEY* 17). The poem, which begins with a conceit of "colonists embarking," represents the late-Puritan heritage and progressivist ethos that Eliot would soon resist.

15. Charlotte Eliot, "The Wednesday Club." Howarth quotes from the poem in *Notes*, 24. Though there is no date on the typescript, the work dates itself. "The twentieth century dawns . . ."

16. As I've suggested in Chapter 1, Eliot's reading of Poe abetted and complicated this process.

17. "These are the days when women must be wise / And crown their effort with self-sacrifice" (Charlotte Eliot, "The Wednesday Club").

18. T. S. Eliot, "A Commentary" (April 1933), 469. I would question the interpretation of *dédoublement* given by the learned Eliot scholar, A. D. Moody, insofar as he suggests that Prufrock succumbs to, while Eliot overcomes, this psychic split: "By a *dédoublement* of personality . . . the poet assumes a double presence, being at once the actor and the consciousness of his action. Moreover, as his consciousness develops in the poem, it alters from detached observer to an active, directing will. Thus he does not yield to his fate, as Prufrock does, but deliberately orders his feeling according to his vision. This is a love song in which the love and the poetry become a form of moral life" (A. David Moody, *Thomas Stearns Eliot, Poet*, 38). Moody finds that Eliot is both the actor, Prufrock, and the consciousness of his action; as the poet's apperception expresses itself or achieves form, it too becomes an actor, with the result that, from the author's standpoint, the initial *dédoublement* is healed by the creative will. I would suggest that, from the opening line to the final moment of drowning, Eliot's own self-division is the occasion of Prufrock's monologue.

19. T. S. Eliot, "The Little Passion From 'An Agony in the Garret'" (*IMH*, 57). In his masterly edition of Eliot's *Inventions of the March Hare: Poems, 1909–1917*, Christopher Ricks uses this title for both poems; but as he notes, this second poem (ii) is untitled, "in pencil on a separate sheet laid in" (*IMH*, 58). He does not date either poem.

After the Berg Collection of the New York Public Library acquired Eliot's early manuscripts from the heir of John Quinn, the New York lawyer and patron of the arts, a curator transferred the poem into the notebook from a miscellany of twenty-nine "loose leaves." I infer that the library transferred "Of those ideas in his head" into the notebook because "The Little Passion from 'An Agony in the Garret'" is a revision of its middle strophes. For the history of the notebook and the "loose leaves," see Donald Gallup, "The 'Lost' Manuscripts of T. S. Eliot"; and *IMH*, xi–xviii. I follow Ricks in his reading: "Of those ideas in his head"; Gallup has "Of these ideas. . . ."

20. See Gordon, *Eliot's Early Years*, 43; and John T. Mayer, *T. S. Eliot's Silent Voices*, 41.

21. See Mario Praz, *The Romantic Agony*, 291–303.

22. Bercovitch, *American Jeremiad*, 14 (quote), 11–16.

23. Charlotte Eliot, "God's Kingdom Is at Hand. Repent!" stanzas 1 and 3. The rhyme of "Judaea" and "clear" demonstrates that Charlotte's own accents were "strong and clear" and of New England; young Tom Eliot spoke with a Missouri drawl.

24. George Santayana, *George Santayana's America*, 99; originally published in "Walt Whitman: A Dialogue," in the *Harvard Monthly* of May 1890.

25. W. DeLoss Love Jr., *The Fast and Thanksgiving Days of New England*, 534.

26. Kenner observes the biblical echo in *Invisible Poet*, 12.

27. Compare "White flannel ceremonial / With cakes and tea'" in "Goldfish (Essence of Summer Magazines)" (*IMH*, 28). Eliot would remark that his parents took part in the monthly Unitarian communion but did not see to it that he did so (T S. Eliot to William Force Stead, February 2, 1927).

28. Samuel Taylor Coleridge, *Collected Works of Samuel Taylor Coleridge*, 71:260. William Wordsworth, *Wordsworth's Literary Criticism*, 210.

29. Compare the recent Emerson biography, by Robert D. Richardson Jr., who says that Emerson, in an unpublished 1842 lecture, "traced the New England character back to Puritan times, remarking . . . that the religious aspirations of the seventeenth century are 'the most creative energy in our experience'" (Robert D. Richardson Jr., *Emerson: The Mind on Fire*, 385).

DENIS DONOGHUE

Beginning

I

I can't remember when I first read "Prufrock" (as I'll call it for short). It wasn't at school, I'm sure of that. I was born in Tullow, a small town fifty miles southwest of Dublin, but I grew up in Warrenpoint, a town not much larger, in County Down, just across the border into Northern Ireland. For secondary education I attended the Christian Brothers' School in Newry, five miles away. The Brothers, as we called them, were and still are an order dedicated to giving lower-middle-class Irish Catholic boys a working education, nothing fancy, elaborate, or expensive. For English literature we had anthologies of stories, plays, poems, and essays. I recall with something approaching satisfaction *The Poet's Company*, an anthology predicated on the lighter Yeats as an introduction to music might have been predicated on the lighter Elgar. I don't think we were ever told what literature was or how we might know a literary work when we saw one. A poem could be recognized by the fact that its words stopped short of the margin and each line began with a capital letter. I grew up thinking that poetry must be intimate with "the blue and the dim and the dark cloths / Of night and light and the half-light." The only alternative to early Yeatsian pathos was rollicking verse, preferably in anapestic tetrameters, easy to memorize. I can still recite the first stanzas of Byron's "The Destruction of Sennacherib," a featured poem in *The Poet's Company*:

From *Southern Review* 34, no. 3 (1998): 532–49. Copyright © 1998 by Denis Donoghue.

The Assyrian came down like the wolf on the fold,
And his cohorts were gleaming in purple and gold;
And the sheen of their spears was like stars on the sea,
When the blue wave rolls nightly on deep Galilee.
Like the leaves of the forest when Summer is green,
That host with their banners at sunset were seen:
Like the leaves of the forest when Autumn hath blown,
That host on the morrow lay wither'd and strown.

"Strown" was hard to deal with. Our English teacher, Brother Cotter, allowed us to turn it toward "strewn." Reciting the poem in class, I introduced for effect a pause—which I did not know enough to think of as rhetorical—between "deep" and "Galilee."

The Poet's Company did not include any of Eliot. I suppose he was still regarded as foreign, difficult, and vaguely unpleasant. He didn't come into the reckoning till I went to university in Dublin. It is my impression, trusting the lies of memory, that I first read "Prufrock" in the National Library, Kildare Street, my home-from-home. I knew it was a different kind of verse from Yeats's or Byron's and that I would never forget it. My criterion for poetry at that time was necessarily simple: unforgettability. In default of knowing what poetry was, I settled for the experience of having a poem take possession of my mind. "The Destruction of Sennacherib" was easy to remember, but I had to decide to commit it to memory; it didn't seize my imagination. There was some satisfaction in reciting it with Assyrian speed, but nothing much remained. The choice poems took hold without any decision on my part. "Prufrock" was one such. At first reading it took up residence in my mind, and I've never changed my opinion of its achievement or doubted that Eliot is a major poet, distinctive and indelible.

I've often wondered about some poets I enjoy reading and much admire: why do their poems not lodge in my mind? Why do they become poems for me again and again, but only when I take up the books? Between readings, they sink into the vagueness of their reputation. I've read most of John Ashbery's poetry and reviewed several of his books, but I couldn't recite two lines of his work if my life depended on it. When I go back to "Self-Portrait in a Convex Mirror," I assent to a cultivated voice as it leads me from one line to the next, but when I've finished the poem, nothing of the voice stays with me except a dim echo. If it is a superb poem—as I think it is—its quality is consistent with a culture that reads with the eye and keeps the ear idle. It presupposes the silent experience of journal or book. Someone recently wrote to *The New Yorker*, challenging readers of Jorie Graham's poetry to recite any four consecutive lines of it. I admire Graham's poems while I'm reading them, but I couldn't take up the challenge. A few years ago, when the BBC turned my memoir *Warrenpoint* into a television program, I had occasion to recite for the camera a stanza from a Seamus Heaney poem: it wasn't too difficult, but I had to work at it. To recite a passage of Eliot, Yeats, Stevens, Frost, Ransom, Lowell, Larkin, or Hecht, on the other hand, would hardly challenge me at all. Does this matter? If we think of poetry as memorable speech, it does.

"Prufrock" initially seemed to me a poem about one's dread of being no good, second-rate, a loser, victim of unemployable gifts. Later readings have made me think it is about spiritual panic, the mind whirling in a void, or the penury of one's being in the world. No one instructed me to think of the poem in relation to Alien Tate's assertion that "in Mr. Eliot puritan obligation withdraws into private conscience." Now that "Prufrock" seems to be the only Eliot poem young people in America read, I find that my undergraduate students at New York University take it as an uncanny description of themselves, their distress, their fear of making the wrong choices and ruining their lives. They don't see that Prufrock has already failed and is brooding in mock-epic terms on his failure. In Ireland, where in my time there were no choices and one was lucky to get a job of any kind, I was more likely to internalize the poem's theme and find Prufrock already defeated. There is an Irish film called *Eat the Peach*, directed by Peter Ormrod. Two pals, factory workers out of a job, build a Wall of Death in the dreary bogland of Westmeath or some such county and hope to make their fortune doing stunts with a motorbike. When I saw the film, I fancied that the young men were students of mine at University College, Dublin, and that I changed their lives by assigning "Prufrock." Eat the peach; or, as Americans say, Go for it.

Knowing no Italian, I could make nothing of the epigraph to *Prufrock and Other Observations* or the further one to "Prufrock." I'm still puzzled by the epigraph to the poem, but for different reasons. In *Inferno*, canto xxvii, Dante questions Guido da Montefeltro, confined in a single flame of punishment for having given false counsel to Pope Boniface. Guido answers Dante: "If I believed that my reply would be to someone who would return to earth, this flame would remain without further movement; but since no one has ever returned alive from this abyss, if what I hear is true, I answer you without fear of infamy." It's not clear what bearing this has on "Prufrock." In the "No! I am not Prince Hamlet" passage, Prufrock speaks of himself as if he were Polonius, but he doesn't confess to having given the king fraudulent advice. Perhaps the epigraph has him saying: I'll tell the whole truth, however humiliating it turns out to be. Or it may be Eliot's device to clear a space for himself, ridding the reader's mind of extraneous matter, all the more effectively because the epigraph is in a foreign language; or his way of insisting that what follows is a made poem, not what it might seem, a transcript of someone's monologue.

Eliot tended to link epigraphs to their poems by congruity or contradiction: either way, he enjoyed the latitude of keeping readers on their toes. I note, incidentally, that in his recording of the poem, he didn't include the epigraph; he started straight into "Let us go then . . ."

Like most of Eliot's early poems, "Prufrock" seems to have started as a bundle of unrelated fragments, bits of verse he wrote under the force of impulses amounting to inspiration and put aside till a certain loose affiliation among them might suggest a possible poem. Many years ago, when transcribing one of Yeats's notebooks for inclusion in his *Memoirs*, I was shocked to find that he started a poem by sketching the argument in a sentence or two. He then picked a word here or there, jotted down its nearest rhymes, and set about turning the prose into verse. A rudimentary argument plus "colt," "dolt," "jolt," and "bolt" turned into "The Fascination of What's Difficult." It seemed a scandalously mechanical method, not difficult enough, though I recognized that in the process of revision his genius asserted itself, as it did in giving him the uncannily apt word "indignant" in "The Second Coming." But Eliot's method was much more bizarre. In the early poems he didn't start with a theme or subject. By his account, what came first was a shard of rhythm, a motif he felt impelled to stabilize in a few words. Those words might suggest a few more—or might not—and the fragments would be set aside. Sometimes he failed to find a future for them; but on happier days, he would put one piece beside another and stir some energy or reverberation between them. "Prufrock," even at a relatively late stage, was called "Prufrock Among the Women" and included a different epigraph, from *Purgatorio*, canto xxvi, and a section of thirty-three lines called "Prufrock's Pervigilium." In its final form it includes three rows of dots, dividing one sequence from the next, as if to acknowledge their origin as fragments.

The first line is odd, though I had to read it many times to see *how* odd. Who is speaking? J. Alfred Prufrock, presumably. But who is he? Hugh Kenner calls him a name plus a voice: "He isn't a 'character' cut out of the rest of the universe and equipped with a history and a little necessary context. . . . He is, once more, the name of a possible zone of consciousness where the materials with which he is credited with being aware can co-exist." Surely he's more than that. But Kenner is right in maintaining that Prufrock isn't the man next door or a character let loose from a novel. We are not to think of him as someone who exists, as we fancy that Leopold Bloom and Stephen Dedalus exist, before and after the novel in which they appear. Prufrock begins and ends with what he says: if he seems to extend beyond, it is because his words do, moving out from their context in Eliot's *Collected Poems*. But the words don't repose upon an implied character or a personage. Who on earth would say to his friend, "Let us go then, you and I"? But Prufrock isn't quite on earth, nor is he quite "he." The problem is that Eliot's language here, and in the early poems generally, refers to things and simultaneously works free from the reference. He seems always to be saying, "That is not what I meant; that is not it at all."

Let us agree that Prufrock and his friend set out on a foggy evening in October to visit an important lady-friend. Prufrock may make a proposal, or he may postpone it:

> The yellow fog that rubs its back upon the window-panes,
> The yellow smoke that rubs its muzzle on the window-panes,
> Licked its tongue into the corners of the evening,
> Lingered upon the pools that stand in drains,
> Let fall upon its back the soot that falls from chimneys,
> Slipped by the terrace, made a sudden leap,
> And seeing that it was a soft October night,
> Curled once about the house, and fell asleep.

Two present-tense verbs—the same word, "rubs"—yield to a sequence of verbs in the past tense—"Licked . . . Lingered . . . Let fall . . . Slipped . . . made . . . and fell asleep." But the relation of the language to its ostensible referents is equivocal. The lines do not say that the fog and smoke were like a cat. Nor do they quite describe a city under fog. The scene belongs to and inheres in Prufrock's state of mind; the apparently objective manifestations bring that scene forth, but do not establish it as independent of Prufrock. There is no commitment to externality or to stability of reference. The plural nouns—"corners . . . pools . . . drains"—generalize the impression and release the language from the mundane duty of attaching to something in particular: no specific corner, pool, or drain is intended. Cat and fog do not hold their places, as they would if a definite relation between them were in view. The verbs—"made a sudden leap" and "curled"—point to a cat, but "Licked its tongue into the corners of the evening" is more fog than cat. The effect is to keep the reader among the words and their internal relations, as if the apparent local meanings were an unfortunate but necessary distraction, a gesture toward an outside world that had to be placated, short of being granted its independence. We are not allowed to escape from the words into a coagulated sense of them.

There is also a minor difficulty with "you." Eliot told Kristian Smidt that the "you" is "merely some friend or companion, presumably of the male sex, whom the speaker is at that moment addressing, and that it has no emotional content whatever." But in a 1962 interview he said that Prufrock was a man of about forty, and in part himself, and that he was using the theory of the split personality. This is a better hint, especially as it allows us to take the "you" as a deeper, second self—as in Conrad's "The Secret Sharer"—fulfilling another mode of being, admonitory though silent. It is typical of Eliot to exert critical pressure on the matter in hand by establishing another perspective. But some of the invocations to "you" are perfunctory; they hardly mean more than "one." It is difficult to believe that the "we" at the end, "We have lingered . . . ," includes more than Prufrock's sole self. I take it as a last flourish of the plural of majesty before the drowning.

When I first read the poem, I winced at "etherised." No one was etherized in a poem by Yeats. I didn't know Jules Laforgue's "Jeux"—"Morte? Se peut-il pas qu'elle dorme / Grise de cosmiques chloroformes?" I had only the vaguest notion of Eliot's being an American Baudelaire, determined to make poetry out of distinctively modern experience, good, bad, indifferent; willing to live on his nerves. I didn't appreciate that the new literature Eliot and Baudelaire exemplify is an affair of cities—London, Paris, Dublin, Prague— and that the friction, the crowds, and the desolate charm of urban life are its chief provocations. I knew nothing of Eliot's debts to Dante, Baudelaire, Dostoevsky, Laforgue, Apollinaire, André Salmon. Théophile Gautier, Tristan Corbière, and a hundred other writers. Nor did I see that Eliot's procedure in "Prufrock" is to refute Wordsworth. If Romanticism was—as F. W. Bateson called it—the shortest way out of Manchester, Eliot's early poems send the poor pilgrim back to Manchester. Instead of celebrating a spousal relation between people and the landscapes of their lives, Eliot sets figures adrift in a modern city and makes them inhabit the confused exchange of energy between inanimate and animate states. Instead of taking human feeling for granted, he shows it dispersed as if promiscuously between people and the streets through which they move. In "Prufrock" we read of the *muttering* retreats of restless nights, of streets that *follow* like a tedious argument, of a fog that *rubs its back*, smoke that *rubs its muzzle*, eyes that *fix* you in a formulated phrase, arms that *wrap* about a shawl, mermaids *combing* the white *hair* of the waves blown back. The transfer of feeling from scene to agent is most complete in the following lines:

And the afternoon, the evening, sleeps so peacefully!
Smoothed by long fingers,
Asleep . . . tired . . . or it malingers,
Stretched on the floor, here beside you and me.

The effect is to remove the sentient privilege from human beings, or to show the desperate intensity with which we project our little grammars and dictions upon an objective life that is, so far as we know, indifferent to our yearnings. Isn't it pathetic to see Prufrock's mind lavished on such puny epiphanies?

For the moment, I'm concerned to note the poem's pervasive cadence, a tentative afflatus followed by inevitable collapse: these strivings rise, shine, evaporate, and fall. "All" is their leitmotif, as prevalent here as in *Paradise Lost*—"For I have known them all already, known them all." The rhythm of rise-and-fall begins with the rhyme of "streets" and "retreats" and the repetition of "Streets"—

> Streets that follow like a tedious argument
> Of insidious intent
> To lead you to an overwhelming question . . .
> Oh, do not ask, "What is it?"
> Let us go and make our visit.

The most complete fall comes when Prufrock's language breaks down—"It is impossible to say just what I mean!"—and the next sentence barely gets to its feet with the helpless, "But as if a magic lantern . . ." Again, this:

> Should I, after tea and cakes and ices,
> Have the strength to force the moment to its crisis?
> But though I have wept and fasted, wept and prayed,
> Though I have seen my head (grown slightly bald) brought in
> upon a platter,
> I am no prophet—and here's no great matter;
> I have seen the moment of my greatness flicker,
> And I have seen the eternal Footman hold my coat, and snicker,
> And in short, I was afraid.

"Should I?" joins other vain questionings: "'Do I dare?' and, 'Do I dare?'"; "Do I dare / Disturb the universe?" "And should I then presume? / And how should I begin?" "Shall I part my hair behind?" The most heartbreaking of these is "Shall I say," as if saying or not saying made any difference. The verbal wondering collapses nearly as soon as it begins: "Shall I say, I have gone at dusk through narrow streets / And watched the smoke that rises from the pipes / Of lonely men in shirt-sleeves, leaning out of windows?"—and the feeling declines upon lowly, primordial certitude: "I should have been a pair of ragged claws / Scuttling across the floors of silent seas." That at least would have entailed an appropriate relation. But for the time being, the afflatus is permitted: associations with John the Baptist, Salome, and King Herod allow Prufrock to indulge himself in "the moment of my greatness"

before it flickers and dies in the unloving arms of Death, the eternal Footman. "And in short, I was afraid." "In short" retains a smidgen of dignity,
like Buster Keaton before he sinks, his body majestically upright, beneath
the waves. What is compelling in this passage is the force of rhythm, the
inevitably controlling cadence; not just the rise and fall but the getting up
again, such that the dying fall in "I am no prophet—and here's no great
matter" is followed at once by another heroically blustering lift of feeling—"I
have seen the moment of my greatness flicker, / And I have seen the eternal
Footman hold my coat." That second "And I have seen" mimes the futile but
not ignoble gesture of pulling oneself up, starting over. It is the hero cheer-
ing himself down, as R. P. Blackmur said.

The supreme afflatus comes at the end of the mermaid passage, which
begins as an astonishing change of reference:

> Shall I part my hair behind? Do I dare to eat a peach?
> I shall wear white flannel trousers, and walk upon the beach.
> I have heard the mermaids singing, each to each.
> I do not think that they will sing to me.
> I have seen them riding seaward on the waves
> Combing the white hair of the waves blown back
> When the wind blows the water white and black.
> We have lingered in the chambers of the sea
> By sea-girls wreathed with seaweed red and brown
> Till human voices wake us, and we drown.

In "Song," Donne gives a list of impossible achievements of knowledge and
power:

> Go and catch a falling star,
> Get with child a mandrake root,
> Tell me where all past years are,
> Or who cleft the Devil's foot,
> Teach me to hear mermaids singing,
> Or to keep off envy's stinging,
> And find
> What wind
> Serves to advance an honest mind.

But Donne doesn't ask that the mermaids sing to him, as Prufrock does.
Claiming to have achieved one impossibility, Prufrock rises to another and
asks that the singing be in his sole favor. No wonder the courage of his fancy

fails him. His description of the mermaids is a further claim to distinction, but it exhausts itself in the telling. This little Ulysses can't get back to Ithaca, and besides, no Penelope awaits him. In the first version of the poem, "sea-girls" was "seamaids." The change was an inspiration, making pathetically erotic the relation between the siren-singers and the love-singer of the poem in our hands.

There has been much discussion of the "overwhelming question," though many critics end up claiming there's no point asking what it is. They may be right, but I see no reason to assume that Prufrock doesn't know. His gesture of impatience need not be a device to conceal ignorance. William Empson once remarked that Hamlet keeps his secret by telling everyone that he has one. The comparison with Hamlet is worth pursuing, given that Prufrock glances at it. J. Peter Dyson has argued that since everything Prufrock aspires to appears in the poem as an echo of something else, the overwhelming question is an echo of Hamlet's: "To be or not to be, that is the question." He reads the relevant line as if Prufrock were saying: "No! I am not Prince Hamlet, nor was meant to be or not to be, *that* is the question." It's an attractive suggestion, but I wish Dyson had gone further with it. He thinks "Prufrock" is "a poem about the difficulties of realizing one's nebulous potentialities." It seems to me much more than that.

If Prufrock is a dying fall from Hamlet, we should ask what Eliot thought Hamlet's problem is. His 1919 essay is a confused account of the play, but it reveals a great deal about himself:

> Hamlet (the man) is dominated by an emotion which is inexpressible, because it is in *excess* of the facts as they appear. And the supposed identity of Hamlet with his author is genuine to this point: that Hamlet's bafflement at the absence of objective equivalent to his feelings is a prolongation of the bafflement of his creator in the face of his artistic problem. Hamlet is up against the difficulty that his disgust is occasioned by his mother, but that his mother is not an adequate equivalent for it; his disgust envelops and exceeds her.
>
> It is thus a feeling which he cannot understand; he cannot objectify it, and it therefore remains to poison life and obstruct action.

Hamlet's buffoonery—his levity, repetitions of phrase, and puns—is "the buffoonery of an emotion which can find no outlet in action." In more general terms,

> The intense feeling, ecstatic or terrible, without an object or exceeding its object, is something which every person of

sensibility has known; it is doubtless a subject of study for pathologists. It often occurs in adolescence: the ordinary person puts these feelings to sleep, or trims down his feelings to fit the business world; the artist keeps them alive by his ability to intensify the world to his emotions. The Hamlet of Laforgue is an adolescent; the Hamlet of Shakespeare is not, he has not that explanation and excuse. We must simply admit that here Shakespeare tackled a problem which proved too much for him. Why he attempted it at all is an insoluble puzzle; under compulsion of what experience he attempted to express the inexpressibly horrible, we cannot ever know.

I don't understand what Eliot intends by "intensify the world to his emotions." I suppose him to mean that artists work up their sense of the external world to the pitch of intensity at which it seems to justify their own passions, however violent. I don't know under what compulsion Eliot attempted to express, in "Prufrock," an emotion that could otherwise find no outlet in action. I can only say that Prufrock is Hamlet still further removed than in Shakespeare or Laforgue from the tolerable state of having found an "objective correlative" for his feelings. What corresponds to Hamlet's buffoonery is Prufrock's rhythm of rise-and-fall: it takes the form of self-regarding irony, dandyish repetitions of phrase, amplitudes of interrogation—"And would it have been worth it, after all"?

But it shouldn't be assumed that Prufrock's problem is merely the lack of a sustaining context, the fact that he comes into the world—to whatever extent I can say this without being fanciful—bereft of parents, wife, or children, without a station in life, indeed with only a few minor possessions and an oppressive desire that he can't express. Eliot's 1930 essay on Baudelaire warns us against thinking that Prufrock's predicament might be relieved by a course of treatment from a decent psychiatrist. In Baudelaire's "Le Balcon," we find "all the romantic idea, but something more: the reaching out towards something which cannot be had *in*, but which may be had partly *through*, personal relations."

Again resorting to general terms, Eliot writes: "Indeed, in much romantic poetry the sadness is due to the exploitation of the fact that no human relations are adequate to human desires, but also to the disbelief in any further object for human desires than that which, being human, fails to satisfy them." In the years between the essay on Hamlet and the essay on Baudelaire, Eliot had come to believe that the finding of an objective correlative for one's feelings is not enough, if that correlative is merely a human relation. After his formal embrace of Christianity, he could not have believed otherwise.

II

The practice of committing poems to memory is now rare, I gather, but while it lasted it had consequences good and bad. Among the good ones for me: it allowed me to take pleasure in the sway of syllables and rhythms, variations of tone, changes of inflection. I was willingly kept among the words. Only with difficult pieces like "Prufrock" was it necessary to ask what the poem was about or what was going on, and even there it was unnecessary to ask who was speaking: the words seemed to have an acoustic presence that need not be distinguished from their presence of mind. The merit of memorizing was that I didn't reduce the poem to the implied crux of the speaker and lose it there, supplanting the poem with the predicament. It may be thought that in what I've said about "Prufrock" I have come close to replacing the poem by Prufrock's predicament, as Eliot replaced *Hamlet* by its hero's problem. In earlier years, the risk I took was that I might find it easy to detach the words not only from an implied speaker but from their referents. "In the mountains, there you feel free": that line could become a tune in the head, endlessly evocative but evoking nothing in particular; it could be let loose from its provenance in *The Waste Land* and turned upon whatever mood in me elicited the words. Long before I read Walter Pater's *The Renaissance*, I thought that poetry must be in an intimate relation to music, and I was dismayed if I found a poem that was bound more deeply to journalism. Later on I was happy to believe in a theory of inspiration, however unfashionable such a model was. Especially when Eliot's poems were in question, I thought of the words as preceding or provoking the feelings that somehow emerged from their conjunctions. I felt he had recourse to writings in French, Italian, Sanskrit, Latin, and Greek not to learn how to write better but to force himself into the recognition of strange verbal combinations and therefore into the possession of corresponding feelings. He seemed to have found the words first and the feelings a split second later. Words were not, for him, the servants or vicars of his emotions or instruments for their delivery according to a theory of literature as communication. They were feelings already inscribed, it seemed, in pencil or invisible ink, and they might be changed later to satisfy some formal requirement; but they appeared to have come first, or at some opportune moment after the inaugurally compelling rhythm or motif. It was pointless to assume that certain feelings, silently established, preceded them and awaited with patience their expressive opportunity. In this respect, Eliot's sense of language differed from Yeats's. It was an enabling moment when Yeats engaged with Donne's poems—it gave him another range of tones—but I don't think he discovered new feelings in himself by finding the words for them in Donne. He read widely, but mainly to extend his field of reference and to find further adepts of the traditions—mainly the neo-Platonic—he valued. Eliot was a much more learned poet than Yeats, but he didn't read to get ideas or enlarge his intellectual fellowship; he read to make himself so familiar with ideas that he could become immune to their claims.

He had another reason for studying the poets. For many years it was common to say that Eliot was a cold, bloodless person. Bertrand Russell seems to have started this easy piece of lore, and Virginia Woolf sent it abroad through Bloomsbury. Michael Hastings's *Tom and Viv* is an extreme version of it. I can't speak to the issue with any authority. I met Eliot only once, by appointment, in his room at Faber & Faber, 24 Russell Square, London. The year was 1960 or '61. We began with desultory conversation about my domestic life: was I married, had I children, how many children?—"Ah yes, a Roman Catholic." Eliot then recalled with pleasure his first visit to Dublin—January 1936—to give a lecture at University College, to address the inaugural meeting of the College's English Literature Society, and to see the U.C.D. Dramatic Society perform *Murder in the Cathedral*: they did the Chorus, he said, better than the professional actors in London had. Then we turned to talk about George Herbert, on whom Eliot was writing an essay for the British Council. The meeting ended in his asking me to send him the essays on Herbert I'd alluded to—one by L. C. Knights in *Sewanee Review*, one by Kenneth Burke in *Accent*. Eliot said nothing especially memorable, except for the minor reflection upon my personal life. He was not cold, but he evidently saw no reason for being warm. Nevertheless, I am convinced that in early years he had been a man of exceptionally intense and probably dangerous feelings. He feared for his sanity, and had cause to. His public demeanor was palpably a mask to conceal the passions he lived in dread of. I see him as a character in a Dostoevsky novel.

If I am right, it follows that Eliot's theory of Impersonality, elucidated in "Tradition and the Individual Talent" and elsewhere, comes from acute personal need: "Poetry is not a turning loose of emotion, but an escape from emotion; it is not the expression of personality, but an escape from personality. But, of course, only those who have personality and emotions know what it means to want to escape from these things." I take those sentences literally, and wonder what part the reading and writing of poems played in Eliot's desired escape. In this context I've been puzzling over an early essay, the second of his "Reflections on Contemporary Poetry" (1917). One of his most detaining pieces, it begins innocently enough with a comparison between the poetry of Harold Monro and that of Jean de Bosschère (sometimes called de Boschère). "Both poets are concerned with this thesis," he wrote, "the intimacy of the relationship between a man and his personal property." But in Monro the man's utensils "are provided with adjectives which connect them with human emotions—'the gentle Bed,' 'the old impetuous Gas,' 'the independent Pencil,' 'you my well-trampled Boots.'" Eliot didn't advert to the fact that in his own poems—and notably in "Prufrock," as I have remarked—not the man's utensils but the constituents of his world (evening, streets, fog) are provided with adjectives that connect them with human emotions. In the "Reflections" he draws a contrast between Monro and de Bosschère, quoting "Homère Mare" to show that the latter makes no pretense "of a quasi-human relationship," and "never employs his thoughts and images in decorating ordinary human sentiments." I'll quote the first lines of the poem:

> Homère Mare habite sa maison de planches.
> La maison est attachée à la montagne comme le nez à la face
> abrupte.
> Sur la roche il plante des herbes alpines;
> Sur la terrasse, une vigne et des pavots.
> Il n'est pas un prophète ni un critique.
> Chaque matin il met lui-même le feu dans l'âtre.
> Tout le jour
> Il est l'époux du feu,
> L'aimé des flammes.

Eliot makes the point that neither "époux" nor "aimé" has "any sentimental associations." He continues:

> M. de Bosschère is in fact almost a pure intellectual; leaving, as if disdainfully, our emotions to form as they will around the situation which his brain has selected. The important thing is not how we are to feel about it, but how it is. De Bosschère's austerity is terrifying. A poet is not a pure intellectual by virtue of any amount of meditation or abstractness or moralizing; the abstract thought of nearly all poets is mediocre enough, and often second-hand. It is better to go to the "De Anima" than to the "Purgatorio" for a theory of the soul. A poet like M. de Bosschère is an intellectual by his obstinate refusal to adulterate his poetic emotions with human emotions. Instead of refining ordinary human emotion (and I do not mean tepid human emotion, but human however intense—in the crude living state) he aims direct at emotions of art. He thereby limits the number of his readers, and leaves the majority groping for a clue which does not exist. The effect is sometimes an intense frigidity which I find altogether admirable.

"Adulterate" is a forceful word: similar force is required to turn "frigidity" into a virtue. The difference between "ordinary human emotion" and "emotions of art" is hard to explain, but I'll try.

What Eliot admires in "Homère Mare" is the bold designation from which every trace of human feeling has been excised. It is as if de Bosschère drafted poems with the usual complement of adjectives and adverbs, only to remove those parts of speech in revision. The result is a sequence of nouns linked by the simplest grammar. Each noun is surrounded by a space through which conventionally human associations may not pass: it is a condition of its being retained that it has given up all yearning for the plenitude of domesticity. De Bosschère anticipates Robbe-Grillet and the Nouveau Roman. Homère travels, takes on the color of every place he visits. He is never himself and never feels the loss of himself:

> Pendant quatre saisons, Homère voyage
> Et dans chaque ville il est un autre personnage;
> Bleu sous le ciel bleu, gris à Londres,
> Recueilli à Paris, perverti à Rome
> Parmi l'ordre de la tombe des tombes.
> Byron dans les iîles, et Shakespeare encore
> Dans la poussière d'hommes de Rome
> Mais jamais il n'est Mare.

As for the difference between ordinary emotions and those of art, I can only suggest that words, in the poems Eliot cared for, had already come through; had escaped the claims of feeling to the extent of their achieved style. I am free to like or dislike de Bosschère's poems, but they are what they are; they are not evidence of their having failed to become something else. The intense frigidity that Eliot admired—and surely envied—is the force of their standing apart from the passions that might have been expected to lay a claim upon them. De Bosschère writes about the appurtenances of ordinary life—house, garden, hearth, travel—but he presents Hombre as a man who remains notionally intact by lending himself to whatever invitations come along: but his sensibility is only on loan. Meanwhile, no everyday human emotion is permitted to be importunate. Reading de Bosschère's poem, we feel the pressure of all the desires his Hombre has set aside so the nouns of his chosen life may stand out boldly and unassertively against those enticements. Surely this device would be even more necessary to sustain a life like the early Eliot's, beset on all sides by panic and fright.

III

"Lune de Miel" is the early poem in which Eliot has most completely resorted to this device. In that respect it prefigures his more systematic dealings with Gautier in "Burbank with a Baedeker: Bleistein with a Cigar" and the other quatrain-poems.

It is well known that Eliot wrote a few poems in French at a time when he was blocked in English. The foreign language released him from the oppression of his own. Few readers have taken the French verse seriously, though Eliot held it in enough esteem to include it in his *Collected Poems*. Usually, "Lune de Miel" has been read as a relatively crude satire on the triviality of modern tourism and sex. At first sight, and perhaps second, this interpretation seems reasonable. The poem and the quatrain-poems to which it points have something of the power of caricature that Eliot ascribed to Jonson, and even more of the tragic farce he found in the last act of Marlowe's *Jew of Malta*. Eliot's honeymooners are lodging for the night in a bug-ridden hotel in Ravenna before setting off for Padua, Milan, Switzerland, and France. Eliot's procedure appears to be what Kenneth Burke called "perspective by incongruity," a silent form of judgment by which incompatible images are brought to bear upon each other: the result is a judgment that includes them both. So we have the ironic relation between "les Pays-Bas" and "Terre Haute"; between the Last Supper in Milan and the cheap restaurant—"Où se trouvent la Cène, et un restaurant pas cher." We have, brought together in one line, "la sueur aestivale" and (rhyming with "Ravenne") "une forte odeur de chienne." The couple are reduced, dismembered, to backs and knees and "quatre jambes molles tout gonflées de morsures." Only a few miles outside Ravenna there is "Saint Apollinaire / En Classe, basilique connue des amateurs / De chapitaux d'acanthe que tournoie le vent." But the relation of the honeymooners to those lovers of acanthus capitals turned by the wind is a matter for interpretation: it need not operate entirely in favor of art historians and aesthetes. William Arrowsmith has noted that Eliot is alluding to a passage in *The Stones of Venice* where Ruskin writes of Byzantine sculptures and of "the leaves drifted, as it were, by a whirlwind round the capital by which they rise." But Eliot's allusion is complex: he recognizes Ruskin's splendor, but also the dismal sense in which he represents Christianity diminished to its aesthetic quality. He thinks of Ruskin as cousin to Arnold, who assumed he could retain of Christianity only its beauty, and yet be saved.

In the second stanza Eliot proceeds as if he were paying tribute to de Bosschère: "the important thing is not how we are to feel about it, but how it is." Not an adjective in sight:

Ils vont prendre le train de huit heures
Prolonger leurs misères de Padoue à Milan
Où se trouvent la Cène, et un restaurant pas cher.
Lui pense aux pourboires, et rédige son bilan.
Ils auront vu la Suisse et traversé la France.

But then, in a characteristically powerful change of tone, Eliot turns back
to Saint Apollinaire:

Et Saint Apollinaire, raide et ascétique,
Vieille usine désaffectée de Dieu, tient encore
Dans ses pierres écroulantes la forme précise de Byzance.

It is a flourish of the grand style. The force of feeling, accrued from the
earlier invocation to the church in Classe, is restrained in "raide et ascétique"
and the parenthetical "Vieille usine désaffectée de Dieu," then asserts itself
at the end of the line with "tient encore," is held back again by "Dans ses
pierres écroulantes," only to take command with "la forme précise de Byzance," rhyming authoritatively with "France." The perspective of judgment is
enforced by such incongruities that a reading of the poem as satire appears
irresistible: satire, caricature, farce, the readiest means by which escape from
ordinary emotions may be effected.

But Arrowsmith's interpretation must be reckoned with. Tender toward
the honeymooners, he sees them as pilgrims, unconsciously turning toward the
light of spiritual being. The bedbugs that plague them are brought into the same
poetic field as the bites, in Dante's *Paradiso*—"Tutti quei morsi"—that "have
power to make the heart turn to God." Instead of reading the juxtaposed details
as enforcing "perspective by incongruity," Arrowsmith takes them as intersecting
and therefore as making possible the striving of the Many toward the One:

Thus in Eliot a *restaurant pas cher* is the worldly counterpart of the
Last Supper; an ordinary cocktail party becomes a shadow play of
the Communion. . . . Reality for [the honeymooners] is just this
misery of sensual repetition; the ideality to which it unknowingly
aspires is represented by the saint's hard, conceptual rigor. But,
however diminished, that ideality—that unsatisfied craving for a
completeness beyond themselves—*inheres* in them just as the form
of the basilica still *holds* (*tient*) in the crumbling stones.

The point here, according to Arrowsmith, "isn't merely the desperate
opposition of lovers and saint, but the fusion implied by their opposition."

F. H. Bradley, on whose theory of knowledge and experience Eliot wrote his Harvard dissertation, is called upon for authority:

> Where a whole is complete in finite beings, which know themselves to be "elements" and members of its system, this *is* the consciousness in such individuals of their own completeness.... It is the self-realization of each member ... to be himself, he must go beyond himself, to live his own life he must live a life which is not *merely* his own, but which, none the less, on the contrary all the more, is intensely and emphatically his own individuality.

Hence the aspiration, which Arrowsmith ascribes to the honeymooners, toward the wholeness of spiritual unity, as if it were Christendom or the "mind of Europe," which according to Eliot's description has not superannuated Shakespeare, Homer, or the rock drawing of the Magdelenian draftsmen.

I wish I could find this reading of "Lune de Miel" convincing; it would be such a relief, after living so long with the image of those wretched honeymooners extending their misery from Padua to Milan. But Arrowsmith's interpretation seems applicable to "Ash-Wednesday" rather than to "Lune de Miel." For one thing, the couple do not know—are not allowed to know—that they are "elements" and members of a system. They are having a terrible wedding trip, which might have been improved had they been able to lodge in clean hotels. In 1917, Eliot was in the punitive stage of his talent, still exasperated by much he'd experienced as a tourist in Europe. After "Prufrock"—written in 1910–'11 and published in 1915—he seems to have felt compelled to engage new emotions, harsher than those of "Prufrock" and "Portrait of a Lady." He had to get the quatrains into his art before getting their cognate feelings out of his system for good. The good is in the tone of "Ash Wednesday" and the Ariel poems, especially "Marina."

IV

But meanwhile there was "Prufrock." In a lecture at the Library of Congress on January 23, 1956, R. P. Blackmur remarked that "the reason why 'Prufrock' is *now* a popular poem (though it was a very difficult poem for most people for its first twenty years of life) is that the analogies with which it is composed have had time to sink in." In my case it was not that the analogies had sunk in but that the tunes, the rhythms, had proved enchanting. They intuited not the world I otherwise inhabited but a possible other realm in which a dandy—self-possessed within the constraints of his nervous system—walked the streets attended by an overwhelming question. What

more beguiling fancy could I ask? Later I had trouble distinguishing him
from Baudelaire's Constantin Guys—except that Guys did something, drew,
painted—or from an irregular image of the dandy, close kin to Pater, Wilde,
Beardsley, and Nabokov, princes of the town, traveling *incognito* the while.
I saw him or his shadow everywhere. Listening to other poets reading their
work, I saw him slide into the back row and wait, departing without fuss
when the question period started: he had his own besetting question, and
there was no need of another. Surely he was at Stevens's reading when the
large red man read "Le Monocle de Mon Oncle" and committed himself to a
primitive desire: "I wish that I might be a thinking stone." A thinking stone
didn't strike me as nearly so resourceful as a pair of ragged claws scuttling
across the floors of silent seas. As if that were not enough, Stevens asked:
"Shall I uncrumple this much-crumpled thing?" I felt as Humbert Humbert
felt while he played tennis with Dolores in the pure air of Champion, Colo-
rado, and an inquisitive butterfly passed, dipping, between them.

RONALD BUSH

In Pursuit of Wilde Possum: Reflections on Eliot, Modernism, and the Nineties

Introduction: Eliot, Modernism, and the Nineties

One of the ongoing concerns of Eliot studies, at least since the 1980s, has been to explore the increasingly apparent "disparity," to quote Colleen Lamos, between the literary progenitors that Eliot acknowledged and the figures in Decadent England and America (principally Walter Pater, Charles Swinburne, Oscar Wilde, and Walt Whitman) whose influence he passively or actively "suppressed."[1] Nearly a hundred years after Eliot's emergence as a poet, we are only beginning to reconstitute his temperamental and intellectual connections with the generation that shaped his earliest verse.

Readers have turned most recently to examining the sexual politics underlying Eliot's reluctance to speak about his Decadent heritage, but not always in a way that does justice to the complex relations between life and art. Take the striking story of Eliot's secondary residence starting in 1923 in Burleigh Mansions on Charing Cross Road. According to Virginia Woolf, Clive Bell, and the Sitwells, Eliot took to wearing green face powder during private parties in the rooms—according to Osbert Sitwell, face powder "the colour of forced lily-of-the-valley."[2] Since the color green was a common emblem of the aesthetic movement—as for instance in Oscar Wilde's subtitle ("A Study in Green") to his sketch of the Pater-like author Wainewright in the essay "Pen, Pencil and Poison"—Eliot's makeup would seem to signify some kind of willful effort to identify himself with the culture of the nineties.[3] But must

From *Modernism/modernity* 11, no. 3 (September 2004): 469–85. © 2004 by the Johns Hopkins University Press.

we conclude with Carole Seymour-Jones in her recent biography of Vivien Eliot that the powder was in fact a statement of Eliot's sexual preference and that the Burleigh House pied-à-terre was a venue for homosexual assignations—"the hub of [Eliot's] secret life"?[4] Seymour-Jones, after all, offers no evidence beyond the face powder, and Peter Ackroyd, who first discovered Sitwell's memoir, argues that the powder was merely a gesture of solidarity with Eliot's artist friends. ("It is significant that the only people who noticed his make-up, and probably the only ones in whose company he wore it, were writers and artists ... wearing face powder made him look more modern, more interesting, a poet rather than a bank official."[5])

The public/private valence of Eliot's gesture, furthermore, is as unclear as its symbolism. Did Eliot intend the face powder as a public statement? Or, given the short-lived and private nature of the evenings, did it represent a half-censored rebellion against his own social reserve? The latter is more likely, as is the possibility that Eliot's relations to the 1890s were less a matter of conscious strategy—a willingness to "traffic in ... homoerotic rhetoric in a private context [but] not a public forum"—than the expression of a genuine and unresolved personal conflict.[6]

Since the 1980s, though, literary and cultural historians have glossed Eliot's relation to the 1890s by explicating his elaborately constructed prose style, with its plainspoken display of rational control, as the calculated censorship of a foresworn emotional expressivity. First Sandra Gilbert and Susan Gubar in 1988 explained Eliot's exaggerated rationality as a way of resisting the growing influence of literary women at the turn of the twentieth century. More recently, Cassandra Laity, Colleen Lamos, Ann Ardis, and others have contextualized it as a response to what Richard Dellamora has called the "crisis of sexual identity and male privilege" that started in the generation of Pater.[7] Most of this criticism assumes, in Ann Ardis's words, that Eliot evaded identification with the 1890s by a "deliberate erasure" (68), and Ardis herself specifies that Eliot's criticism deliberately transformed gendered discussions of self and poetry into a "highly abstract figuration" of literary genealogy (69).

This promising work, I think, needs to be qualified in several respects. As I have argued elsewhere, while it seems reasonable to argue that modernist poetics represents a gendered reaction to post-symbolism's emphasis on the poetry of the body, one should recognize that the definitive move in that reaction took the form not, as Ardis suggests, of a public turn against Decadent softness in art and life, but of the echoing consequences of imagism's instinctive and fundamental redefinition of rhythm and image as expressions of thought.[8] More pertinently here I would add that by overemphasizing Eliot's deliberate suppression of the 1890s, we blur not only the complexity of his response but the way the prose of the English Decadents also deployed masculine markers to hedge the issue of gender, and thus we further exaggerate the break between the Decadent and the modernist generations. In this perspective, Eliot's style only sustains his predecessor's ambivalence. In his own criticism, Wilde frequently employs the rhetoric of manliness to criticize literary Decadence, as he does in "The Rise of Historical Criticism," an essay steeped in the authority of reason and science. There Wilde dissociates himself specifically from "that refined effeminacy, that overstrained gracefulness of attitude" that infects "the sphere of history" in Euripides and Swinburne[9] and praises Polybius by noting that "perhaps there is no passage in the whole of ancient and modern history which breathes such a manly and splendid spirit of rationalism" as Polybius's remarks on the decay of population (*CW*, 1226).

Is it possible that by overstating and then discounting the modernists' conscious dissociation from their predecessors, we may now in a strange way actually be replicating the modernist myth of a break from the 1890s rather than clarifying their genuinely conflicted relations with aestheticism? Eliot's residual emotional ties to the 1890s, I argue in part four of this essay, continued to be a source of discomfort and distress well into the years of his fame and maturity, and his account of the chasm between himself and Wilde's generation was a central instance of that distress.

Eliot and Wilde?

I begin by reexamining Eliot's relation to Oscar Wilde, whom Eliot specifically acknowledged as the leading figure of English Decadence. Without diminishing the temperamental differences between Eliot and Wilde or disregarding the differences between their attitudes toward nature, morality, and religion, I want to call attention to ways in which Eliot derived some of his most famous pronouncements from Wilde. I then wish to explore several insufficiently interrogated accounts in which Eliot fixed the origins of his own literary genealogy in the moment of Wilde's disappearance from the literary scene.

How much did Oscar Wilde mean to the young Eliot? Wilde was not, we may safely say, one of those "dead authors" with whom Eliot openly acknowledged a "profound kinship, or rather . . . a peculiar personal intimacy." ("The usefulness of such a passion is various. . . . We may not be great lovers; but if we had a genuine affair with a real poet of any degree we have acquired a monitor to avert us when we are not in love. . . . We do not imitate, we are changed; and our work is the work of the changed man; we have not borrowed, we have been quickened, and we become bearers of a tradition."[10]) Nor was he the kind of technical innovator who answers to Eliot's comment that besides the debts of "capital importance one has other debts, innumerable debts, to poets, of another kind. There are poets who have been at the back of one's mind, or perhaps consciously there, when one has had some particular problem to settle, for which something they have written suggests the method."[11]

Or are these things so very clear after all? It now seems difficult to read Eliot's just quoted remarks about art, love, and even "tradition" without noticing their Wildean erotics and their equally Wildean delight in paradox. Nor, as the work of Christopher Ricks, Ronald Schuchard, and Richard Shusterman has shown, can one completely dismiss the likelihood that, before his life-changing encounter with Jules Laforgue, Wilde and the 1890s had already impressed an indelible mark on the shaping of Eliot's early poetic self.

Certainly, Eliot as a young man was familiar with Wilde's work. A letter from his mother lists Wilde's "[The Ballad of] Reading Gaol" as one of the books he carefully stored away when he left St. Louis, and his own letter to Scofield Thayer recalls their time at Oxford together, when Thayer lived in Magdalen (Wilde's college) and affected Wilde's manners.[12] The latter reminds us of how recently (1878) Wilde had left Oxford and how strong his shadow yet remained. Eliot, on his part, reminds Thayer of the latter's reputation as a "connoisseur of puberty and lilies" and recalls the bond between them by quoting by heart from Wilde's *The Picture of Dorian Gray*: "'To cure the soul by means of the senses, and the senses by means of the soul!'"[13]

Nor, though Eliot once described *Dorian Gray* as perhaps "perfect rubbish," was his ability to produce a passage of the book from memory out of character.[14] Annotating Eliot's poetic notebook, "Inventions of the March Hare," Christopher Ricks points to more than a dozen recollections of Wilde in Eliot's early verse, including five to the "Ballad of Reading Gaol" and eight to *Dorian Gray*, with many of the latter falling in crucial moments either in the excised "Pervigilium" section of "The Love Song of J. Alfred Prufrock" or in the equally important early poem "The Love Song of St. Sebastian."[15] The most striking resemblance may be to this passage from chapter seven of *Dorian Gray*, which resonates through a half-dozen of Eliot's major early poems, above all in "Prufrock" and "Prufrock's Pervigilium":

> He remembered wandering through dimly-lit streets, past gaunt black-shadowed archways and evil-looking houses. Women with hoarse voices and harsh laughter had called after him. Drunkards had reeled by cursing, and chattering to themselves like monstrous apes. He had seen grotesque children huddled upon doorsteps, and heard shrieks and oaths from gloomy courts.[16]

The sum of these poetic recollections point to Wilde as an important source for the strain of psycho-sexual-spiritual distress in Eliot's published and unpublished early verse. Referring to the 1890s more generally, Ronald Schuchard goes farther and contends that the 1890s' "admixture of religious and sexual emotion" represents Eliot's real *point de depart* and that Eliot later covered his links with the 1890s by stressing affinities with Baudelaire rather than with the English followers of Baudelaire he read as a young man. The impact of Wilde and his circle on Eliot, Schuchard holds, was therefore "more substantive than aesthetic;" his "deepest emotional affinity was with the English poets" and he shared their "morbid fascination with the conflicts of desire and beatitude, body and soul, flesh and Absolute." Little wonder, he continues, that Eliot later affirmed that the poets of the 1890s are "'nearer to us than the intervening generation . . . the fact that they were interested in Baudelaire indicates [our genuine] community.'"[17]

Wilde and Eliot's Poetics

It is true, of course, that Eliot's poetic recollections of the 1890s do not always concern Wilde, and that in his poetry he may have turned more frequently to other English Decadents, especially Swinburne and Lionel Johnson. When we examine to Eliot's critical prose though, Wilde's significance seems preeminent. Eliot's borrowings here extend well beyond his early aestheticist stress on poetry "as poetry and not another thing" and crucially include an emphasis on the poet's self-conscious modernity; a deliberate and provocative turn away from emotional sincerity and its allied notions of the natural and the real; the championing of impersonality and poetic artifice; and a notion of tradition that while apparently highlighting literary continuity in fact strongly stresses poetic revolution.[18]

Eliot read Wilde's essays carefully and expressed his admiration on a number of occasions. In the course of lectures he gave on Victorian literature for the London County Council for the fall of 1917 he devoted a full lecture to the aestheticism of Pater and Wilde and during that year he conducted tutorials for the same authority on "Modern English Literature" that included a major section on "The 'Nineties.'" The latter featured Wilde as the first among equals, required that the students read his critical essays in *Intentions* as well as *The Importance of Being Earnest* and *The Ballad of Reading Gaol*, and recommended for supplementary reading Arthur Ransome's intelligent *Oscar Wilde: A Critical Study*, which had been published just five years before.[19] Then, in a 1922 essay discussed at length below, Eliot went as far as to write that the "best of Wilde" was to be found in the critical volume *Intentions*.[20] Still later, in his teaching notes for English 26 ("Contemporary English Literature, 1890 to the Present Time"), which Eliot taught to undergraduates at Harvard in the Spring of 1933 (and for which he likely elaborated his 1917 lecture notes), Eliot made recurrent (though not always complimentary) reference to Wilde, calling him in the first lecture the "*chef d'école*" of the 1890s, and in lecture 4 praising the "Wilde group" for reacting against Victorian association of art with social causes and moral teaching. (Intriguingly, Eliot either suppressed or never produced the notes for a scheduled lecture that would have covered the aesthetic movement. His Harvard notes indicate but do not include a lecture 3 between lecture 2's discussion of Kipling and lecture 4's treatment of the Fabians in the generation that followed Wilde.)[21]

Given Eliot's well-documented attentions to Wilde though, it is still startling to be reminded of how many of the fundamental formulations of Eliot's poetics can be traced to *Intentions'* central essays—"The Decay of Lying" and "The Critic as Artist." Consider the assertion so often advanced by Eliot and also Pound, that the poet first must identify what the modern age lacks and then supply it from the style of a different time or place—the famous "historical sense," which "involves a perception, not only of the pastness of the past, but of its presence" and which "makes a writer most acutely conscious of his place in time, of his own contemporaneity" (*SW*, 49). It was the historical sense, Eliot had written the year before, that not only allows Pound's work to get "the spirit of Provençal, or of Chinese, or of Anglo-Saxon, as the case may be," but to have perceived "what *they* have that *we* want;" such a sense is only obtainable by "an organised view of the whole course of European poetry from Homer."[22]

Behind Eliot's idea ultimately stands Baudelaire's "The Painter of Modern Life," which holds that the ideal of timeless beauty has been exploded and that the artist now understands that every age must recreate beauty in a new "historical envelope." It is the first duty of the modern artist, Baudelaire contends, to identify those formal conventions that are no longer tenable and to invent new ones suitable to the age. But since this requires understanding the histories of style, it also means that art belongs not to the amateur but to the connoisseur-practitioner who can understand the "form[s] of modernity."[23] In 1918 and 1919 though, Eliot did not derive these ideas directly from Baudelaire, but from Wilde, whose "The Rise of Historical Criticism" traces the rise of our "historical sense" (*CW*, 1227), and whose "The Critic as Artist" concurs with Baudelaire that the first duty of the modern artist is the critical task of defining for his own generation the form of modern beauty (the "highest criticism . . . criticises not merely the individual work of art, but Beauty itself") (*CW*, 1127).

Eliot's praise of the poet's "historical sense" has two parts. The first involves an assertion that the artist is a critic before he is a creator. This idea forms the core of Wilde's "The Critic as Artist," which, as Lawrence Danson notes, develops it by reversing Matthew Arnold's "The Function of Criticism at the Present Time" (1865), which had praised the critical character of his age but also lamented that modern criticism has stifled artistic creation (*WI*, 128–9). Wilde signposted his reversal when he first published the essay in the July and September 1890 issues of the *Nineteenth Century* under the pseudo-Arnoldian title, "The True Function and Value of Criticism." In the words of Wilde's mouthpiece, Gilbert, the essay argues that "Creation is always behind the age. It is Criticism that leads us" (*CW*, 1154). Gilbert then explains that "Without the critical faculty, there is no artistic creation at all worthy of the name" (*CW*, 1118) and that "the work that seems to us to be the most natural and simple . . . is always the result of the most self-consciousness" (*CW*, 1118). It is these last passages that Eliot echoes in 1924 in a pseudo-Arnoldian essay of his own, "The Function of Criticism," which replicates Wilde's argument: "Matthew Arnold . . . overlooks the capital importance of criticism in the work of creation itself;" "[no] great artist is an unconscious artist."[24]

The second part of Eliot's account of the artist's "historical sense" also comes from Wilde, this time from "The Rise of Historical Criticism." Wilde explains that historical discourse goes beyond underlining our differences with the past and emphasizes the method of "comparison" (*CW*, 1240) that identifies the past's contemporaneity. Wilde's essay, drawing on Hegel and resisting the tendency of nineteenth-century historicism to emphasize the past's singularity—what Eliot calls the "pastness" of the past—holds that the historical sense is in fact part of "that complex working towards freedom" which may be described as part of our own "revolt against authority" (*CW*, 1198). It was based on such assertions that Pound and Eliot placed historical perception at the heart of the contemporary poet's critical modernity.

Wilde's anticipation of Eliot's modernism, moreover, runs deeper still. In Wilde's wake, Eliot challenges the two most important premises common to both Romanticism and realism—that art must grow out of spontaneous, "natural" feeling, and that art should imitate the truth of nature around us. Tellingly, both writers in their moments of greatest seriousness engage with reality within discussions of realist literature. Regarding Wilde, Lawrence Danson usefully identifies the debate about literary realism—and especially about the naturalist Zola—as "the contemporary polemical context in which ["The Decay of Lying"] is to be understood," and quotes Linda Nochlin to remind us that "although the Realist refrained from moral comment in his work, his whole attitude towards art implied a moral commitment, to the values of truth, honesty, and sincerity" (*WI*, 47). Against this, Wilde's "The Decay of Lying" holds that realist art is stifling, because it bases its portraits on the Victorian's sham, outdated, and potentially suffocating notions of that "dreadful universal thing called human nature" (*CW*, 1076). Wilde's alternative to this "unimaginative realism" is an "imaginative reality" of the kind Swinburne found in Balzac's novels, which "reduces our living friends to shadows and our acquaintances to the shadows of shades" (*WI*, 55).

Wilde's comments lead inescapeably to Eliot's jazz play, *Sweeney Agonistes*, and spur Eliot's unfaltering attempts to discredit realist drama. Hence Eliot insists in his 1919 essay, "Ben Jonson," that Jonson's drama succeeds because it grows out of a poetry "of the surface" (*SW*, 105). It is "not human life" Eliot tells us, that informs Jonson's characters, "but it is energy of which human life is only another variety" (*SW*, 109). His "art of caricature" involves, therefore, "a brutality, a lack of sentiment, a polished surface, a handling of large bold designs in brilliant colours" (*SW*, 120–1). Eliot's animus against "sentiment" here reprises Wilde's dislike of "human nature." Abhorring the lies we accept as "reality," it opposes to the realist theatre's presentation of those lies Jonson's purely imaginative and "titanic show" (*SW*, 121).

The family resemblance between Eliot and Wilde can also be discovered in their responses to the realist assumption that art imitates the truth of a nature that is to be found all around us. In the other major essay in *Intentions*, "The Decay of Lying," Wilde devotes himself to disproving this "truth" by exposing the artificiality of everything we assume to be natural. In the dialogue, Vivian famously holds that far from art imitating nature, nature imitates art. He argues, as Danson notes, that

> What we call 'nature' is not natural, not (that is) an inescapable given of existence. Society made what society now worships as the thing which made it: Nature is no great mother who has borne us. She is our creation ... [Therefore, when] so-called nature poses as nature—that is, inevitable rather than imitative or social—[it] traps us into imitating it. In quest of the natural we spend our lives imitating an imitation ... Not only 'All bad art' but, by implication, all bad social conditions, come 'from returning to Life and Nature, and elevating them into ideals.' The liar heroically refuses to accept the inevitability of conditions that pose as natural facts: the 'beautiful untrue things' he tells are the things that have not entered our repertoire of repetitive, imitative, gestures. (*WI*, 44–5)

This line of reasoning, starting with the apparent paradox that art is more natural than nature, would lead Eliot repeatedly to lament the death-like grip of the cliché of the real in contemporary letters. In one case Eliot even adopts Wilde's characteristic form, the philosophical dialogue. In a sketch entitled "Eeldrop and Appleplex" (1917), Appleplex (modelled after Ezra

Pound) explains that "the majority of mankind live on paper currency: they use terms which are merely good for so much reality, they never see actual coinage." To this Eliot, in the voice of Eeldrop, replies: "'I should go even further than that . . . The majority not only have no language to express anything save generalized man; they are for the most part unaware of themselves as anything but generalized men. They are first of all government officials, or pillars of the church, or trade unionists, or poets, or unemployed; this cataloguing is not only satisfactory to other people for practical purposes, it is sufficient to themselves for their 'life of the spirit.' Many are not quite real at any moment.'"[25]

Although this last citation signals that Eliot could sometimes alter Wilde's premises in fundamental ways, it suggests no irreconcilable break. Wilde's animus against the humanist mystification of uplifting sentiment is grounded in the conviction that "the only thing that one really knows about human nature is that it changes" ("The Soul of Man Under Socialism," *CW*, 1194). Less radical than Wilde, Eliot ultimately redefines the "death" and "unreality" that Wilde discovers in the Victorian's repetition of outdated imitations of life in specifically Christian terms, connecting them to a divorce from spiritual life. Nevertheless, Eliot's influential early criticism, insistently focussed on aesthetic issues, seamlessly continues Wilde's deconstruction of humanist clichés. Also, albeit at lower volume, Eliot continues to appropriate the energies of paradox—the motor of Wilde's deconstruction of the "natural" in art and life—to erect the teasing reversals at the heart of his poetry and prose: Not only, we remember, do Eliot's core paradoxes include "creation" and "criticism" and "the present" and "the past," but also "life" and "death," "personality and impersonality," "tradition" and the "individual talent," "theft" and "originality," and so on. As in Wilde, all these oppositions target a delusion about "nature" and "reality" that distorts contemporary society and contemporary art.

This focus is perhaps easiest to see in relation to Eliot's observation on "impersonality." It is but a short step from Gilbert's denunciation in "The Critic as Artist" of "genuine feeling," from which "all bad poetry springs" (*CW*, 1148), to Eliot's more famous insistence in "Tradition and the Individual Talent" that "poetry is not a turning loose of emotion, but an escape from emotion; it is not the expression of personality, but an escape from personality" (*SW*, 58). In Wilde no less than in Eliot, artifice becomes a tool for discrediting the clichéd sentiment that society regards as "genuine" so that the form of art may recreate feeling in a more intense form. And so in his discussion of poetic theft, Eliot says that "the good poet welds his theft into a whole of feeling which is unique, utterly different from that from which it was torn" (*SW*, 125). Wilde and then Eliot emphasize stylization in poetry and drama because, apparently more artificial than "natural" speech, it is in fact less tainted by cant and more useful for strong expression. This idea founds the theory of masks propounded by poets from Wilde to W.B. Yeats to Pound to Eliot: speaking through the artifice of a mask, whether simply a second self or a voice distant in space, culture, and time, the poet cleanses himself of those clichés that masquerade as true emotions and takes on a language that is strange enough to require that it be charged by its aesthetic context to mean anything at all.

A more pointed example of the same principle involves poetic theft. Eliot's provocative proclamation that "Immature poets imitate; mature poets steal" (*SW*, 125) reminds us that no less than Wilde he flaunted the way he pieced his writing together from material drawn from others. Wilde too, we remember, was notorious for his so-called plagiarism. In fact, as Josephine M. Guy has shown, Wilde's most radical originality can be discovered in the way he appropriated other poets' work, especially in individual sections of *Intentions* and *Dorian Gray* and even in what appears to be his most innovative creation, *Salome*.[26] Working in a culture that would not countenance radical cultural or literary innovation, Guy argues, Wilde's solution was to invoke and then appropriate traditions so flagrantly that his appropriations became marks of his own originality (*BA*, 142–3). Hence, his apparently outrageous assertion that "it is only the unimaginative who ever invent . . . the true artist is known by the use he makes of what he annexes, and he annexes everything" (*BA*, 142).[27] Eliot's "Immature poets imitate; mature poets steal" shocks us in the same way and for the same reasons—because we associate poetry with a false ideal of originality, we assume that nothing that is not "original" can be poetic.

Finally, Eliot's equally paradoxical but more consequential invocation of "tradition" stems from Wildean premises and reveals itself as no less individualistic.[28] To assert one's originality by arguing that innovation flows from the voices of one's predecessors has deep roots in Wilde, whose practice explains both the historical context of the assertion and the reaches of its iconoclasm. To again invoke Josephine Guy:

> Pater and Morris invoked a tradition in order to disguise or deny the innovative aspects of their thinking; in this sense traditions lent authority to Pater's and Morris's idiosyncratic (and subversive) views about the nature and function of art and literature by appearing to invoke historical precedents for those views. Wilde, on the other hand, uses exactly the same strategy, but he does so in order to *exhibit* his originality: what Pater and Morris had disguised, he holds up for general inspection. Wilde claimed that

in the hands of the 'true' artist all traditions were transformed into something new, and that they had authority only in so far as they 'bore the signature' of the artist who interpreted them. . . . Far from possessing a normative function, for Wilde, traditions were merely the 'suggestion' for an entirely new creation . . . traditions were nothing more than the artist's 'raw materials'; and it was the artist's unique handling of them—the extent to which he transformed them through the exercise of his personality and therefore his style—which was of primary interest. (*BA*, 142–3, 145)

Backward Glances

The preceding brief account, constructed to bring out Eliot's Wildean foundations, serves I hope at least to suggest the point of the "Wilde" in my title. What remains is to think about how and why "the Possum," while retaining the force of Wilde's core paradoxes, replaced Wilde's provocations with a more Arnoldian style of apparently disinterested prose and obscured Wilde's part in the formation of his modernist vision.

Richard Shusterman would have it that Eliot turned his back on Wilde for reasons of decorum and highmindedness—that he "learned from Wilde's bitter experience that even the artist who is alienated and critical of society must make some sort of peace with society," and that he resolved not to "belie the seriousness and importance of his thought . . . by too frivolous expression" ("WE," 141). Like most of Eliot's critics, that is, Shusterman assumes that driving both was the kind of serious moral "thought" that caused Eliot to substitute moral life for sexual identity as the principal field on which he opposed nature. On the other hand, the line of what Ann Ardis identifies as the "new modernist studies" suggests that the converse may be true, and that Eliot's "thought" was the product of his policy rather than its cause. Both, however, speak of deliberate strategy and a clear generational change.[29] What I have intimated above, and would now like to entertain more seriously, is the possibility that Eliot's apparent social and literary conformity with the discourse of his time marks not a break but a continuity with Wilde's own literary practice of subverting while appearing to conform to the temper of Victorian and post-Victorian Britain, in a context in which the openness of a Francophile cultural avant-garde was simply not permitted.[30] I would also like to raise the question of whether Eliot's style might have been, rather than a calculated effort to efface Wildean sexual expression, a not always successful act of self-censorship.

To address these issues fully would require a nuanced psychological reading of Eliot's career based on information about his private life that is not currently available. But the beginning of a response may be deduced from three fugitive essays in which Eliot, more candidly than was his usual custom, reconsidered the significance of his own work. All three of these essays rehearse an inside history of modern literature, and all three were triggered by Eliot's uncomfortable intuition that he was, in ways that he had not yet acknowledged, connected to the other great English poet of his moment, William Butler Yeats and therefore also to the Wilde circle from which Yeats had emerged.

In 1922, soon after Yeats had published *The Trembling of the Veil*—that section of his *Autobiographies* that concerns the 1890s—Eliot published two short pieces that acknowledge the essential importance of Wilde and his circle to Eliot and to American modernism. Eliot's "Lettre D'Angleterre," first published in French in *La Nouvelle Revue Française* for March 1922 and then in English in the November 1923 *Vanity Fair* as "A Preface to Modern Literature," goes as far as to assert that "English Literature at the present time"—a state of affairs that includes "a very small number of writers who will represent this time fifty years hence, but who are, at the moment, rather a part of the future"—begins "about the date of the trial of Oscar Wilde" ("PML," 44).

Eliot comments,

> The effect of [the Wilde] trial upon English literary society was fatal. Here was a small group of English people, who had succeeded in the midst of Victorian society, in acquiring a high degree of emancipation from the worst English vices; which was neither insular, nor puritanical, nor cautious; a public scandal disposed of its social leader for ever; the broken group lost all influence upon English civilization. Wilde and his circle stood for something much more important than any of the individual members: they stood for the end of a type of culture. In general, they represented urbanity, Oxford education, the tradition of good writing, cosmopolitanism; they were in contact with the continent, and some of their most important members were Irish.[31]

First note here that, far from casting aspersions on the frivolity of the 1890s, Eliot associates it with some of his own highest values—"urbanity," "culture," "civilization," "cosmopolitanism," and freedom from English "insularity" and "puritanism." Nor it seems is he damning with faint praise, holding back still grander accolades having to do with high moral seriousness, for he adds to his tribute the further comment that "the greatest merit of this group of people is, to my mind . . . a moral quality apparent in the group as a whole"—a moral quality that Eliot defines in perhaps surprising terms

("PML," 44). The Wilde group, Eliot insists, ("serious writers" possessing "intellectual dignity") "had a curiosity, an audacity, a *recklessness* which are in violent contrast with that part of the present which I denominate as the already dead" ("PML," 44).

Eliot's aversion to the "already dead" here is, I think, telling. Along with the phrases "intellectual dignity" and "cosmopolitanism," it attributes to Wilde and his group a critical temperament capable of dissociating the great cultural shibboleths of "Victorian society" associated with a false understanding of life in human nature and in art. Because of the loss of that critical temperament, Eliot goes on, the inevitable course of early twentieth-century cultural history, "after the collapse of the society in which Wilde was the most prominent member," was to produce a situation where "English literature is in a state of disintegration into at least three varieties of provincialism"—English, Irish, and American—with dire consequences for all three and for the whole of which they had once formed a part ("PML," 118). The Wilde trial, Eliot says, produced a "chasm," with the result that "the long tradition from Ben Jonson" was broken ("PML," 118). Consequently, Eliot argues, English provincial literature has collapsed into journalism, and Irish provincial literature, no longer having London as a safe "exile," has turned in on itself in the manner of Synge ("PML," 44). (Wilde's fall, Eliot says, may have in this way been momentous enough to have "led to the constitution of the Irish Free State" ["PML," 118]). Meanwhile, Eliot and the live members of his generation who wish to continue the line for which "Walter Pater, in an earlier epoch, was an heir of Arnold and Ruskin, and Wilde the heir of Pater," find themselves "very much alone" ("PML" 118).

Yet Eliot concludes that this situation, on its face utterly discouraging, has had its compensations. American literature, for example, in "the absence of any new creative effort in England," has been able to burst forth with provincial energy even though it retains a "commonplace" quality that derives from its lack of historical sense ("PML," 118). And, he implies, he, James Joyce, and Pound (the heirs because of their critical acumen and "audacity" of the lost generation of the 1890s and also the beneficiaries of the new opportunities opened to American writing by the sudden gap in live literature) have already managed to repair the break in a way that no critic in the interim generation of George Bernard Shaw and H.G. Wells could have foreseen.

Eliot extends his ruminations about the "chasm" caused by the fall of Wilde in an essay entitled "The Three Provincialities" which appeared in the Spring 1922 number of *Tyro*. "The Three Provincialities" most significantly develops Eliot's thoughts about the current place of American literature.[32] Still insisting on the provinciality of contemporary American literature, and still holding a place for Joyce, Pound, and himself as the true heirs of Wilde's cosmopolitan exploitation of the English language, Eliot nevertheless stresses that "the advance of 'American literature' has been accelerated by the complete collapse of literary effort in England" and that, given the model of one of the "greatest and least local" American writers, "Edgar Poe," there exists at least the possibility that America may "in time develop a superior language" upon which might be elaborated "a separate American literature—contingent, probably, upon the disappearance or sufficient degeneration of the English language in England."

Together, then, "A Preface to Modern Literature" and "The Three Provincialities" provide testimony to Eliot's sense of his own origins that is I think nowhere else available in Eliot's prose. Not only are they unequivocal about the importance of Wilde's cosmopolitan and anti-puritan "audacity" (and about the significance of his loss), they also clearly state the extent to which Eliot holds himself the descendant of Wilde's combination of seriousness and "*recklessness*." As such, the articles serve to support the evidence supplied by Eliot's critical prose that he maintained both the substance and the subversive stance of Wilde's aesthetics, as for example in the slyly antiauthoritarian slant of his remarks on tradition.

It is true that Eliot acknowledges in these essays in no uncertain terms the fact that the end of the Wilde group was caused by an act of social repression. Unlike Yeats, who in *The Trembling of the Veil* traces the demise of Wilde and his group primarily to the individuals themselves (sometimes suggesting moral flaws and elsewhere that they were tragically born at the wrong place in the wrong time), Eliot places the blame squarely on the "public scandal" of "the trial of Oscar Wilde." Nor are the implications of this conclusion unclear, though Eliot does not spell them out. If the task of his own generation is both to restore Wilde's cosmopolitan culture and to resist the obviously potent forces of English insularity, cautiousness, and puritanism, then the "very small number of writers" destined to accomplish this task must somehow both maintain Wilde's "recklessness" and consciously defend themselves against the powers that so recently created the "chasm" of modern literature. No less that Joyce's Stephen Daedalus in *A Portrait of the Artist as a Young Man*, they must, Eliot implies, practice "silence, exile, and cunning."[33]

Eliot, that is to say, by 1922 had long since imagined his career as a conscious and calculated negotiation through a "vicious," "provincial" "insular," "puritanical," and "cautious" English milieu from which genuine "emancipation" was not a real possibility. To a considerable degree, there is justice in assuming that the distance Eliot put between the 1890s and his modernist colleagues was a "deliberate" strategy. Nevertheless and most curiously, however, Eliot in the same argument expresses a continuing need to practice Wilde's audacity rather than—as both Shusterman and Ardis would have it—refining it out of existence. Note also the odd exaggeration in Eliot's remark that Wilde had faltered while attempting to "emancipate" himself, and compare this to Josephine Guy's revisionary insistence that Wilde did not try to escape from Victorian conventions so much as he strove to subvert them quietly from within. Wilde fell, that is, not because he had defied Victorian Britain but because his protective coloration let him down. Eliot's retrospective account, though, needs to make Wilde's rebellion even more extreme than it was. Partly, this is to distinguish it from his own. Partly, however, Eliot's exaggeration of the heroic nature of Wilde's generation seems to express a genuine longing to have been part of an "emancipated" culture that never existed—a longing that strangely matches the survivor's guilt voiced in both essays when Eliot speaks of the opportunities opened up to American literature.

Whatever calculation there was in Eliot's response to Wilde's tragedy then, also was complicated by psychic tension. It is therefore fascinating to see Eliot elaborate this strong but ambivalent identification with Wilde and his circle in another personal testimony later in his career. I refer to a passage which calls attention to itself precisely because of an urgency that vastly exceeds its argument. It is something that Eliot wrote fourteen years after "A Preface to Modern Literature," at a time when he was already forty-three years old and was convinced the best part of his career was behind him. The occasion for his remarks was Eliot's first visit to Dublin in January 1936, in the course of which he listened to an address by the Reverend Burke-Savage on "Literature at the Irish Crossroads" and then twice addressed the English Literary Society of University College, Dublin.[34] Eliot's second response, entitled "Tradition and the Practice of Poetry" and only published in the 1980s, shows Eliot again attempting to formulate his place in English letters and again lingering over his relation to Yeats. In it Eliot continues to propound a notion of genuinely "modern" art based on Hegel and Baudelaire in which the "revolutionary" or "reactionary" terms of the truly modern writer are dictated by the "need of [the artist's own] time and place" ("TPP," 11). In this view, Eliot explains, though the artist as poet is not always conscious of it, "the perpetual task of poetry is to *make all things new*. Not necessarily to make new things" ("TPP," 11), and the principal means of that renewal are to be found in a literature's "new contact with an older period of itself" ("remote enough to be of use") or "by contact with a foreign literature" ("TPP," 13). It is at this point that Eliot, invoking his "own experience," adverts to his contact with the 1890s.

Eliot's history, more than usually suave, when read carefully turns out also to be exceedingly odd. For one thing, he begins, returning to the idiom of the remarks with which I began this essay, by telescoping poetic influence with the erotics of personal intimacy. Literary history, he says, is a matter of "fertilization" by the languages of different cultures, and:

> The fertilization of which I am talking goes much deeper than the exact receptions of ideas: just as we may be deeply influenced, in our private lives, by someone whom we understand very imperfectly indeed. ["TPP," 13]

Eliot at the same time begins to describe his own encounter with the literature of another language (French Symbolist poetry) not in terms of his reading of that literature, but by a narrative of his relations with the English poets of the 1890s, who never really absorbed the French and yet somehow are allowed to remain the center of Eliot's attention:

> I am neither a scholar nor a philosopher, and I can perhaps be most useful in these matters in sticking to my own experience. I cannot help wondering how my own verse would have developed, or whether it would have been written at all, supposing that the poets [i.e., the Irish poets] of the generation of the nineties had survived to my own time and had gone on developing and increasing in power. Perhaps they were men who could not have developed further, but I am making that assumption. I certainly had much more in common with them than with the English poets who survived to my own day—there were no American poets at all. Had they survived, they might have spoken in an idiom sufficiently like my own to have made anything I had to say superfluous. They were in contact with France, and they might have exhausted the possibilities of cross-fertilization from Symbolist Poetry (as they called it) before I had a chance. What happened was that they made it possible for me to discover those poets. . . . When one reviews one's own writing, as when one reviews one's own life, how much there is that bears the appearance of mere chance! One has been dependent upon one's predecessors for what they did not do, as much as for what they did! The one poet of that period, the youngest and the greatest, who survived, was of course Yeats; and it happened that in my own formative period Yeats was in his most superficially local phase, in which I failed to appreciate him. ["TPP," 13–4]

Especially interesting here is the personal horror that Eliot's summoning up of the 1890s arouses ("I cannot help wondering . . . whether [my own verse] *would have been written at all*"; "They might have spoken in an idiom suf-ficiently like my own *to have made anything I had to say superfluous*"). This is a reaction almost as pronounced as Virginia Woolf's when she reflected in 1928 that her father might have lived long enough to stifle her work: "Father's birthday. He would have been 96. 96, yes, today; & could have been 96, like other people one has known; but mercifully was not. His life would have entirely ended mine. What would have happened? No writing, no books;—inconceivable."[35]

Eliot's remarks, though, shed light not on parental relations, but on amorous ones. And though he fixes in a similar way on the possibility of being closed down and closed off, his account enlarges Woolf's terror that "anything I had to say" might have been stifled before the fact by associating it with a very different kind of anxiety, a fear that he would have been denied a great intimacy—the experience "of cross-fertilization"—the way a lover is denied access to his beloved, by an older and potentially threatening suitor. (In this case the suitor is imagined as one who might have gone on "increas-ing in power.")

But why attribute this menacing power, even in the past, to the poets of the 1890s and to them alone? And why weight with such a heavy charge a deprivation that had never occurred? Eliot, after all, by 1936 had carried on twenty-five years of unimpeded interchange with French verse. Surely by then he felt no real fear of a broken connection?

Contemplating this intense and complex anxiety (mocked, to be sure—but also confirmed—by the comedy in Eliot's comment about "mere chance"), one has to wonder about the lurking and unnamed relation that Eliot implies had NOT been allowed—a relation that seems to have been closed down by Eliot himself. If Eliot, that is, focuses on the 1890s when the occasion required a serious glance not at England but at France, he does so because his real deprivation seems to have been not from France (access to which he was never deprived) but from "the generation of the [English] 'nineties,'" whose presence Eliot calls up as if in a séance and then fails to substantively address.

Eliot's strongly felt but unspoken anxiety here, inherent in his strange mention of the potentially increasing power of the 1890s and in the strong inhibition that keeps him from addressing the poets of the 1890s in a concrete way, testifies to the deep and uncomfortable roots of his relations with Wilde and his circle. Such roots sink deep enough to color Eliot's argument, I would suggest, more definitively than any conscious career strategy. Though Eliot's efforts to distance himself from the 1890s are undeniable, they seem less to have stemmed from a steady resolution than to have enacted a vacillating ambivalence, for which the language of deliberation does not fully account.

Part of that ambivalence undoubtedly involved a sexual component—else why Eliot's recourse to the erotics of influence?—but there is no need to assume that the impulse amounts to a cover-up of real-life sexual experience. If we read Eliot's desire for and guilt about his identification with the English Decadents as overdetermined and unconscious, the continuing force of that identification becomes much more interesting.

Notes

1. Colleen Lamos, *Deviant Modernism: Sexual and Textual Errancy in T.S. Eliot, James Joyce, and Marcel Proust* (Cambridge: Cambridge University Press, 1998), 69. Lamos (27–34) usefully cites a growing list of studies by Richard Poirier, Gregory Jay, Graham Hough, and others, of Eliot's debts to Pater, Swinburne, and Whitman.

2. Quoted in Peter Ackroyd, *T.S. Eliot: A Life* (New York: Simon and Schuster, 1984), 136.

3. Josephine M. Guy, *The British Avant-Garde: The Theory and Politics of Tradition* (London: Harvester, 1991), 146; hereafter abbreviated *BA*.

4. Carole Seymour-Jones, *A Painted Shadow: A Life of Vivienne Eliot* (London: Constable, 2001), 344.

5. Ackroyd, *T.S. Eliot: A Life*, 136–37.

6. Ann Ardis, *Modernism and Cultural Conflict 1880–1922* (Cambridge: Cambridge University Press, 2002), 63; hereafter abbreviated *MCC*.

7. See Sandra Gilbert and Susan Gubar, *No Man's Land: The Place of the Woman Writer in the Twentieth Century. Volume 1: The War of the Words* (New Haven: Yale University Press, 1988); Richard Dellamora, *Masculine Desire: The Sexual Politics of Victorian Aestheticism* (Chapel Hill: University of North Carolina Press, 1990), 217 and *passim*; Eve Kosofsky Sedgwick, *Epistemology of the Closet* (Berkeley: University of California Press, 1990), 169; Cassandra Laity, *H.D. and the Victorian Fin-de-Siècle* (Cambridge: Cambridge University Press, 1996), 9–17; Colleen Lamos, *Deviant Modernism*, 17–117; Ann Ardis, *Modernism and Cultural Conflict*, 45–71, especially 63–4 and 68–71.

8. See Ronald Bush, "Imagist Poetics and the Cultural Politics of Modernism: A Note," *Ambassadors: American Studies in a Changing World. Proceedings of the Seventeenth Biennial International Conference of the Italian Association for American Studies*, ed. by Massimo Bacigalupo, forthcoming.

9. *The Complete Works of Oscar Wilde* (London: Harper Collins, 1994) hereafter abbreviated *CW*. For "The Rise of Historical Criticism," see *CW*, 1198–1241, especially 1224.

10. "Reflections on Contemporary Poetry [IV] *The Egoist* 6.3 (July 1919), 39.

11. "What Dante Means to Me" *To Criticize the Critic* (New York: Farrar, Straus & Giroux, 1965), 127.

12. *The Letters of T.S. Eliot*. Ed. Valerie Eliot. Vol. I (New York: Harcourt Brace Jovanovich, 1988), 398, 137–38; hereafter abbreviated *LTS*.

13. For a fuller account of the aestheticism that Thayer affected and Eliot and Vivien shared, see Seymour-Jones, *A Painted Shadow*, 138–9. Eliot's letter is also discussed in Ardis, *Modernism and Cultural Conflict*, 63–4, 69.

14. "A Preface to Modern Literature: Being a Conspectus, Chiefly of English Poetry, Addressed to An Intelligent and Enquiring Foreigner. By T.S. Eliot, Author of 'The Waste Land.'" *Vanity Fair* for November 1923, 44, 118. See 44; hereafter abbreviated "PML".

15. *The Inventions of the March Hare: Poems 1909–1917,* ed. Christopher Ricks (London: Faber and Faber, 1996), 149–50, 173, 180, 183–6, 223, 264–5, 268, 272, 275–6, 289, 301. For yet other examples, see Richard Shusterman, "Wilde and Eliot," *T.S. Eliot Annual I* (London: Macmillan, 1988), 117–44, especially 123–5; hereafter abbreviated "WE".

16. The resemblance between this passage and various of Eliot's poems is noted both by Ricks in *Inventions of the March Hare,* 180 and by Shusterman's "Wilde and Eliot," 123.

17. Ronald Schuchard, "The Dark Angel," *Eliot's Dark Angel: Intersections of Life and Art* (New York: Oxford University Press, 1999), 3–24, especially 8, 9, 19.

18. Citation from *The Sacred Wood* (New York: Methuen, 1966), viii; hereafter abbreviated *SW.* Eliot's connections to Wilde's criticism have been previously discussed by Shusterman's "Wilde and Eliot," 126ff. and more briefly by Lawrence Danson, *Wilde's Intentions: The Artist in his Criticism* (Oxford: Oxford University Press, 1997), 39; hereafter abbreviated *WI.*

19. Ronald Schuchard, "In the Lecture Halls," *Eliot's Dark Angel,* 25–51, especially 40, 43–44.

20. "A Preface to Modern Literature," 44. Arthur Ransome makes the same point in the book that Eliot recommended to his mature students, *Oscar Wilde: A Critical Study* (London: Methuen, 1923), 139: "[*Intentions*] is, in my opinion, that one of Wilde's books that most nearly represents him."

21. Eliot's lecture notes are preserved in the Harvard University Archives. For a fuller account, see Ronald Bush, "'As if You Were Hearing it from Mr. Fletcher or Mr. Tourneur in 1633': T.S. Eliot's 1933 Harvard Lecture Notes for English 26 ('Introduction to Contemporary Literature')," *ANQ* XI.3 (Summer 1998), 11–19. (A list of Eliot's lectures is given on p. 12.)

22. "A Note on Ezra Pound," *To-day,* London, IV.19 (Sept. 1918), 3–9, 4–5.

23. Charles Baudelaire "The Painter of Modern Life," in *Selected Writings on Art & Artists,* 390–435, especially 402–3.

24. T.S. Eliot, *Selected Essays* (London: Faber and Faber, 1951), 29–30; hereafter abbreviated *SE.*

25. T.S. Eliot, 'Eeldrop and Appleplex I' in *The Little Review Anthology,* ed. Margaret Anderson (New York: Horizon Press, 1953), 104–5.

26. See Guy, *The British Avant-Garde,* 139, which comments on the obviously "derivative" quality of even Wilde's most innovative work, and traces, for example, Wilde's *Salome* to Joris-Karl Huysman's *À Rebours* and Laforgue's *Moralités Légendaires,* Stéphane Mallarmé's *Hérodiade,* Gustave Flaubert's *Hérodias* and Jules-Émile-Frédéric Massenet's *Hérodiade,* Maeterlinck's *La Princesse Maleine,* and Victor-Marie Moreau's painting, *The Apparition.*

27. From a book review cited in Richard Ellmann, *Oscar Wilde* (London: Penguin, 1988), 358.

28. For a reading that argues that Eliot's invocation of tradition though inconsistent more "objective" than Wilde's, see Shusterman, 138–41.

29. Ann Ardis, *Modernism and Cultural Conflict,* 7.

30. As Josephine Guy points out in *The British Avant-Garde*, "the rejection of *Salome* in Britain and its enthusiastic reception in France and Germany" testifies to "the uniqueness of the intellectual conditions for avant-garde activity in Britain; what was an 'appropriate' form of opposition in France, was simply unacceptable in Britain" (141).

31. ("PML," 44) See above, note 14. (The French version of "PML" was published as "Lettre D'Angleterre" in *La Nouvelle Revue Française* for March 1922, 617–24.) Shusterman ("Wilde and Eliot," 144) and Ardis (*Modernism and Cultural Conflict*, 46) make brief reference to the English version, but, neither does justice to its richness.

32. "The Three Provincialities," *Tyro* 2 (Spring 1922), 11–3.

33. James Joyce, *A Portrait of the Artist as a Young Man*, ed. Chester G. Anderson (New York: Viking, 1968), 247.

34. "Tradition and the Practice of Poetry" [hereafter abbreviated "TPP"] was only belatedly published in 1985. See A. W. Litz's transcription and annotation of the essay, first in the 1985 Southern Review and then in *T.S. Eliot: Essays from the Southern Review*, ed. James Olney (Oxford: Oxford University Press, 1988), 7–25. Schuchard ("The Dark Angel," 8–9) takes Eliot's remarks on the nineties in the essay at face value.

35. Virginia Woolf, diary entry for 28 November, 1928. *The Virginia Woolf Reader*, ed. Mitchell Leaska (New York: Harcourt Brace & Company, 1984), 317.

JOSEPH JONGHYUN JEON

Eliot's Shadows: Autography and Style in The Hollow Men

Locked up in an archive at Princeton University and sealed by order until 1 January 2020, the letters of Thomas Stearns Eliot to Emily Hale, upwards of a thousand, currently sit gathering dust. Hale was an intimate of Eliot's, who Ronald Bush ambiguously describes as "more than a companion, less than a fiancée" (185), and as a result these letters seem to offer a whiff of scandal more than any currently available Eliot document. Likely against Eliot's wishes, Hale donated them to the library, compromising by having them sealed for fifty years. They are of such great interest that they were displayed boxed and banded in 2000 at a Princeton Library exhibit showing off its collections.

The unavailability of such documents pertaining to this pillar of twentieth-century poetry has sparked some predictable speculation. In a 1973 biography, for example, T.S. Matthews imagines Hale's response to Eliot's first marriage in terms befitting a soap-opera: "This was a rude interruption of their intimacy, but no more than an interruption" (140). At the end of Martha Cooley's 1998 novel, *The Archivist*, the protagonist, who is entrusted to safeguard the letters, burns them (after reading them of course). In general, the letters salaciously seem to promise Eliot's most private thoughts and feelings regarding the developing problems with his first wife, Vivienne

From *Yeats Eliot Review* 24, no. 4 (Winter 2007): 12–24. Copyright © 2007 by Joseph Jonghyun Jeon.

Haigh-Wood, perhaps in relation to his conversion to Anglicanism in 1927. And although they reportedly cover a broader period of time, they seem to promise a glimpse of Eliot in his weakest moments.

With its emphasis on shadows in its final section, *The Hollow Men* (1925), I suggest, adumbrates what the Hale letters seem to promise, the revelation of the secret, private Eliot. Originating in extracts from *The Waste Land* (1922) and free from the editorial hand of Pound, *The Hollow Men* offers shadowy expressions of extremely personal emotions, though never in autobiographical form. For the poet who famously described poetry as an "escape from emotions" and "an escape from personality" ("Tradition" 58), however, this sort of self-revelation cannot be direct so, instead of confessing scandalous secrets, the poem reveals the private Eliot through its style. In general, style is an aspect of writing that resists definition. When we speak of style, as E.B. White writes in his famous style guide, "we leave solid ground" (66). This departure not only resonates thematically in *The Hollow Men*—since the lack of solid ground is exactly what frustrates the hollow men—it also characterizes Eliot's mode of personal revelation in the poem. Eliot foregrounds style by making it crucial to the central drama of the poem, and gradually a shadowy sense of Eliot himself emerges as the poem shifts away from its central figures, away from the hollow men, and toward style itself.

Published in its final form in 1925—before Eliot's conversion to Anglicanism and after the great success of *The Waste Land*—*The Hollow Men* is a profoundly personal poem without being an autobiographical one. The poem does not provide, secretly or explicitly, any new facts about Eliot's life. Rather, *The Hollow Men* partakes in something like "autography" as H. Porter Abbott has described it with respect to Beckett: "what autography also means in Beckett's case is an art of extreme vulnerability. Instead of an artist above his work, paring his fingernails, we have an artist seeking to approach unmediated contact" (21). Style is the preferred mode of autography for *The Hollow Men*, because it allows for personal revelation while satisfying Eliot's intense concern for privacy. This stylistic procedure resonates with Abbott's distinction between autography and autobiography:

> Autobiography in the sense of a memoir or life story is something Beckett had few illusions about, and the inadequacy of life stories is a theme that recurs throughout his oeuvre. So a better term than "autobiography" is "self-writing" and, better still, "autography," which avoids not only the implications of historical narrative in "bio" but also the semantic baggage of "self," a term as problematical for Beckett as the term "story." Preferable to all these is the coinage

"autobiographical action," for it concentrates attention on the text, both as "self-writing and as immediate action taking place as it is written." (x)

Abbott's reasoning for Beckett certainly applies to Eliot, the great proselytizer of impersonal poetics. His term expresses at once the compulsion toward self-expression, or "self-writing," while acknowledging the hesitations before the autobiographical mode.

Figured most powerfully by the shadows in the final section, Eliot's style in *The Hollow Men* is restrained and quiet, but tortured by the tensions that pervade the poem's milieu. It is elliptical and ecliptic. Eliot's shadows, however, do more than simply obscure and hide and provide an enabling criterion that recalibrates the otherwise meaningless whispers of the hollow men. The poem begins just as it famously ends, not with a bang but a whimper. The spoken words of the hollow men are "meaningless" and thus weak. "We are the hollow men / We are the stuffed men," they proclaim, announcing the collective chorus that voices the lines (*Complete Poems and Plays* 56).[1] In part an allusion to the straw bodies burned in effigy on Guy Fawkes Day in England mentioned in the poem's epigraph, this couplet seems rife with contradictions. "Stuffed" is an antonym of "hollow," but the two words function here more as synonyms. Unlike the phrase, "I am," which usually aspires to announce individual identity, the correlating pronoun–verb combination here, "We are," denies any claims about individuality; these are empty figures. This gesture, which seems to signify the lack of identity, makes hollowness the very basis of identity, they are "the hollow men" and not just "hollow men." That they lack substance makes them somehow substantive, and the lines thus foreground and efface identity simultaneously. The hollow men try unsuccessfully to imagine the existence of a divine and a world that depends on such a figure, and accordingly, their voices fail to register in any effective manner. In the final section, the shadows redress the problem of meaning in the previous sections by making meaning dependent not on an ideal governing structure, but rather, on the smaller relationships of affinity and difference that one can only see when one abandons such foundational and prohibiting idealizations. In this sense, the poem's oft-quoted finale, "This is the way the world ends . . . / Not with a bang but a whimper," treats whimpers, not as meaningless utterances that vanish in the abyss between heaven and earth, but as shadowy murmurs that have no meaning until they are considered in relation to one other (59). The key is scale. A whimper among gods is a meaningless sound; a whimper among whimpers is a language.

Agency and Orthodoxy

The autography of *The Hollow Men* is born out of, at best, ambiguity and, at worst, confusion. In the years after the publication of *The Waste Land* and before his conversion to Anglicanism in 1927, Eliot's increasing ideological commitment to orthodox thought came in conflict with his earlier belief in the transformative ability of poetry. This ideological shift however hides a continuity in his criticism visible as early as "Tradition and the Individual Talent" (1919) and as late as *After Strange Gods* (1934), in which Eliot consistently demonstrates a tendency to muddy the relationship between individual agency and orthodoxy. The Clark Lectures (1926), delivered the year after the final version of *The Hollow Men* was published, clearly demonstrate this tension. As Eliot became more wedded to political conservatism, his ideas about a poet's individual agency did not so much disappear as they lingered. Rather than dovetailing, Eliot's poetic and political beliefs became increasingly adversarial in this period.

In "Tradition and the Individual Talent," Eliot famously develops his notion of the individual poet's role through an analogy. Poetic impersonality, he suggests, enables the poet to become a "catalyst" or "medium" by which the "mind will digest and transmute the passions which are its material" (54). The poet is like a platinum catalyst, without which the reaction is impossible. In chemical terms, a new compound is produced; in poetic terms, a new unity results, which alters nothing less than the course of tradition itself. Among other commentators, F.R. Leavis notices how poorly this analogy holds together, precisely at the point where the poet enters the reaction. He notes that the comparison both relies on and omits the poet's creativity:

> How we get from a "liberty to enter into new combinations" to "the mind which creates" Eliot does nothing at all to explain; it is surely a long way—it is in fact a yawning gap in his theory or diagram. . . .
>
> Nothing is done to supply the absent something answering to the verb 'create' (the mind which 'creates') by the reference, a couple of sentences later, to the 'intensity of the artistic process, the pressure, so to speak, under which the fusion takes place', for Eliot does nothing to explain or suggest what the process is, or where the pressure could come from. (180)

Leavis points out that the notion of authorial creativity becomes completely supplemental to the logic of the analogy despite the fact that Eliot's entire point depends on it. Without it, the argument loses the agency that is precisely the payoff for writing impersonally. On one hand, the analogy maintains the individual creative power of the poet who is capable of changing the existing order of history through his literary production, and, on the other, it imagines that power to be not individual at all, so that it might claim universal rather than personal significance.

In *After Strange Gods*, Eliot imagines the poet's function much differently, but a similar problem lingers. Whereas in "Tradition," he maintains the possibility that the poet might transform culture, in the later essay, he calls for poetry to serve the demands of orthodox values, which, he describes as having an absolute value whether anyone in a given period believes them or not. Orthodoxy takes the place that tradition had earlier occupied; it becomes the point of access for a poet to universal values. The poet here aims less towards transformation, and more toward the confirmation of these orthodox values. Oddly, however, he characterizes "blasphemy" in unexpectedly favorable terms:

> blasphemy is not a matter of good form but of right belief; no one
> can possibly blaspheme in any sense except that in which a parrot
> may be said to curse, unless he profoundly believes in that which
> he profanes. . . . It is certainly my opinion that first-rate blasphemy
> is one of the rarest things in literature, for it requires both literary
> genius and profound faith . . . I am not defending blasphemy; I am
> reproaching a world in which blasphemy is impossible. (56)

What is important to Eliot about "first rate blasphemy" is not its subversive potential, but the manner in which it indicates a latent commitment to orthodox values. True blasphemy, he writes, is rare in his era because the era lacks true faith; evidence of blasphemy, ironically, thus becomes evidence for hope to the orthodox thinker. Eliot's logic once again has become equivocal at precisely the point at which individual agency comes into question, lost again in Leavis's "yawning gap." Blasphemy at once marks the possibility of faith as well as the blasphemer's attempt to undermine the orthodoxy to which faith might cling. Although he poses the example as hypothetical and general, Eliot's blasphemer is oddly specific, and has a distinct personality trait. Specifically, he is conflicted: as if a believer in disguise, he seems to act contrary to his own beliefs. One might venture that he is not so much a lapsed believer as he is a repressed one. Ultimately, Eliot's version of blasphemy satisfies no one since it fails to accomplish the will of either the blasphemer or the orthodox thinker entirely: one interested in real blasphemy would inevitably fail in the task, since blasphemy simply confirms the primacy of orthodox values, and one truly interested in upholding these values might certainly find better means. The moment in Eliot's text is nonetheless striking because it reveals how poetic agency lingers even as the explicit purpose of poetry, the confirmation of orthodox values, seems to require its suppression.

We can see such conflict more clearly in Eliot's Clark Lectures, delivered in 1926 at Cambridge University. In these lectures, he takes up an analysis of the same tradition he had earlier addressed in "The Metaphysical Poets" (1921) and privileges poetry that can fuse "sense with thought" (*Varieties* 58). The great hero of these lectures is Dante who "always finds the sensuous equivalent, the physical embodiment, for the realization of the most tenuous and refined intensity . . . of experience" (57). Poetry here refuses the task of change and instead seeks to find poetic equivalents for already lofty abstract ideas. A great poet differs from ordinary ones, not in his capacity to change, but to increase the intensity of experience and thus endeavors to validate rather than transform a given view of the universe. Importantly, this new criterion for poetry makes Eliot's task as a twentieth-century poet immediately problematic, since he lives in a time completely different than that of his hero, one in which lofty ideas have lost their prominence.[2] If Dante is exemplary, his example becomes impossible to follow.

> I have not in any way advocated a return to the thirteenth century, whatever that might mean, but only the eternal utility, in a world of change, of any achievement of perfection. . . . The "disintegration of intellect" of which I speak was, so far as I can tell, an inevitable process. The process of knowledge and the process of history go on relentlessly, and it is always "up to" the human being to adapt himself to the alterations for which he is but partially responsible. Having achieved a unity on a basis which, so far as we can see, was partial and inaccurate, we can only go on and wait for luck to provide another. (222–3)

Though faced with an era that he would deem in need of transformation, one already suffering from the "disintegration of intellect," Eliot admits that the ideal thirteenth-century model of Dante is unavailable. The problems of the twentieth century are inevitable. Eliot tries to minimize this issue by foregrounding the benefits of "perfection," but cannot disencumber his logic from the problem posed by the tension between, on one hand, the exemplarity of Dante's belief system and, on the other, the constraints imposed one by one's own era, however impoverished it might be. Though he would like to write like Dante, the primacy of his own historical era insures that he cannot accomplish what he deems most fundamental about the greatness of Dante's writing.

This complex of thought stems from a mind on the fence between two different conceptions of poetry's social function. On one hand, Eliot is becoming the voice of *After Strange Gods* who is more concerned with the confirmation of orthodox values than with upsetting them. On the other, in order to perform this affirmation, he would need the kind of poetic ability to transform described in "Tradition;" he infers that to arrive at such a confirmation, modern society requires change, since these values are no longer the predominant ones.[3] Eliot regards Dante as exemplary because of his ability to make "sense" confirm the orthodox values of his age, but the troubling task becomes how to recover the orthodox values that are unavailable to poet's own era. The act ceases to be one of *confirmation* and necessarily becomes one of *transformation*. Although the political commitments become clearer for Eliot in this period, the relationship of poetry to politics does not. So the backdrop for *The Hollow Men* that the Clark Lectures provides is not only the endorsement of "the medieval wisdom of Richard St. Victor, Aquinas, Cavalcanti, and Dante" (83), as Bush suggests, but also the conflict of demands that such an endorsement produces in Eliot's poetics. Dante is both exemplary and impossible to follow. *The Hollow Men* fashions this conflict into its central concern by placing the task of confirming orthodox values in the feeble voices of the hollow men and the burden of transformation on style and in shadows.

In between shadows, shadows in between

J. Hillis Miller interprets the shadows in the final section of the poem as "the paralysis that seizes men who live in a completely subjective world" and the poem as "an eloquent analysis of the vacuity of subjective idealism" (181). Like many readers of the poem, Miller identifies how the shadows negate. Shadows, after all, generally hide and obscure: evil, monsters, and shame tend to be the sort of unscrupulous residents that they attract. Miller's subsequent account of the "fleeting glimpse" of hope in the poem thus seems far-fetched:

> Eliot's hollow men understand dimly that if they endure the death which is to preclude rebirth they have some hope for salvation. Though Eliot's language is deliberately ambiguous, it implies that the sightless eyes of the hollow men may see again, and confront the divine eyes which are "The hope only / Of empty men" and will reappear as "the perpetual star / Multifoliate rose" of heaven itself. The idealists of "The Hollow Men" have stepped out of themselves into the barrenness of an external world, and the fragments of the Lord's prayer ("For Thine is / ... For Thine is the") which they

mutter at the end of the poem are moving appeals to a God who
may be infinitely distant, but who is independent of their minds
and therefore may have the power to save them. (182)

Miller returns to the idea of salvation as a possibility for the hollow men.
Miller can thus place the poem on a trajectory toward Eliot's later artistic
efforts: "The movement of reversal and self-sacrifice begun in 'The Hollow
Men' culminates with the humility of 'Ash-Wednesday,' and is completed
in the affirmations of the 'Four Quartets' and the plays. These affirmations
are both a new means of personal salvation and a new definition of the role
of poetry" (184).

But God is not merely distant in this poem; God is radically absent
even as an idealization. Justified by the allusion to Dante, Miller supplements
the "Multifoliate rose" with his own description, "of heaven itself," but such
an implication is precisely the hope that the poem works so hard to cancel.
When the hollow men look to the stars for evidence of divinity and the hope
of salvation, they see only more emptiness in places that resemble their own
too much to offer any solace. The poem is too committed to demarcating a
ground for meaning that the absent divine figure cannot provide. Eliot makes
clear that the hollow men have no agency, and hence are incapable of self-
sacrifice. It is central to the poem's project to render such a place as heaven as
either inaccessible and inconceivable or proximate, and thus unable to live up
to any promise of transcendence.

Elisabeth Schneider privileges confusion itself as central to the poem. She
calls attention to the ways in which the poem fails to cohere: "But problems
arise from the recurring "words and their associations"—"eyes," "death," "kingdom," "a fading star," and words having to do with drought—which dominate
the poem" (102). She goes on to list the varieties and permutations of these
terms that abound in the poem before explaining her line of reasoning:

> I list these not in mockery but to indicate the perplexity of the
> house-dog, who will not go to sleep because he has had a sniff of
> meaning, because, in fact, the poem is enclosed within the very
> precise "meanings" of the drumbeat beginning and end. In between,
> however, the "meanings and associations" of the words become
> increasingly indeterminate, equations left insoluble by the presence
> of too many variables; and the result is not so much "suggestive" in
> the Symbolist sense as it is amorphous. (102)

The increasing indeterminacy of meaning, for Schneider, results in a poem
that shows its seams. She goes on to admit that she "cannot escape the

impression of its having been put together primarily out of thrift, as an ingenious means of preserving and making something out of short lyrics which never quite crystallized as lyrics and yet were too attractive to discard entirely" (106). The trick of the first four sections, however, is to present the thoughts and dreams of the hollow men as if they made sense or were governed by logic and, in so doing, demonstrate the opposite to be true. Their thoughts are all expressed simply and seem to build on one another as if simple steps to solving a larger complex problem. Rather than offering "meaning," they indeed only offer a "sniff" as Schneider complains.

The final version of *The Hollow Men*, published in November 1925, begins with a description of the hollow men and the sad state of affairs that causes their suffering. The status of voice in the poem puts the reader in a problematic relationship to the very words on the page, asking the reader to understand their declarations while paradoxically marking them as unintelligible: "Our dried voices, when / We whisper together / Are quiet and meaningless / As wind in dry grass / Or rats' feet over broken glass / In our dry cellar" (56). Accordingly, the short-lived re-emergence of the first-person singular in the second section is coupled with its own subsequent erasure: "Eyes I dare not meet in dreams"; "Let me be no nearer"; and "Let me also wear / Such deliberate disguises. . . . Behaving as the wind behaves / No nearer" (57). In these excerpts, the entrance of the negative after each verb cancels the first-person's attempts to assert and wish. The speech of the hollow men thus comes in voices whose ability to communicate vanishes; fleeting assertions of self give way quickly to retractions.

Just as the poem undermines the ability of the individual voice to announce and define itself, the poem also undercuts the reliability of any clear organization of place. Specifically, the poem's effort to make geographic delineations gradually gives way to geographic confusions. This drama begins with a meditation on the relationship between "us" and "Those who have crossed," in which the latter are separated from the former by space:

> Those who have crossed
> With direct eyes, to death's other Kingdom
> Remember us—if at all—not as lost
> Violent souls, but only
> As the hollow men
> The stuffed men. (56)

The stanza suggests two sets of distinctions, between "Those who have crossed . . ." and "us" and between "lost violent souls" and "the hollow men." By declaring that "Those who have crossed / With direct eyes, to death's other Kingdom / Remember us," the poem seems to authorize the memory of "Those who have crossed" in determining the value of "us." It reads as a gesture of humility that defers to the superior judgment of those that occupy a better place. But the closer one looks, the more this authorization becomes appropriately hollow. In addition, the sense of the verb, "remember," wavers between two very different options either suggesting a simple statement of fact (it is true that "Those who have crossed" remember us) or, alternately, an imperative desire, asking to be remembered in a certain manner (please do not remember us as violent souls, but as hollow men).

Although the poem begins to imagine an idealized heaven by mapping the place of the hollow men with respect to a series of "other" kingdoms, these geographic distinctions gradually gave way to indeterminacy.

> Eyes I dare not meet in dreams
> In death's dream kingdom
> These do not appear:
> There, the eyes are
> Sunlight on a broken column
> There, is a tree swinging
> And voices are
> In the wind's singing
> More distant and more solemn
> Than a fading star. (57)

Grammatical subjects in these lines sit in uncomfortable relationships to their predicates. The first of these subjects, "Eyes," suffers two lines of qualification before meeting its resolution, "do not appear," but not before reiteration by "These." The firm promise of the colon after the phrase, "These do not appear," in the third line above is broken because the lines before and after it fail to resolve into grammatical or spatial clarity. Other indicators of place, the strong mentions of "There" in the fourth and sixth lines, made emphatic by the caesura that follows each, ultimately fracture the sentences that they pretend to modify. The first threatens to hide the sentence's actual grammatical subject ("the eyes") in a subordinate clause. The second nearly flows through the comma that prevents "There, is a tree swinging" (nearly a question) from becoming "There is a tree swinging" (a clear descriptive statement). The stanza reads as if it were a pantheon of nouns competing for the role of antecedents for the pronouns, "There" and "These." More importantly, the attempt to clarify location in these lines meets with a troubled fate. The second and seventh lines ("In death's dream kingdom" and "In the wind's singing") unsuccessfully attempt to specify the place of action (or lack thereof). It is unclear in the first two lines of the section where the speaker dares not meet the "Eyes." Is "in dreams" synonymous with "in death's dream kingdom"? Do all dreams take place there or not? Similarly, it is uncertain whether the speaker wishes to use the phrase, "in the wind singing," as an apposition or to complete the predicate. The stanzas leave behind a fundamental confusion uncured by conspicuously absent punctuation.[4] Eliot's geography thus proliferates by way of chaotic cartography.

We also witness this drama of imprecision in the manipulation of demonstrative pronouns (here, there, these, those, this). Markers usually employed to delineate and organize space are instead used to obfuscate.

> This is the dead land
> This is cactus land
> Here the stone images
> Are raised, here they receive
> The supplication of a dead man's hand
> Under the twinkle of a fading star
>
> It is like this
> In death's other kingdom . . . (57)

The differences between "death's other kingdom" and "the dead land" and between this land and the "other" one break down under scrutiny. The various uses of the deictic, "this," fail miserably to indicate distinctiveness. In fact, all the markers of place in this passage serve to complicate rather than clarify just where "this dead," "cactus" land might be located with respect to "death's other kingdom," especially since the latter seems not altogether different from "this land": "It is *like* this / In death's other kingdom." Since the poem poses difference not between life and death, but this dead land and death's other kingdom, the burden of differentiation falls not on the adjective "dead," but on the nouns "land" and "kingdom." Here, adjectives fail to mark difference, and nouns must take up the slack. And that which seemed most central to the characterization of each place, death, becomes a shared trait and not a point of distinction.

Whatever the difference between these places, it must be marked in terms of an incremental logic instead of an oppositional one. Otherness becomes no longer a matter of difference, but of affinity, which in turn troubles any hope for the hollow men. The first stanza above depicts an act of religious appeal: "the stone images / Are raised, here they receive / The supplication of a dead man's hand / Under the twinkle of a fading star." But, hope for transcendence is squashed: this last entreaty by an abject figure located at a monumental distance from a vanishing star falls on deaf ears. Furthermore, the second stanza, set in "death's other kingdom," offers an equally empty scene as the alternative: "Waking alone / At the hour when we are / Trembling with tenderness / Lips that would kiss / Form prayers to broken stone." This "other" place offers no promise that one might expect from a location that is offered as the opposite of a "dead land." It fails as an idealization. God has not only abandoned the hollow men, but heaven as well.

The other kingdoms in the poem represent not places of wholeness in which one finds what one once lacked, but places that have too much in common with the land occupied by the hollow men to offer them any compelling imaginary promise. They become places understood within the system imposed by the poem and not as idealized other places outside this system. This progression culminates in the fourth section. By this point, we have lost track of any organizing logic for place, and words like "here" and "there" exacerbate rather than curb this trend.

> The eyes are not here
> There are no eyes here
> In this valley of dying stars
> In this hollow valley
> This broken jaw of our lost kingdoms (58)

By placing an undue burden on the accompanying adjectives to mark difference (adjectives whose failure to perform this task we have already witnessed), the descriptions of distinct locations with the same nouns ("stars" and "kingdoms" are associated with both here and there) fail to clarify any criteria for difference. We come to doubt the finality of this "last of meeting places" because we have long ago tossed away our maps. In the final stanza above, we arrive at the site where Miller saw hope. Indeed, the equivocation, "unless," after the stated problem, "sightless," seems to validate Miller's optimism. But if the problem were sightlessness, then one would hope that the reappearance of "the eyes" might bring vision, sight, and indeed insight. The reappearance of the eyes, however, does not exactly promise the experience of seeing; rather, the eyes emerge as themselves an objective sight to behold, "As the perpetual star / Multifoliate rose." The promise here is not of transcendent vision, but of witnessing the objectified image of seeing itself, which is very much at home in the system of objects the poem establishes. These at last eyes fail to bring any insight.

Schneider's frustrated reader thus has a legitimate complaint, but ultimately her bafflement arises from too close an identification with the hope for transcendence that the poem implodes. The "other" idealized places in the poem lose their potential value as sites of religious transcendence or salvation, since one fails not only to locate them, but also to imagine them at all. The distinction, between "here" and "there," collapses in this drama of failed deictics. All that remains from this progressively indeterminate exploration of spatial coordinates is an imperative to refuse such categories as structures for thought. There is no heaven here or anywhere and neither is there salvation because the difference between "here" and "there" itself breaks down. Instead, the universe expands into undifferentiated space, inhabited by souls doomed in different degrees.

In addition, the first four sections of the poem perform the failure of individual agency by severing the hollow men from any context in which their thoughts or voices might have meaning while persistently offering the hope that they might succeed. As we witnessed in the opening section, their speech produces content only in the suggestions of eidetic images: "Our voices, when / We whisper together / Are quiet and meaningless / As wind in dry grass / Or rats' feet over broken glass / In our dry cellar." In these quick lines, however, the similes link meaninglessness with a surprising excess. The sound of whispers opens onto the perceptions of an eye capable of attending to small, seemingly irrelevant details. *The Hollow Men* is filled with velleities, which it locates in eidetic images, as if the careful effort to locate the place of things (wind in dry grass, rats' feet over broken glass in a dry cellar) might serve as a small solace for the crisis of signification that pervades the poem. These eidetic images complicate the meaninglessness of the hollow voices by gesturing, however slightly, toward an all but invisible content. So while semantic signification fails, the similes that describe this failure leave images that mark the velleities that linger in voices otherwise devoid of volition. The substance, which the hollow men lack when trying to announce their subjective identities, becomes associated with minuscule objects that supplement their meaningless whispers.

Although these whispers give way to whimpers in the poem's final section, the most prominent figures in this finale are the shadows. Taking his cue from Eliot's allusion to Shakespeare's Brutus, Hugh Kenner describes the shadow in terms similar to Miller's. He suggests that the Shadow's fall consistently cuts and impedes like an executioner's ax (an image he invokes just previous to the following excerpt). It thereby ends any aspiration to enact a plan, as in the case of Guy Fawkes, or, as for Brutus, it causes suffering "between the acting of a dreadful thing / And the first motion."[5]

Brutus undertook, and carried through, an action not unlike Guy Fawkes', and on principles equally high; though an action less

abstract; bearing a knife is a more personal crime than lighting a
fuse beneath victims one cannot see. The "dream" for Brutus was
an interim stage, to be passed through. The Shadow that fell for
Fawkes took the form of sudden scruple among certain of his
co-conspirators. He was detected and hanged. The Shadow for
the Hollow Men falls apparently in the faculty of the will itself,
impeding themselves alone; no one will know, in the absence of
a produced "reality," that there ever was an "idea." They may lead,
presumably, blameless lives. But they are neither worse than Brutus,
or Fawkes, nor better. (192–3)

For the hollow men, according to Kenner, the falling Shadow threatens to
cut short the will, filling in the interim stage between the conception of the
idea and its execution. Gathering a good deal of momentum from the twin
stories of failed or painful insurrections, Kenner identifies the Shadow as a
force that negates or at very least hinders. This seems a reasonable conclusion given that this section follows such a thorough dramatization of the
failure that pervades the lives of the hollow men.

A. David Moody and Ronald Bush share the view that the shadows in
the poem's final section represent a figure of obfuscation, of ambiguity itself.
Moody writes, "The Shadow is, of course, indefinable" (126), while Bush
claims that it "would be a mistake to push the moods to any conclusion other
than the ambivalence expressed in the ambiguity of 'Shadow'" (101). Both
are right to foreground the final section and its troubling shadows as crucial,
since they dramatically break from the thematics worked though in the first
four sections, replacing a consideration of the hollow men with a puzzling
taxonomy of vague concepts that seems divorced from the previous, more
direct, elaboration of voice and place. While the earlier sections attend to the
pathetic condition of enfeebled would-be subjects, the final section concerns
itself with abstractions in a more distant manner. On the other hand, this
last section also acts as the culmination of the poem because of the finality
claimed by its grandly authoritative tone, most notably in the final lines, "This
is the way the world ends / Not with a bang but with a whimper." The finality
of tone, its position as the final section, and its seeming unwillingness to lead
the reader beyond ambiguity thus produces an odd friction, promising, but
refusing, to clarify and finalize the development of the first four stanzas.

The first four sections attempt to accord human thought as figured by the
hollow men with orthodox belief, but the available structures ultimately fold
in on themselves. The failure of the many binary differences in these sections
also means the impossibility of salvation because an ideal place like heaven
and a divine figure become unimaginable. The only intelligibility that remains

after the collapse of such idealizations is the affinity between increasingly pro-
liferating places. The final section, and the last to be added to the poem for
publication in its final form, however, removes the quest for meaning from any
religious context and reorients it toward a vision of poetic language, in which
velleities become intelligible, not by according individual voice any additional
meaning, but by shifting the criteria of meaning itself. Whereas the first four
sections offer a sniff of meaning that ultimately disappoints, the final section
tries to move subtly toward clarity. If the world of the hollow men fails to
deliver on its promises, the final section attempts to make redress.

In both form and theme, this final section foregrounds the middle, the
space in between fragments and ideas. As for its form, it begins and ends
with a modified version of the children's song, taking the lines, "Here we
go round the mulberry bush" and "This is the way we clap our hands," and
changing them into "*Here we go round the prickly pear*" and "*This is the way
the world ends.*" Obviously, the children's song becomes burdened here with
more adult images and themes. Four stanzas fall in between this frame, the
first three about the shadow's fall. In between each of these four stanzas,
the poem offers two allusions. The fragment from the Lord's Prayer, "*For
Thine is the Kingdom,*" appears twice, between the first and second of the four
and between the third and fourth. Finally, Eliot places an allusion to Joseph
Conrad's *An Outcast of the Islands* (1896), "*Life is very long,*" in the very center
of this final section of the poem with exactly fifteen lines before and after it.
One can imagine how Eliot might have thought of his poem and identified
with the novel's protagonist when reading sentences like the following: "He
struggled with the sense of certain defeat—lost his footing—fell back into
the darkness. With a faint cry and an upward throw of his arms he gave up as
a tired swimmer gives up: because the swamped craft is gone from under his
feet; because the night is dark and the shore is far—because death is better
than strife" (80–1).

At the very center of this final section then, Eliot places an odd auto-
graphical moment. In Conrad, the words are spoken to a man named Willems
by a seaman named Lingard who is Willems's mentor. Willems has just been
caught stealing from his employer and cast out of his house by his wife. Not
at all a sympathetic character, he has despised his wife for years and in fact
beat her. Sensing that Lingard cares too much about the feelings of his wife,
Willems initiates the following exchange, from which Eliot's line derives.

"Your compassion is all for my wife, Captain Lingard," said
Willems moodily. "Do you think I am so very happy?"
"No! No!" said Lingard, heartily. "Not a word more shall pass
my lips. I had to speak my mind once, seeing that I knew you

from a child, so to speak. And now I shall forget; but you are young yet. Life is very long," he went on, with unconscious sadness; "let this be a lesson to you." (42)

The line that Eliot borrows from Conrad is meant to comfort an outcast; that life is very long gives Willems more chances perhaps to make better choices. Place in the very middle of the final section, the allusion references Eliot's own marital problems, but only in an obscurity manner. The line from Conrad is far from memorable and does not explicitly mention anything to do with troubled marriages. So as we witnessed earlier in the poem, the concerns of the individual are both asserted and retracted in this allusion.

The section in fact is a series of allusions, and, much of it borrowed, little if any of the language here seems to derive from a central poetic persona. Despite this fact, the section is not simply a cold rehearsal of allusions. Rather, it stages the very same conflicted thinking witnessed in the Clark Lectures, epitomized here by the tension between the Lord's Prayer fragment and the reference to Conrad: the concern for the individual competes with reverence for God. The intelligence of the section is thus not found in profundity of statement; from this standpoint, the poem is not even original. Rather, the tone and affective register of this section are effects of style. The strategies of arrangement and collage and the manner in which the poem assembles the borrowed fragments combine to represent a personal struggle. The language here simultaneously reveals and obscures. It cites other contexts by way of allusions, but treats them ambivalently, shedding innocence from the children's song and reverence from the Lord's Prayer fragment.

Style in this poem claims the same position as the shadows, the place in between. And if the hollow men fail to speak in a meaningful way because their reliance on divine governance fails, then the shadows re-conceive semantics itself. The relationship of affinity that confused the previous efforts to clarify geography here opens in language sites of possibility, interstitial spaces in between words and ideas, which might make sense of otherwise meaningless utterances.

For Thine is
Life is
For Thine is the (59)

Notice the competing contexts in this penultimate stanza, which are presented as parallel sentence fragments: between an orthodox context, "For Thine is," and a more ambiguous context, "Life is." Though presented in similar gnomic patterns, these fragments have opposing implications. The first, "For Thine is" functions as a deliberate elision and refusal, omitting the obvious nouns from the Lord's Prayer that name and confirm divine authority, "the Kingdom and the Power and the Glory Forever." The choice to leave out the second half of the sentence seems tantamount to blasphemy. The elision of the description "very long" from Conrad's sentence, in contrast, does not significantly change the force of the statement. The force of the former is obvious, calling attention to the enormity of what has been cut, while that of the latter is more ambiguous.

Instead of a failed idealization of heaven and earth, this section describes an idealized vision of language mapped out in space. The oppositions between which the Shadow falls, follow the course of all oppositions in this poem: first, because the Shadow's fall marks the space in between the poles, not as empty, but as markable space. Secondly, the odd range of criteria that determines these poles makes us wonder if they are oppositions at all. One could conceive of "idea" and "reality" as antonyms, but "motion" and "act" seem somewhat synonymous or at least different degrees of the same action. "Conception" and "creation" perhaps mark different chronological points in a process. "Desire" and "spasm," along with the pair of "potency" and "existence," seem opposites in some senses and similar in others. "Essence" and "descent" seem paired for their phonetic kinship as much as any other. Ultimately, these pairings cannot share the same criteria for difference; each term within each pair has alternative connotations sufficient to unsettle any categorical account of how the couplings work in general.

The idealized space of language described in this final section is thus not represented as a place of unity or fusion. It does not eradicate difference, but rather, arranges relationships of difference such that the reader experiences difference not categorically, but separately. What emerges out of these relationships is an invitation to imagine language not as a representation of its own failure, but as a struggle that demands engagement. Inscribed in this idealization of language is thus an imperative to redress the problem of meaning by adding a third point of reference, the fall of the shadow, to the binary logic that proved so faulty in the poem's earlier sections. The failure of the opposition becomes a faith in triangulation as a way to recover meaning in language. This imperative shifts the question of meaning away from an orthodox context, "For Thine is," to livable experience, "Life is." It re-directs the mental energy from the effort that the first four sections put into an understanding of a self-imploding conception of heaven and earth to an attempt to build meaning, not through a mastery of language, but through the experience of language's ambiguities.

The shadows thus perform a similar effect as the gnomons from the poem's first section: "Shape without form, shade without colour, / Paralysed force, gesture without motion" (56). Although these lines tempt us to read them as simple negations, they also give rise to a series of related questions: how might one possibly conceive shape without form?; what is shade without color?; what sort of energy can a "paralysed force" muster? In so doing, they ask us first to find difference in what seems a pair of synonyms and then to imagine a third term that might result. Instead of occlusions, we see eclipses. These shadows not only function to obscure, but more importantly, to indicate. The shadows both refuse the accepted meanings of the words they fall between, as the negations did in the earlier section, and point to velleities that escape the common meaning while invoking them at the same time. Just as the subtractions of the earlier section invited the reader to imagine what the remainder might mean after such an ostensibly complete subtraction, the shadows in this section ask the reader to seek meaning through alternate criteria. The shadows defamiliarize our expectations with regard to language and then ask us to think about meaning through the relationships between words that have suddenly become peculiar. The shadows literally fall, as if they were figures of weight. Unlike the voices of the hollow men, which seemed light by comparison, "As wind in dry grass / Or rats' feet over broken glass," these shadows have a decisive gravity. As we have seen, God is absent from the landscape of the hollow men. The same is true in this final section. The fragment of the Lord's Prayer, "For Thine Is," refuses divine power. The implied question behind such a prayer then becomes, what is prayer when not addressed to God?

The answer that this poem provides is that prayer without God is poetry. The only description associated with God in this stanza is "The Kingdom," a term which the poem has already over-determined and rendered meaningless. The semantics of this final section claim for poetry a mobility of thought impossible to conceive in terms of orthodoxy. It substitutes a failed religious hope with a faith in language, not by a reliance on an external God to offer transcendence, but through the construction of a belief system that replaces God as a means for understanding the universe, which maintains the weight of the system it replaces; what led to impossibility and futility earlier for the hollow men here become virtues. *The Hollow Men* refuses to make the religious leap of faith and insists on dwelling within the shadows, so much so that it replaces religious faith with a faith in ambiguity and doubt. This tension is even more significant because the ideological commitments under attack derive from Eliot's own beliefs. The dramatized conflict pits a mind against itself. The poem is so powerful because it demonstrates the conflict in Eliot between conservative political beliefs on one hand, and a separate belief in the power of poetry on the other. In this poem, the two struggle for prominence, but however personally committed to orthodox values Eliot might have been, he simply could not write an orthodox poem at this point in his career, not even disguised in the regalia of orthodox blasphemy.

The ecliptic style of this poem reveals the personal emotions that many expect to find in the Hale letters. Even if Eliot did labor in his writing to escape personality, in *The Hollow Men*, we see how personally these evasions end up registering. I think that it is no coincidence that Eliot chose from Conrad words of comfort offered to a man who has just been cast out by a wife that he had come to despise. The most forceful representation of suffering in the poem, however, does not come through a buried allusion, but rather, through the tension between the radical failure of the hollow men in the first four sections and the passive aggressive assertion of style in the finale. Whimpers for Eliot in this poem carry the force of bangs. Whimpers in the end are not retreats. This is what Eliot offers up for public consumption, his distaste for publicity notwithstanding, in his deepest and darkest shadows.

Notes

1. All quotations from *The Hollow Men* come from this volume and will hereafter be parenthetically cited with page number only.

2. Early on in the lecture series, Eliot had confessed more than an academic interest in the study of the metaphysical tradition: "My attitude is that a craftsman who has attempted for eighteen years to make English verses, studying the work of dead artisans who have made better verses. The interest of a craftsman is centered in the present and immediate future: he studies the literature of the past in order to learn how he should write in the present and the immediate future; and no matter how profound and disinterested his studies, they will always so to speak come out at the finger tips, and find their completion in the action of the chisel, the brush or the typewriter" (44).

3. See Asher: "What the Clark lectures provide is evidence of the transition from classicism to orthodoxy, though as I have tried to indicate this is really just an adjustment of a constant set of values rather than a break with the past" (21). As a statement about Eliot's politics, Asher's account offers a strong case for this claim. But as a statement about Eliot's poetics, it ignores the internal complexities around the question of poetic agency which are crucial not to a decision about Eliot's ideological commitments, but to the value of Eliot's thought for contemporary theory and criticism. His description of Eliot's break—"Radical individualism and reliance on one's inner voice is still anathema, but the charge of romanticism is evolving into that of heresy"—is attentive to Eliot's revised diagnosis of problematic poetry, but overlooks the complicated terrain poetic agency must now occupy in his new model. The shift towards orthodoxy places a more intense pressure on this poetic agency, which does not disappear as much as it becomes more problematic.

4. See Eliot *Letters*. In a letter to John Quinn dated 9 May 1921, Eliot writes, "I see reason in your objection to my punctuation; but I hold that the line itself punctuates, and the addition of a comma in many places, seems to me to over-emphasize the arrest. That is because I always pause at the end of a line in reading verse, which perhaps you do not" (451). But one need only to listen to Eliot's own recorded

reading of *The Waste Land*, particularly to the portions of "The Fire Sermon" that are structured not unlike these lines from *The Hollow Men* to see that this is indeed not his practice, even when reading aloud.

   5. Kenner quotes from *Julius Caesar* II.i.63–4.

WORKS CITED

Abbott, H. Porter. *Beckett Writing Beckett: The Author in the Autograph*. Ithaca: Cornell University Press.

Asher, Kenneth. "Poetry and Politics in T.S. Eliot's Clark Lectures." *Yeats Eliot Review* 15.1 (1997): 18–23.

Bush, Ronald. *T.S. Eliot: A Study in Character and Style*. New York: Oxford University Press, 1983.

Conrad, Joseph. *An Outcast of the Islands*. Garden City, NY: Doubleday, Page, 1926.

Cooley, Martha. *The Archivist*. Boston: Little, Brown and Company, 1998.

Eliot, T.S. *After Strange Gods: A Primer of Modern Heresy*. New York: Harcourt Brace, 1934.

———. *The Complete Poems and Plays, 1909–1950*. New York: Harcourt Brace, 1952.

———. *The Letters of T.S. Eliot, 1898–1922*. Ed. Valerie Eliot. Vol. 1. Harcourt, Brace, Jovanovich, 1988.

———. "Tradition and the Individual Talent." *The Sacred Wood: Essays on Poetry and Criticism*. London: Methuen, 1920.

———. *The Varieties of Metaphysical Poetry: The Clark Lectures at Trinity College, Cambridge, 1926, and the Turnbull Lectures at the Johns Hopkins University, 1933*. Ed. Ronald Schuchard. New York: Harcourt Brace, 1994.

Kenner, Hugh. *The Invisible Poet: T.S. Eliot*. New York: Harcourt, Brace and World, 1959.

Leavis, F.R. "T.S. Eliot as Critic." *Anna Karenina and Other Essays*. London: Chatto & Windus, 1967.

Matthews, T.S. *Great Tom: Notes Toward the Definition of T.S. Eliot*. New York: Harper and Row, 1973.

Miller, J. Hillis. *Poets of Reality: Six Twentieth-Century Writers*. Cambridge: Harvard University Press, 1965.

Moody, A. David. *Thomas Stearns Eliot, Poet*. 2nd ed. New York: Cambridge University Press, 1994.

Schneider, Elisabeth. *T. S. Eliot: The Pattern in the Carpet*. Berkeley: University of California Press, 1975.

Strunk, William, Jr. and E. B. White. *The Elements of Style*. 4th ed. Boston: Allyn and Bacon, 1979.

JOHN H. TIMMERMAN

The Aristotelian Mr. Eliot:
Structure and Strategy in The Waste Land

Agnostic though he was at the time, T.S. Eliot undoubtedly was searching for some degree of spiritual direction in his Waste Land Cycle of poems.
His thoughts might well have been incarnated in Gerontion's words:

> I have not made this show purposelessly
> And it is not by any concitation
> Of the backward devils.
> I would meet you upon this honestly.[1]

The pronoun "this" in the final line is strategically ambiguous. Does it refer
to his earlier deliberation on the vacuity of human history and the soul-
robbing lack of passion in the modern age? Or, more likely, does it refer to
the immediate subject of the stanza in which it appears—the spring (appearance or leap) of the tiger in the new year (spring)?

* * *

Since Eliot did consider "Gerontion" as a prefatory poem to *The Waste Land*,
the questions are not without merit, both in their criticism of the modern
age and also their search for the meaning of Christ in an age without

From *Yeats Eliot Review* 24, no. 2 (Summer 2007): 11–23. © 2007 by John H. Timmerman.

apparent meaning. "Gerontion" sets against each other, in a tension typical of *The Waste Land*, the Logos of the Gospel of John, the sign already given, and a search for answers located within the age itself. Thus, while "Christ the Tiger" is divided in a profaned sacrament by such people as Mr. Silvero, the profanation itself causes the tiger to leap and snap our hollowness under its jaws. The pivotal passage on human intellectual history—"After such knowledge, what forgiveness?"—that also expresses Gerontion's own rationalist defense against passionate commitment, whirls apart in mere words when the tiger springs.

Spiritual stultification marks Eliot's modern wasteland. The individual self remains impotent to reach beyond itself in any directed commitment. The inhabitants of the waste spaces peer into mirrors, unable to escape the pitiless stare of their shrunken passion. *The Waste Land*, with its sustained deliberation on self-gratification and urgency, welds together the bleakness of modernism and the tense uncertainty of a culture mired in spiritual quicksand. Yet, *The Waste Land* also points toward a way out of the wasteland.

Many readers have recognized the lyrical and symbolic suggestiveness of Section V and have related it as a response to earlier sections. Only partially explored is the careful way in which the thunder's commands respond to the debased trinity of earlier sections. Essentially, Eliot establishes a three-fold devolution in which passion becomes mere urgency, the quest for the divine becomes immediate gratification, and civilization becomes the Unreal City. In each of these patterns, moreover, Eliot carefully adapts the philosophy of Aristotle to nuance his analysis of the modern human condition. Particularly important to this study are Aristotle's use of the *via negative*, his analysis of animal and human distinctions in *Partibus Animalium* and *De Anima*, and his ideological ethics in *Nicomachean Ethics*.

Aristotle, Aquinas, and the *Via Negativa*

Eliot's acquaintance with Aristotle was lengthy and profound already by the time of *The Waste Land*. Sections of his dissertation lauded Aristotle for his ability to combine realism and idealism in the *Physics*. In a 1916 essay on Leibniz, Eliot appreciated this balance of Aristotle: "Aristotle is too keen a metaphysician to start from a naive view of matter or from a one-sided spiritualism."[2] In "The Perfect Critic" (1920), an essay that addressed the modern schism between intelligence and sense perception, Eliot turns again to Aristotle: "He was primarily a man of not only remarkable and universal intelligence; and universal intelligence means that he could apply his intelligence to anything. . . . There is no method except to be very intelligent, but of intelligence itself swiftly operating the analysis of sensation to the point of principle and definition."[3] This modulation of intelligence and sensation to a syncretic whole became something of a lifelong creed for Eliot, affecting his life, essays, and poetic theory.

Aquinas' undertaking of the synthesis of Aristotelian philosophical system with Christian theology arose from Averroes' earlier translation of Aristotle, which, Aquinas believed, was invalidated by Averroes' commentary that cast Aristotle in a distinctly Moslem slant. Moreover, Aquinas believed that Averroes had misrepresented Aristotle's method altogether, thereby giving a twisted echo rather than a true translation. Thus, Aquinas set out not only to reappropriate that system for the west, but also to "baptize" Aristotle's First Mover[4] as the Christian God. In this process he adopted Aristotle's method of negation to serve his own ends.[5]

The effort was intrinsically difficult, for Aristotle's First Mover is aloof, impersonal, and distant. Yet, one can know certain things about this Being by excluding those qualities limited to human sensory and verbal experience. These could not be properties that define the Unmoved Mover since our senses are always at variance. Although we will return to the qualities of the First Mover itself later in this study, it is important to recognize here that distinction between sensory and verbal experience and the epistemology acquired by mind (the Aristotelian *Nous*) and will. To this end the *via negativa* is essential.[6]

For both Aristotle and Aquinas, the idea of the *via negativa* begins with two characteristics of humanity—dependence and limitation. Only God is essential being. His nature is to exist. All creation depends upon and stands in relation to this higher cause. Furthermore, whatever we describe of God is anthropomorphic and linguistically limited. Our difficulty in knowing God, Aquinas points out, is that "any term that denotes perfection modified by a creaturely limitation cannot be predicated of God except in the manner of simile and metaphor."[7] Consequently, human knowledge of God is often by means of analogy. We can at best describe what God is *like*, given the limitations of experience and language.

But at this point the logical progression of the *via negativa* comes to aid. The way of negation denies that we can know God's essence; only God himself knows that. Nonetheless, there are certain qualities that we can deny of God. We know, for example, that he is not material, else he would be confined to time and space as we know it. The more qualities we can deny of God, then, the better we can isolate qualities that we do understand.[8] The value of the *via negativa* lies precisely in the fact that human knowing is so cluttered with sensory and experiential data that our tendency is to make truth claims based on those data. We "know" by self-reference.

The *via negativa* leads to epistemological conclusions. In this way also *The Waste Land* in its entirety may be read as a *via negativa*, exposing the way of negation by which one lives in the modern age, excluding those as avenues of epistemological certitude, and drawing from them signs toward a positive way. Eliot offers two options: the ceaseless burning of the fire sermon, or the rumble of thunder. The burning of desire is wholly self-inclusive while the rumble of the thunder calls one away from self. Moreover, as this essay examines that conflict, it also becomes apparent that the very structure of the poem mirrors the dialectic.

To arrive at a full understanding of those directions, however, one has to follow Eliot's precarious way of negation. If one can identify and exclude qualities of the age that are not, or work against, enduring values, then one can begin to define those values that do endure and that are redemptive of the age.[9] Seen in this way, *The Waste Land* is not one long lament over the desolation of the modern age, but a vigorous intellectual searching for a remedy to that desolation. This may be seen further in the primary structure of trinities upon which Eliot builds the poem.

The Debased Trinity

Passion

Prior to *The Waste Land*, Eliot's characters often represent the absence of any gratification because of immobilizing stasis. For example, Prufrock's imagination leads him "to an overwhelming question," but also to a multiplicity of answers to the question. Consequently, he is paralyzed by inaction through his fear of others and what their responses might be. He typifies, as Eliot wrote in *The Hollow Men*, "Paralyzed force, gesture without motion."

Similarly, Gerontion stands as one who has "lost my passion." In his case, however, passion has been lost to the spinning gears of rationalization. "Inquisition" is necessitated by "terror," but what is lost is beauty. The vortex of the rational mind is figured in the spinning apart of the "fractured atoms" at the end of the poem. The substantive difference from Prufrock is the fact that Gerontion genuinely laments his state with its lost opportunities.

The Waste Land opens with the narrator's sensual yearning, the April rain stirring "memory and desire" out of the dead land of winter. Section I, as Lyndall Gordon has argued, takes the form of a spiritual confessional, where fragmentary and deliberately incomplete entries "demand a reciprocal effort" from the reader.[10] From the outset, then, the poem demands that the reader join in the spiritual discovery of the poem: "The point lies not in their [spiritual confessions] context so much as in the reader's act of self-discovery and judgment."[11] If so, the attendant question is what self-discovery appears to be made in the narrator and reader in regard to passion? Are we simply mired again in Prufrock's social fear or in Gerontion's rational cage?

In *The Waste Land* the narrator suffers from a sensual passion that is self-consuming rather than transcending. His passion fails to find an end outside of self, but exists only to gratify the self. Even at this early point, Eliot's understanding of and appreciation for Aristotle comes to bear upon the poem.

In the *Nicomachean Ethics*, Aristotle argues that "neither the virtues nor the vices are passions" simply because virtue and vice are choices, while passions are matters of character.[12] The question central to *The Waste Land* is whether characters act out of choice or passion. Making a determination on that issue leads directly toward uncovering Eliot's philosophy of ethics in the poem.

In his inventive and fascinating study *The Parts of Animals*, Aristotle argued that humans most nearly resemble animals in sensual passions. Consequently, he locates the source for sensual passion in the weighty, lower extremities. He reserves the source of intellect and choice in the head that deliberates and hands that enact.

Aristotle makes his clearest distinctions between animals and humans in *De Anima*, however. Common to each are the nutritive soul and reproductive soul, the basest qualities in all living things. In humans, as with animals, these may be manifested as pure appetite not governed by the will. Humans are distinguished by possessing, beyond nutrition, reproduction, and sensation, the power of mind or intellect, the highest form of soul, and that which allies us with the First Mover.[13] This is a distinction he returns to in *Metaphysics*. In his prefatory discussion (Book I), Aristotle varies his premise only slightly: "The animals other than man live by appearance and memories, and have but little of connected experience; but the human race lives also by art and reasoning."[14] One advances through sensation, memory, experience, and art, to theoretical knowledge, the essential for a study of being and substance. At its highest level, then, theoretical knowledge brings us into relationship with absolute being and substance—the First Mover.

In *The Nicomachean Ethics*, Aristotle casts his entire theory in ethical terms, and those are more precisely applicable to *The Waste Land*. If we say that nutrition and reproduction are intrinsic characteristics of all living beings (plant, animal, and human), humanity adds to these the capacity of theoretical knowledge. While in metaphysical matters this is capacity for knowing God (the First Mover), in ethical matters it is the power of virtuous choice: "Virtue, then, is a state of character concerned with choice, lying in a mean, i.e. the mean relative to us, this being determined by a rational principle, and by that principle by which the man of practical wisdom would determine it."[15] Aristotle's claim that virtue constitutes a mean sounds problematic, suggesting relativity to individual inclination. Such is not the case. There are actions, Aristotle insists, that are intrinsically bad:

But not every action nor every passion admits of a mean; for some have names that already imply badness, e.g. spite, shamelessness, envy, and in the case of actions adultery, theft, murder; for all of these and suchlike things imply by their names that they are themselves bad, and not the excesses or deficiencies of them. It is not possible, then, ever to be right with regard to them; one must always be wrong. Nor does goodness or badness with regard to such things depend on committing adultery with the right woman, at the right time, and in the right way, but simply to do any of them is to go wrong.[16]

As Aristotle develops his theory, it becomes clear that any action that is "self-indulgent," or purely for gratification of sensual desire, is a vice. At one point, Aristotle's condemnation of vice sounds eerily like one of the thunder's commands: "For it [self-indulgence] consists in two things, deficiency in giving and excess in taking."[17] On the contrary, the virtue of justice "does what is advantageous to another."[18]

In *The Waste Land*, sensuality devolves into an increasingly negative pattern. In Section II, "A Game of Chess," lust burns from the upper class woman to the pub-women. Some argue that three classes, including middle class, are represented in this section; the point, however, appears to be the social inclusiveness of gratification of mere desire. In the same pattern Tiresias, the mythic icon of debased sexuality, witnesses the seduction of the typist and a sequence of seductions on the Thames.

THE DIVINE

The second major pattern of debasement, also introduced in Section I, involves a spiritual quest. Although universalized as the Grail Quest in Section V, it is introduced here as the same need for immediate gratification when the narrator stops at Madame Sosostris to have his fortune told.[19] Rather than seeking some sense of the divine outside himself, he seeks an immediate sign as psychological solace. Such is also the case with Gerontion's "Christ the Tiger." This divine sign, introduced in "Gerontion" as the *Logos*, has been given. Modern humanity debases the sign to the need for immediate answers.[20]

Just as passion can either be debased to merely sensual gratification or direct humanity toward answers outside the self, so too the search for the divine can either be stripped to immediacy or direct humanity to transcendent sources. These dialectics also correspond with Aristotle's aligning of humanity with the First Mover.

It has been suggested that Aristotle's philosophy may be summarized by two words—quality and quantity. The more properties a thing or being shares, the fewer of those things or beings exist. There are fewer animals, for example, than plants; fewer of different sorts of men such as slaves, "mechanics" or laborers, or husbandmen; and fewer still of masters, intellectuals, and rulers. The pyramid tops out with the First Mover. While the point is limited, it does encapsulate Aristotle's belief that all life is discrete while the supreme being is unity. In the same way the disjunctive nature of Sections I–IV of *The Waste Land* reveal characters far removed from any sense of a divine source for unity.

While we often turn first to Aristotle's *Metaphysics* to learn of his First Mover and the relation of humanity to it, hints of his theory appear throughout his works like a cohesive thread.[21] *Metaphysics*, particularly Books IV and IX, does two things. First, it provides definition (which for Aristotle is always a process of separation). Second it relates humanity, albeit inconclusively, to the Unmoved Mover in a First Cause / Final Cause relationship—thereby providing humanity something of a teleology. But, since the First Mover is not at all involved in this world, does not really know this world, and has no plan for or ultimate interest in this world, that teleology itself is disturbingly vague. In effect, humanity struggles toward an ideal way of life that the *philosopher* sets out for it.

Aristotle, then, sought a rigidly fixed system, defined by careful parameters, in which the First Cause is also, at once, the Final Cause. The *Telos*, or end, of humanity is to be in accord with this Cause.[22] The issue of humanity's relationship with the divine is much less rigid for Eliot, however. *The Waste Land* dramatizes for the reader the conflicts and choices universal to the human condition. The poem itself is a searching out, rather than a positioning of apodictic and universal truths or values. Indeed, even twisted or debased passions may in themselves become avenues of divine enlightenment. Such, for example, is also the view of Lyndall Gordon in her analysis of the confessional narrative in *The Waste Land*.[23]

The characters of *The Waste Land*, however, lack both a sense of ethical imperative and also a divine source for those ethics. Lacking those, they look to the Madame Sosostrises for immediate signs. It is because they are unknowing and unknown. Yet their fear in this handful of dust that shapes their bodies compels them to look for something. Or, just anything. Precisely there, moreover, lies another example of the way of negation in *The Waste Land*, for if impulsiveness governs self-gratification, so too it governs humanity's search for the divine in the modern age. No sustained, concerted effort guides us, but merely a chasing after chimeras.

"The Fire Sermon," consequently, reveals the divine virtually disappeared from the arid land, reduced to the memory of "The king my brother's wreck / And . . . the king my father's wreck before him." The bones of the spiritual past now litter "a little low dry garret" for the musings of hermits. Not surprisingly, the Fisher King narrates here. His wounded genitalia represent both the absence of a vital life force in the land and also the pronounced separation from spiritual significance figured in the absence of rain, the fouled river, and the blasted aridity of the land.

The City

The third major pattern of debasement, also introduced in Section I, appears with the "Unreal City," which represents modern civilization generally. Thereby, the movement of the three parts fluctuates among sensual experience, the debased spiritual quest, and the disillusionment of modern humanity. The city is unreal precisely because it holds no redemptive force. Rather, it is a force unto itself, an anarchistic mechanism running on its own engine of greed and relentless hurry. The parade of people on London Bridge in Section I is symptomatic. Each individual hurries in the crowd, but finally it is only the crowd, like so many lemmings, that one perceives.

Appropriately, Eliot links this mass of humanity with the sighing dead of Dante's *Inferno*:

> So long a train
> Of people, I never should have believed
> Death had undone so many. (Canto III, 55–57)

The scene also evokes the narrator's acquaintance Stetson, who has buried something in his garden (Christ?) that he wants very much to keep buried. Like the dead without hope in the *Inferno*, sighing without hope, the crowd of humanity plods over London Bridge. Like Stetson, the crowd tries hard to bury the past. The closing line, taken from Baudelaire's "To the Reader," the prefatory poem to *The Flowers of Evil*, both reflects upon the scene of the crowd, and also extends outward to modern humanity. Baudelaire's poem scourges a humanity captive in sin: "Each day we take another step to hell."[24]

The pattern of the "unreal" city, stripped of communal value and purpose, shapes a poetic backdrop that holds the other tensions in place. It is at once setting and central symbol. It is both the background noise of a tinny gramophone and "horns and motors," and also the reflective agent of a people rushing about in tumultuous, pointless hurry. "Teach us to sit still," Eliot implores in *Ash Wednesday*. In *The Waste Land* there is no still point, but only people tumbling around the prickly pear. The unreal city of London introduced in Section I, wrapped in a brown fog in Section II, turns more universal as the poem emerges, including in its symbolic arms civilization generally. We sit with Tiresias by the wall of Thebes; we go with Augustine into Carthage. With the focus on the Grail Quest in Section V, the expanse broadens, for the loss of the Grail represents the loss of civilized values altogether. Now we watch the "falling towers of Jerusalem Athens Alexandria Vienna London Unreal," even as we stumble to the tower of the Chapel Perilous.

In many respects Eliot's portrait of the debased Unreal City in *The Waste Land* also traces to Aristotle, and it is tempting to draw parallels. Similarities to Aristotle's *Politics* exist. For example, for Aristotle (as with other Greek thinkers) the state exists for an end—the supreme good of humanity evidenced in moral and intellectual virtues. The state thereby is a protectorate, insuring what Aristotle calls the "good life," meaning precisely these virtues. All this would comport with Eliot's positive view of civilization as arrived at through the *via negativa* of the Unreal City.

Such a comparison, however, has limitations. These are partly due to the fact that what we have of the *Politics* is considered fragmentary and incomplete, that such portions as we do have—the slave/master relationship or the regulation of property, for example—are directed toward topics of little relevance to our subject.

If the patterns of human and spiritual debasement appear to reflect the imprint of Aristotelian ethics—the substitution of the gratification of sexual impulse for mind and will—then the degradation of the city appears to bear the imprint of Hobbes' concept of government, a theory Eliot believed to be ruinous of modern civilization.

In his essay "John Bramhall," Eliot reconstructed the Archbishop's defense of the faith against Hobbes. Although Eliot takes pains to represent both sides of the argument, he takes few pains to disguise where his sympathies lay. In Eliot's estimation, Hobbes' attitude "toward moral philosophy has by no means disappeared from human thought; nor has the confusion between moral philosophy and mechanistic psychology."[25] Rather, Hobbes' determinism has settled down like a vast, gray fogbank of relativism and fatalism upon the modern age. The tragedy of Hobbesian thinking, in Eliot's mind, is its easy appeal "to gentle people."[26] In effect, the modern age is duped into believing that no alternatives exist to determinism. This attitude leads to Eliot's sharpest criticism in the essay: "His specious effect of unity between a very simple theory of sense perception and an equally simple theory of government is of a kind that will always be popular because it appears to be intellectual but is really emotional, and therefore very soothing to lazy minds."[27] Ease of intellectual effort is the opiate of those who wander the wasteland.[28]

Eliot's critique of Thomas Hobbes, "one of those extraordinary little upstarts,"[29] might almost serve as a compendium on *The Waste Land*, a reflection on the modern moral situation written a decade after the poem. Eliot makes little effort to disguise his contempt for Hobbes—"In Hobbes there are symptoms of the same mentality as Nietzsche: his belief in violence is a confession of weakness."[30] But where, precisely, do Eliot's points of contention lie?

His difficulty with Hobbes arises from two essential points of disagreement—on Hobbes' political thought and, more fundamentally, his moral system. By reducing human will and consciousness to a biological determinism, Eliot argued, Hobbes essentially rubbed out the individual integrity of human nature. Consequently, moral norms and ethical values are shoved out of the human picture. "For Hobbes," Eliot asserts, "all standards of good and evil are frankly relative."[31] Having stripped humanity of free will and ethical norms, then, Hobbes institutes a thoroughly pragmatic government. Instead of enacting justice, for example, the role of this government is merely to keep order. In Eliot's view, "It will be remembered that Hobbes wished to maintain the activity of human legislation in his deterministic universe; so he considered that law acts as a deterrent force."[32] The effect is that "the whole system ceases to have meaning, and all values, including his own value of good government, disappear."[33]

It should be clear that in *The Waste Land* Eliot also exposes the maladies of the modern political age. The self-indulgent qualities manifested personally and spiritually prevail culturally and politically. His own constructive statements on the role of government accompanied his conversion in 1927 and didn't receive full articulation until the mid-1930s through World War II. In the Spring and Summer 1929 issues of the *Criterion*, Eliot defined several contemporary political perspectives and outlined his idea of loyalty to a monarch.

For many years he was quite wary of the church as ecclesiastical body playing any role in politics. In 1934 he wrote that "So long as the Sacraments are provided for the benefit of men, and the service for the glory of God, the Church is doing what is its *essential* business."[34] With the pressing concerns of World War II, however, Eliot's thinking changed dramatically. The reformation of his position insisted that both the ecclesiastic church and individual Christians bear a responsibility to address cultural wrongs.

His vision of a Christian society was developed more fully in "The Idea of a Christian Society" (1939), "Towards a Christian Britain" (1941), "Notes Toward a Definition of Culture" (1948), and "The Aims of Education" (1950). *The Waste Land* asserts the presence of a moral hollowness in culture and politics; the latter essays attempt to construct the framework of an ethically viable culture.

The Directive Trinity

It is fruitful at this point, as we trace the three primary patterns of personal, spiritual, and cultural debasement to the poem's concluding response, to be reminded of the epigraph to the poem. Taken from Petronius' *Satyricon*, Chapter 48, Apollo has granted the prophetess Sibyl as many years of life as she could hold grains of dust in her hand. She neglected, however, to ask for youth to go with it. At this point in the *Satyricon*, Sibyl is but a shrunken, dry form. Therefore, she croaks the words essential to the epigraph: "For I myself, with my own eyes, saw the Sibyl of Cumae hanging caged in a bottle, and when the boys said to her: "Sibyl, what do you want," she answered: "I want to die." Significantly, at this point in *Satyricon* the narrator stands on the threshold of Hades. Thereby the Sibyl's dusty, dry voice reflects the aridity of Eliot's modern wasteland as we, the readers, are led to the threshold of hell. Here, as line 30 has it, lies "fear in a handful of dust."

Is there a way out? Two important patterns suggest that there is. The first of these rests in the structural response of Section V to the rest of the poem.

In terms of the most basic structure of the poem, the common assumption is that Section I, "The Burial of the Dead," relates to the element of earth; "A Game of Chess" relates to air; "The Fire Sermon" to fire; "Death by Water" to water. The fifth section, "What the Thunder Said," appears to break the pattern; all the elements have been cited. But this section, Benjamin Lockerd argues in *Aethereal Rumors*, represents the aether, Aristotle's concept of a distinct element, nonetheless working in consort with the others. It is the spiritual element, not opposed to but commensurate with the physical elements. "Clearly," Lockerd writes, "something happens here [in Section V] which is quite different from what we experience in the first four sections."[35] Indeed, the revelation of Section V, counterpointing the harsh physicality of the first four sections, consists of spiritual directions for a way out of the wasteland.

The second pattern arises from three signs or signals to the wasteland wanderers—the signs of Gethsemane, the Road to Emmaus, and the Holy Grail. I called these "signals" because they point two ways. They are at once reflexive, or responsive to the debased trinity of *The Waste Land*, but also they are directive, pointing ultimately to the command of the thunder.

Even though the concluding lines of *The Waste Land* leave us in the whirling fragments of a self-indulgent age, much as "Gerontion" does, Eliot does formulate his tripartite command to the age as directions out of the personal, spiritual, and cultural desert.

Gethsemane

The first signal occurs when we are suddenly placed in Gethsemane, the garden where Jesus was arrested (Matt 26:36–46). After presiding over the

Last Supper—thus the link to the Grail Quest pattern—Jesus took Peter, James, and John with him to pray. Fully aware of his impending death and in sweating agony, Jesus implored God three times to take the cup (of suffering) from him. Each time Jesus returns to his three disciples to find them asleep. "The frosty silence in the gardens" deeply pains Jesus since he had specifically asked the disciples to "keep watch with me." He is abandoned into the solitary. If solitary, however, Jesus' sojourn in the garden is also selfless. He gives up self to the will of the father: "Yet not as I will, but as you will" (Matt 26:39, 42). The choice lies in precise counterpoint to the self-indulgence of the wasteland, and foreshadows the thunder's command to give selflessly.

The following lines (324–330) quickly summarize the aftermath of Gethsemane. "The agony in stony places" captures the beatings and mockery; "The shouting and the crying" recall the crowd, the popular voice of the people, calling for the release of Barabbas; "Prison and palace" signal the appearance before Pilate. Suddenly, in this compact explosion of drama, the scene shifts to Golgotha. "The reverberation of thunder of spring over distant mountains" recalls the darkness at mid-day, the rending of the temple veil, and the earthquake (Matt 27:45–53). The scene ends with the blunt statement: "He who was living is now dead."

The statement echoes a sequence of deaths in the poem. The narrator wonders if Stetson's corpse, buried in the garden, has begun to sprout in this debased April of the poem. While the Gethsemane agony occurs in "frosty silence," the narrator wonders if Stetson's corpse has been heaved by frost. In "The Fire Sermon" the Fisher King recalls the death of "the king my brother" and "the king my father's death before him." Most notably, the narrator, who has been told by Madame Sosostris to "Fear death by water," hears of the death of Phlebas by drowning in Section IV and believes he is free of the prediction. He isn't, of course, for the Gethsemane scene ends with these lines: "We, who were living are now dying / With a little patience" (329–330). Those in *The Waste Land* are all the living dead, walking through the threshold to Hades, in dire need of rejuvenation and direction. But here "red sullen faces sneer and snarl / From doors of mudcracked houses" (344–345).

The Road to Emmaus

The second major signal arises from another biblical analogue, the appearance of Christ on the road to Emmaus. The scene is recorded in only one of the synoptic gospels, that of the physician/historian Luke. On Resurrection Sunday, the women who had visited the empty tomb ran to where the disciples were gathered to tell them the news. Of the remaining eleven disciples only Peter ran back to the tomb for verification. The other disciples remained skeptical. Two of Jesus' followers, Cleopas and another who is not named, set off for Emmaus, a village about seven miles distant from Jerusalem. On the road Jesus fell in step with them. The crux of the story is that the two walked side by side with the risen Christ but did not recognize him until Jesus explained the fulfillment of Old Testament prophecies about the Christ. He then sat down with them and shared a meal. At this point, "Their eyes were opened and they recognized him" (Lk 24:31). Interestingly, they observe after Jesus leaves that "were not our hearts burning within us while he talked with us on the road and opened the Scripture to us?" (Lk 24:32).

The burning of the self-indulgent wasteland is transmogrified to an inner burning for spiritual answers that ultimately lie outside of self. The process is a stirring of the soul, or in Aristotle's terms the work of the *anima*. Furthermore, it correlates with the thunder's command to sympathize, or have compassion. This is the inward turning from self to others.

Search for the Sacred

The third pattern in Section V is the Grail Quest itself, which represents longing, seeking, and restoration of order. The Fisher King himself is an ironic antitype to Jesus, the fisher of men. The ancient symbol of the *Ikhthos*, the fish, was fashioned by early Christians so that anagramic letters represented Jesus Christ, Son of God, Savior. The figure of the Fisher King, however, is always fettered with irony. Wounded in the genitals, the Fisher King rules a kingdom cast into sterility and drought, a wasteland. He does have knowledge of the Grail's location, but, because of his wasted sterility, he settles into the discomfort of fishing. In Eliot's poem the Fisher King is pictured thus:

> A rat crept softly through the vegetation
> Dragging its slimy belly on the bank
> While I was fishing in the dull canal. (187–189)

He himself lacks the strength to pursue the rejuvenating Grail. He can, however, direct others to it—if only they would ask him.

The Arthurian knights of the legend don't take time to ask. They scour the wasteland in a frenzied quest, not unlike the mindless crowds flowing over London Bridge. Lancelot loses his sanity. Arriving at the Chapel Perilous he finds the way guarded by rampant lions, his own heraldic device. He has to overcome himself to see the Grail—the most difficult quest of all. It is a wasteland out of control. To the modern age the Grail, the representation of Christ's passion and shed blood, is reduced to "the empty chapel, only the wind's home" (389). Those who dwell in the wasteland live by impulse and sensation, unguided by reason and control. Control, as Aristotle argued, is an act of the will guided by reason. As the thunder proclaims, even our giving and sympathy are subject to control.

The wasteland qualities of personal experience guided by self gratification, spirituality debased by the quest for immediate answers, and the unreal city of modern culture are now offset by the suggestive patterns of Gethsemane, the Road to Emmaus, and the Grail Quest. However suggestive, they are not explicit. They lead the narrator to a point of receptivity where he can hear the inarticulate growl of the thunder and translate sounds into signals for a way out of the wasteland. The scene shifts. From wasteland imagery we move to lightning and black clouds. The dry rocks become a jungle, a metaphor for London, humped in silence. Even with the change in locale, however, the "limp leaves / Waited for rain" (96–97). But they are waiting, listening for the sounds that signal renewal. Three commands echo over the jungle.[36]

Each of these positive commands is framed by a negative picture of how they are enacted in the present wasteland. Each positive command, then, is given authority by the way of negation. Thus *datta*, "give," is revealed in the wasteland as mere impulse:

> The awful daring of a moment's surrender
> Which an age of prudence can never retract.

Dayadhvam, "sympathize," has been enacted as mere selfishness. The image of someone willfully locking him or herself into a self-contained prison is chilling. *Damyatta*, "control," fits into the lovely image of the expert sailor permitting the boat its essential freedom before the wind. Control fulfills being, or, in Aristotelian terms, permits entelechy—that condition of a thing whose essence is fully realized. It seems, at first glance, the one positive conjunction of command and image in the series. Yet a tone of wistfulness and loss haunts this image also, for the description continues:

> Your heart would have responded
> Gaily, when invited, beating obedient
> To controlling hands. (421–423)

The use of the subjunctive mood draws attention to what might have happened had we been a people of personal control. Instead, all that we are stands in contrast to the loveliness of the image.

At this stage of the poem, the characters clearly are unable to enact the state of withdrawal from self concern in order to engage the active commands.

But perhaps the thrust of the poem is less an indictment of a miserable condition than a haunting evocation of our fundamental need.[37] From the inward searching of The Hanged Man, albeit ironically figured in the poem, to the fable of the Thunder in the *Brihadaranyaka-Upanishad*, *The Waste Land* sets side by side what we moderns are and what we could be. And if one is mindful of Eliot's admiration for Aristotle, we could add *should be*, for these also echo Aristotle's virtues for the ethical community.[38]

The commands are repeated once more in the poem, as a response to the disorder that the Fisher King perceives in the wasteland (423–432). But their response also carries the sign of a promise—the three-fold *Shantih*.

At the end of the poem, the Fisher King sits huddled before the sordid canal. The arid plains stretch behind him. The cacophony of the wasteland beats upon his ears. He ponders whether he can set his own lands in order, but the various legends of the Grail Quest indicate the futility of his question. His land is under siege; no one pursues the correct questions to remedy the wasteland. In a sense, Eliot's whole poem is a question mark.

That question, in all of its fundamental simplicity, is whether we see anything beyond our immediate perception. Before there can be perception, argued Aristotle in *Categories*, there must be the perceptible: "The object of perception is, it appears, prior to the act of perception. If the perceptible is annihilated, perception will also cease to exist; but the annihilation of perception does not cancel the existence of the perceptible."[39] The denizens of *The Waste Land* have willfully blinded their perception of any existence beyond their own. Their perception is animalistic—of satisfying their own needs only. The impulse is akin to what Eliot described in his Clark Lectures as "Mankind suddenly retires within its several skulls."[40]

That distinction between perception and the perceptible, moreover, marked the development of Eliot's own literary theory. It appears nearly full blown in his essay on Dante, who Eliot prizes for the ability to fuse particular images to a significantly full vision of life. Reacting in part against Paul Valéry's claim that poetry intends to elicit a state of feeling, Eliot counters:

> The true mystic is not satisfied merely by feeling, he must pretend at least that he *sees*, and the absorption into the divine is only the necessary, if paradoxical, limit of this contemplation. The poet does not aim to excite—that is not even a test of his success—but to set something down.... Dante, more than any other poet, has succeeded in dealing with his philosophy ... in terms of something *perceived*. When most of our modern poets confine themselves to what they had perceived, they produce for us, usually, only odds and ends of still life and stage properties; but that does not imply

so much that the method of Dante is obsolete, as that our vision is perhaps comparatively restricted.[41]

Precisely such is the restricted vision of *The Waste Land* inhabitants.

As *The Waste Land* ends, we find ourselves still on the *via negativa*. While no direct answers, like a broad thoroughfare, appear on the desiccated plains, Eliot does nonetheless provide the road signs. The very ambiguity of those signs in the thunder's growl is essential. The way out of the wasteland is not merely corporate. No government can rush in, like Arthur's knights, to reinvigorate and redirect the citizens living in what is defined in "The Hollow Men" as "death's dream kingdom." Any redemptive action begins with a personal choice: the imposition of the intelligent will over sensual gratification. This, in turn, leads to the recognition of ethical and spiritual values that lie outside personal experience. Such values the searching mind apprehends. Only then may the ideal of the orderly city be found.

A just society, Eliot argued with the support of Aristotle, is at once ideal and real—a balanced power. It incarnates such ethical values as justice, kindness, and compassion in concrete actions. The concern of the just state always turns outward, working toward peace and harmony in the citizenry. These values are not just elusive in the wasteland with all its tumbling towers of civilization; they have been willfully abandoned at all levels for personal gratification.

The Waste Land, then, poses a trinity of faults that rive the political unity of the age. These keep the Fisher King, that emblem of renewal, hunched before his canal, face turned from the dry desert wind that sweeps across his back. Personal gratification, reduction of spiritual seeking to the need for immediate answers, the abandonment of ethical values that leads to the decay of modern civilization—these work like hammers to fracture the unity and wholeness of humanity.

But as he sits by the canal, the Fisher King says that "These fragments I have shored against my ruins" (431). The comment has been popularly understood in two ways. In one, the "fragments" refer to the whirling cacophony of the final ten lines, the unfinished thoughts, the jarring of juxtapositions. This view would suggest, then, that fragments are the only thing the Fisher King has to shore his ruins—not a very effective force. The second common view is that "fragments" refers to the entire poem, an even more disconsolate view for the Fisher King as he studies the bleakness of the land.

Perhaps the most significant word in the sentence, however, is not "fragments" but "shored." Read this way, the Fisher King—spiritual spokesman for the poem and a counterpoint to Tiresias—uses fragments to "shore against" ruins. He is constructing a bulwark, props to hold back the tide of destructive living, out of fragments. Then the essential question becomes which fragments? The chaotic lines surrounding the sentence? The whole of the poem? Only in deepest irony, and in thorough resignation to disconsolation, would the Fisher King answer that way. Not unless Eliot is deliberately rupturing the essence of the myth, certainly a possibility. More likely, however, the "fragments" refer to the inarticulate growlings of the thunder, which only the narrator perceives as words. That trinity of words, however, certainly shore against the ruins of the wasteland trinity. Give, sympathize, and control form the Aristotelian ideals that provide transformation for the reality of fragmentary dissolution.

Notes

1. T.S. Eliot. *Collected Poems 1909–1962* (New York: Harcourt Brace and Co., 1963). All quotations from Eliot's poem *The Waste Land* are from this edition. All quotations from *The Waste Land* will be cited in the text by line number.

2. T.S. Eliot. "The Development of Leibniz' Monadism," *The Monist* 26 (Oct 1916). Reprinted in *Knowledge and Experience in the Philosophy of F.H. Bradley* (New York: Farrar, 1964), 188.

3. T.S. Eliot. "The Perfect Critic," *The Sacred Wood: Essays on Poetry and Criticism* (London: Methuen, 1920, 1966): 10–11.

4. Aristotle, *Metaphysics, The Basic Works of Aristotle*, 689. Aristotle uses the term "First Mover" or "Prime Mover" for this absolute. The popular term "Unmoved Mover" is misleading, since, in his cosmological thinking, there may be several dozen of these, each associated with some planetary motion. See *Metaphysics*, Book XII. Although most of our modern understanding of the "First Mover" is taken from the *Metaphysics*, Aristotle laid the groundwork in Books VII and VIII of the *Physics*.

5. Aquinas' fascination with Aristotle, both in logical method and a kindred sensibility, is unquestionable. Among his many volumes, Aquinas wrote commentaries on Aristotle's *Physics, Metaphysics*, and *Ethics*.

6. It should be noted that during the 9th century, John Scotus, uninfluenced by Aristotle, developed his theory of the *via negativa* based upon linguistic limitations. See *On the Division of Nature* (Indianapolis: Bobbs-Merrill, 1976).

7. Thomas Aquinas. *An Aquinas Reader*. Ed. Mary T. Clark (New York: Fordham University Press, 3rd Rev. Ed., 2000), *Summa Theologica*, I, 30. References to the *Summa Theologica* will be cited by textual source. The standard translation is the five volume work by the fathers of the English Dominican Province (Christian Classics, 1981). Its bulk and weight (12 pounds) makes the edition difficult to use. Because of the convenience, reputation, and availability of Clark's edition, I will use its translation and page numbers.

8. See *Summa Theologica*, I. 14: "The chief way to consider divine essence is the way of negation, for by its immensity the divine essence transcends every form attained by our intellect; and so in apprehending it we do not know what it is. But by knowing what it is not we get some knowledge of it, and the more things we are able to deny of it, the nearer we come to knowing it" (139).

9. Some scholars deny that *The Waste Land* contains any intrinsic pattern or plan of renewal. For them, *The Waste Land* is the inextricable modern condition.

See, for example, Eloise Knapp Hay, *T.S. Eliot's Negative Way* (Cambridge: Harvard University Press, 1982), where she argues that "Nowhere in the poem can one find convincing allusions to any existence in another world . . ." (49).

10. Lyndall Gordon. *T.S. Eliot: An Imperfect Life* (New York: W.W. Norton, 1999): 149.

11. Ibid.

12. Aristotle, *Nicomachean Ethics, The Basic Works of Aristotle*, ed. Richard McKeon (New York: Random House, 1941): 957. Compare this passage also to "Gerontion," ll. 45–48.

13. See *De Anima*, Books II and III.

14. Aristotle, *Metaphysics, The Basic Works of Aristotle*, 689.

15. Aristotle, *Nicomachean Ethics, The Basic Works of Aristotle*, 959.

16. Ibid.

17. Ibid., 987.

18. Ibid., 1004.

19. The figure of the fortune teller is ironically patterned upon the figure of Mr. Scogan in Aldous Huxley's *Crome Yellow*. At a charity fair, Mr. Scogan dresses in drag and passes himself off as "Sosostris, the Sorcerer of Ecbatana." The pose itself, man as witch, is a falsification, but so too are the theatrical pronouncements of Scogan/Sosostris. Scogan's closing words, tersely matter-of-fact, work as counterpoint to Eliot's: "Good afternoon. That will be six-pence. Yes, I have change. Thank you. Good afternoon." In both instances, Huxley's and Eliot's, the people swarm the sorcerer's tent. Aldous Huxley, *Crome Yellow* (London: Chatto and Windus, 1921, p. 134).

20. Much has been made of Madame Sosostris' prediction, especially what she does not find—The Hanged Man of the Tarot deck. The allusion functions ironically in the poem. The Hanged Man, the twelfth card in the *Major Arcana*, is thoroughly at peace. It is the card of suspension, not of life or death, where one looks inward in peaceful repose to find spiritual direction. He is at rest, unlike the harried, appetitive people of Eliot's poem. The irony continues in that The Hanged Man's planet is Neptune, or water. Sosostris tells the narrator to fear death by water; yet, no life will spring in the arid land until the commands of the thunder are heeded.

21. See, for example, the definitions of Perception, the Relative, and Substance in *Categories*, Chapter 7.

22. See *Partibus Animalium*, 644^{b}22–646^{a}4, and *De Anima* 408^{a}34–^{b}31–429^{a}10–439^{a}25.

23. See *T.S. Eliot: An Imperfect Life*, Chapter Five.

24. Charles Baudelaire, "To the Reader," *Les Fleurs du Mal* (Boston: D.R. Godine, 1983).

25. T.S. Eliot, "John Bramhall," *Essays Ancient and Modern* (New York: Harcourt, Brace, 1936): 28.

26. Ibid., 36.

27. Ibid.

28. Eliot would take his own pattern of a passion guided by intellect from Blaise Pascal. For Eliot, Pascal represented "the type of one kind of religious believer, which is highly passionate and ardent, but passionate only through a powerful and regulated intellect . . . facing unflinchingly the demon of doubt which is inseparable from the Spirit of belief" (*EAM* 158). Mindful of the fragmentation that occurs in *The Waste Land*, Eliot commends Pascal to "those who doubt, but

who have the mind to conceive, and the sensibility to feel, the disorder, the futility, the meaninglessness, the mystery of life and suffering, and who can only find peace through a satisfaction of the whole being" (*EAM* 168).

29. T.S. Eliot, "John Bramhall," 26.

30. Ibid., 36.

31. Ibid., 35.

32. Ibid., 30.

33. Ibid.

34. T.S. Eliot. "What Does the Church Stand For?" *Spectator* (19 October 1935), 560.

35. Benjamin G. Lockerd, Jr. *Aethereal Rumors: T.S. Eliot's Physics and Poetics.* Lewisburg: Bucknell University Press, 1998: 182.

36. Two of the better studies of the thunder's commands in and of themselves include Jewel Spears Brooker and Joseph Bentley, *Reading "The Waste Land": Modernism and the Limits of Interpretation* (Amherst: University of Massachusetts Press, 1990) and Richard Hanson, "A Grammatical and Idiomatic Analysis of the Sanskrit in *The Waste Land*," *Yeats Eliot Review* 16, 2 (Winter 1990): 34–39. For a general study of the influence of Eastern thought upon Eliot, see Cleo McNelly Kearns, *T.S. Eliot and Indic Traditions: A Study of Poetry and Belief* (Cambridge: Cambridge University Press: 1987).

37. Such, for example, is the view of Robert Crawford who writes in *The Savage and the City in the Work of T.S. Eliot* (Oxford: Clarendon Press, 1987) that "*The Waste Land* is a poem that leaves its readers in darkness" (148). And also, "The 'Shantih' at the poem's end may be simply a way of stopping . . . or it may be comparable to the exhausted collapse after the destruction at the end of 'Gerontion'" (149).

38. See Aristotle, *Nicomachean Ethics*, 1107^a28–179^a6, and *Politics*, 1280^a7–1326^b24.

39. Aristotle, "Categories," *The Basic Works of Aristotle*, 21.

40. T.S. Eliot. *The Varieties of Metaphysical Poetry.* Ed. Ronald Schuchard. London: Faber and Faber, 1993: 80.

41. T.S. Eliot. "Dante," *The Sacred Wood.* London: Methuen, 1928, 1920.

Works Cited

Aquinas, Thomas. *An Aquinas Reader.* Ed. Mary T. Clark. New York: Fordham University Press. 3rd Rev. Ed. 2000.

Aristotle. *The Basic Works of Aristotle.* Ed. Richard McKeon. New York: Random House, 1941.

Baudelaire, Charles. *Les Fleurs Du Mal: The Complete Text of the Flowers of Evil.* Trans. Richard Howard. Boston: D.R. Godine, 1983.

Brooker, Jewel Spears and Joseph Bentley. *Reading* The Waste Land: *Modernism and The Limits of Interpretation.* Amherst: University of Massachusetts Press, 1990.

Crawford, Robert. *The Savage and the City in the Works of T.S. Eliot.* Oxford: Clarendon Press, 1987.

Eliot, T.S. *Collected Poems 1909–1962.* New York: Harcourt, Brace, 1963.

———. "The Development of Liebniz' Monadism," *The Monist* 26 (Oct 1916). Reprinted in *Knowledge and Experience in the Philosophy of F.M. Bradley.* New York: Farrar, Straus and Giroux, 1964.

———. "John Bramhall," *Essays Ancient and Modern.* New York: Harcourt, Brace, 1936.

———. "Lancelot Andrewes," *Essays Ancient and Modern*. New York: Harcourt, Brace, 1936.

———. "The Music of Poetry," *Selected Essays*. London: Faber and Faber, 1932.

———. "The Pensées of Pascal," *Essays Ancient and Modern*.

———. "Review of John Masefield, *The Coming of Christ*." *Criterion*, 4 (June 1928)

———. *The Sacred Wood*. London: Methuen, 1928, 1920.

———. *The Varieties of Metaphysical Experience*. Ed. Ronald Schuchard. London: Faber and Faber, 1993.

———. "What Does the Church Stand For?" *Spectator* (19 Oct 1934).

Gordon, Lyndall. *T S. Eliot: An Imperfect Life*. New York: W.W. Norton, 1999.

Hanson, Richard. "A Grammatical and Idiomatic Analysis of the Sanskrit in *The Waste Land*," *Yeats Eliot Review* 16 (Winter 1999): 34–39.

Hay, Eloise Knapp. *T.S. Eliot's Negative Way*. Cambridge: Harvard University Press, 1982.

Huxley, Aldous. *Crome Yellow*. London: Chatto and Windus, 1921.

Kearns, Cleo McNelly. *T.S. Eliot and Indic Traditions: A Study of Poetry and Belief*. Cambridge: Cambridge University Press, 1987.

Lockerd, Benjamin G., Jr. *Aethereal Rumors: T.S. Eliot's Physics and Poetics*. Lewisburg: Bucknell University Press, 1998.

Schuchard, Ronald. *Eliot's Dark Angel: Intersections of Life and Art*. New York: Oxford University Press, 1999.

Scotus, John. *Periphyseon: On the Division of Nature*. Indianapolis: Bobbs-Merrill, 1976.

Chronology

1888	Thomas Stearns Eliot born September 26 in St. Louis. Youngest of seven children born to Henry Ware and Charlotte Chauncey Eliot (née Stearns).
1909	Receives B.A. from Harvard University.
1910–11	In 1910 receives M.A. from Harvard. Studies in Paris at the Sorbonne.
1911–15	Graduate student in philosophy at Harvard from 1911 to 1914. In 1914, studies at the University of Marburg, Germany; cut short by war. Reads philosophy at Merton, Oxford, 1914–15. Meets Ezra Pound.
1915–17	"The Love Song of J. Alfred Prufrock" published in *Poetry* in 1915. Marries Vivienne Haighwood in 1915. Teaches at High Wycombe Grammar School, London, and then at Highgate School, London, from 1915 to 1917.
1917–19	Employee of Lloyd's Bank from 1917 to 1925. Assistant editor of *The Egoist* from 1917 to 1919. *Prufrock and Other Observations* published in 1917.
1920	*Poems* and *The Sacred Wood*, essays on poetry and criticism, published.
1922	Editor of *The Criterion*, until its closure in 1939. *The Waste Land* published. Wins Dial Award.

1925	Publishes *Poems, 1909–25*. Joins Faber & Gwyer, later Faber & Faber, publishers.
1927–31	Becomes a member of the Church of England and a British citizen in 1927. Publishes *Journey of the Magi* in 1927, *For Lancelot Andrewes: Essays on Style and Order* in 1928, *Ash-Wednesday* in 1930, and *Thoughts After Lambeth* in 1931. Divorces circa 1930.
1932–34	In 1932 publishes *Selected Essays 1917–1932*. Delivers Charles Eliot Norton Lectures at Harvard (publishes as *The Use of Poetry and the Use of Criticism*, 1933), and the Page-Barbour Lectures at the University of Virginia (published as *After Strange Gods— A Primer of Modern Heresy*, 1934). *The Rock* opens in London in 1934.
1935	*Murder in the Cathedral* performed in Centerbury Catherdral before opening in London.
1936	Publishes *Collected Poems, 1909–35*.
1939	Delivers the Cambridge Lectures, published as *The Idea of a Christian Society*. *The Family Reunion* opens in London.
1943	Publishes *Four Quartets*.
1945	Publishes *What Is a Classic?* Visits Ezra Pound at St. Elizabeth's Hospital in Washington, DC. Shares an apartment in London with John Hayward until 1957.
1947	Death of first wife, after long illness.
1948	Awarded the Order of Merit and the Nobel Prize for Literature.
1949	Publishes *Notes Toward a Definition of Culture*. *The Cocktail Party* opens.
1950	Suffers a mild heart attack, in poor health thereafter. Wins New York Drama Critics Circle Award and Antoinette Perry Award for *The Cocktail Party* as best foreign play.
1953	*The Confidential Clerk* opens in Edinburgh and then moves to London.
1956	Lectures at the University of Minnesota. Lecture published as *The Frontiers of Criticism*.
1957	Marries Valerie Fletcher, his personal secretary. Publishes *On Poetry and Poets*.

1958	*The Elder Statesman* opens in Edinburgh.
1962	Publishes *Collected Plays*.Seriously ill.
1963	*Collected Poems, 1909–1962* is published. Visits New York with Valerie Eliot.
1965	Dies at home in London on January 4. Buried in Westminster Abbey.

Contributors

HAROLD BLOOM is Sterling Professor of the Humanities at Yale University. Educated at Cornell and Yale universities, he is the author of more than 30 books, including *Shelley's Mythmaking* (1959), *The Visionary Company* (1961), *Blake's Apocalypse* (1963), *Yeats* (1970), *The Anxiety of Influence* (1973), *A Map of Misreading* (1975), *Kabbalah and Criticism* (1975), *Agon: Toward a Theory of Revisionism* (1982), *The American Religion* (1992), *The Western Canon* (1994), *Omens of Millennium: The Gnosis of Angels, Dreams, and Resurrection* (1996), *Shakespeare: The Invention of the Human* (1998), *How to Read and Why* (2000), *Genius: A Mosaic of One Hundred Exemplary Creative Minds* (2002), *Hamlet: Poem Unlimited* (2003), *Where Shall Wisdom Be Found?* (2004), and *Jesus and Yahweh: The Names Divine* (2005). In addition, he is the author of hundreds of articles, reviews, and editorial introductions. In 1999, Professor Bloom received the American Academy of Arts and Letters' Gold Medal for Criticism. He has also received the International Prize of Catalonia, the Alfonso Reyes Prize of Mexico, and the Hans Christian Andersen Bicentennial Prize of Denmark.

HUGH KENNER taught at several universities during his lifetime and was a frequent contributor to the *National Review*. He was the editor of Prentice-Hall's *T.S. Eliot: A Collection of Critical Essays*. His numerous critical books include *The Poetry of Ezra Pound* and *A Homemade World: The American Modernist Writers*.

CLEO MCNELLY KEARNS is a lecturer at Rutgers University. She is the author of *T. S. Eliot and Indic Traditions: A Study in Poetry and Belief* and *The Virgin Mary, Monotheism and Sacrifice*.

JOHN PAUL RIQUELME is a professor at Boston University and the author of *Teller and Tale in Joyce's Fiction*. He has been the editor of Joyce's and others' works. He also has been the guest editor of various journals.

A.D. MOODY is an emeritus professor at the University of York in England. He is the author of *Thomas Stearns Eliot: Poet* and *Tracing T.S. Eliot's Spirit*, and editor of *The Cambridge Companion to T.S. Eliot*. He also has done extensive writing on Pound.

ANTHONY L. JOHNSON has taught at the Università di Pisa. He is the author of *Sign and Structure in the Poetry of T. S. Eliot*, *The Verbal Art of W. B. Yeats*, and other titles.

LEE OSER is an associate professor of English at the College of the Holy Cross. He has published *The Return of Christian Humanism: Chesterton, Eliot, Tolkien, and the Romance of History*; *The Ethics of Modernism: Moral Ideas in Yeats, Eliot, Joyce, Woolf and Beckett*; and a novel.

DENIS DONOGHUE is a professor at New York University. He is the author of many titles, including *Words Alone: The Poet T.S. Eliot* and *Thieves of Fire: The Promethean Imagination* (The T. S. Eliot Lectures at the University of Kent at Canterbury).

RONALD BUSH has been a professor at California Institute of Technology. His works include *T. S. Eliot: A Study of Character and Style* and *T. S. Eliot: The Modernist in History*.

JOSEPH JONGHYUN JEON is an associate professor at the University of San Diego. He has published *Racial Things: Visuality and Racialization in Avant-garde Asian American Poetry*. He is poetry editor of *Kaya*.

JOHN H. TIMMERMAN is a professor at Calvin College. He has published several titles, including *T. S. Eliot's Ariel Poems* and others on Robert Frost, John Steinbeck, and Jane Kenyon. He also has published short fiction and creative nonfiction.

Bibliography

Austin, William J. *Deconstruction of T.S. Eliot: The Fire and the Rose.* Lewiston, N.Y.: Edwin Mellen Press, 1996.

Barfoot, C. C., and Theo D'haen, eds. *Centennial Hauntings: Pope, Byron and Eliot in the Year 88.* Amsterdam; Atlanta, Ga.: Rodopi, 1990.

Basu, Tapan Kumar, ed. *T. S. Eliot: An Anthology of Recent Criticism.* Delhi: Pencraft, 1993.

Blisten, Burton. *The Design of* The Waste Land. Lanham, Md.: University Press of America, 2008.

Booty, John. *Meditating on* Four Quartets. Cincinnati, Ohio: Forward Movement Publications, 2003.

Brooker, Jewel Spears, ed. *The Placing of T.S. Eliot.* Columbia, Mo.: University of Missouri Press, 1991.

Brooker, Jewel Spears, and Joseph Bentley. *Reading* The Waste Land: *Modernism and the Limits of Interpretation.* Amherst, Mass.: University of Massachusetts Press, 1990.

Chinitz, David E. *T.S. Eliot and the Cultural Divide.* Chicago: University of Chicago Press, 2003.

Clarke, Graham, ed. *T. S. Eliot: Critical Assessments.* London: Christopher Helm, 1990.

Cook, Eleanor. "T. S. Eliot and the Carthaginian Peace." *ELH* 46, no. 2 (Summer 1979): 341–55.

Cuda, Anthony. *The Passions of Modernism: Eliot, Yeats, Woolf, and Mann.* Columbia, S.C.: University of South Carolina Press, 2010.

Cuddy, Lois A. *T.S. Eliot and the Poetics of Evolution: Sub/Versions of Classicism, Culture, and Progress.* Lewisburg, Pa.: Bucknell University Press; London; Cranbury, N.J.: Associated University Presses, 2000.

179

Davidson, Clifford. *Baptism, the Three Enemies and T.S. Eliot*. Stamford, Lincoln-shire: S. Tyas, 1999.

Davidson, Harriet, ed. *T.S. Eliot*. London; New York: Longman, 1999.

Donoghue, Denis. *Words Alone: The Poet T.S. Eliot*. New Haven, Conn.: Yale University Press, 2000.

Hands, Anthony. *Sources for the Poetry of T.S. Eliot*. Oxford, England: Hadrian Books, 1993.

Howard, Thomas. *Dove Descending: A Journey into T. S. Eliot's* Four Quartets. San Francisco: Sapienta Classics/Ignatius Press, 2006.

Jaidka, Manju. *T.S. Eliot's Use of Popular Sources*. Lewiston, N.Y.: Edwin Mellen Press, 1997.

Julius, Anthony. *T.S. Eliot, Anti-Semitism, and Literary Form*. New York: Thames & Hudson, 2003.

Kaplan, Harold. *Poetry, Politics, and Culture: Argument in the Work of Eliot, Pound, Stevens, and Williams*. New Brunswick, N.J.: Aldine Transaction, 2006.

Kermode, Frank. *Selected Prose of T.S. Eliot.* New York; London: Harcourt (Farrar, Straus & Giroux); Faber, 1975.

Khare, R. R. *Shakespeare, Eugene O'Neill, T.S. Eliot and the Greek Tragedy*. New Delhi, India: Mittal Publications, 1998.

Kirk, Russell. *Eliot and His Age: T. S. Eliot's Moral Imagination in the Twentieth Century*. Wilmington, Del.: ISI, 2008.

Lobb, Edward, ed. *Words in Time: New Essays on Eliot's* Four Quartets. Ann Arbor, Mich.: University of Michigan Press, 1993.

Lowe, Peter. *Christian Romanticism: T. S. Eliot's Response to Percy Shelley.* Youngstown, N.Y.: Cambria, 2006.

Maddrey, Joseph. *The Making of T.S. Eliot: A Study of the Literary Influences*. Jefferson, N.C.: McFarland & Co., 2009.

Manganaro, Marc. *Myth, Rhetoric, and the Voice of Authority: A Critique of Frazer, Eliot, Frye, & Campbell*. New Haven, Conn.: Yale University Press, 1992.

Marsh, Alec. "Pound and Eliot." *American Literary Scholarship: An Annual* (2007): 169–93.

McLaughlin, Joseph. *Writing the Urban Jungle: Reading Empire in London from Doyle to Eliot*. Charlottesville, Va.: University Press of Virginia, 2000.

Melaney, William D. *After Ontology: Literary Theory and Modernist Poetics*. Albany: State University of New York Press, 2001.

Menand, Louis. *Discovering Modernism: T. S. Eliot and His Context*. New York; Oxford: Oxford University Press, 2007.

———. "T. S. Eliot and Modernity." *New England Quarterly: A Historical Review of New England Life and Letters* 69, no. 4 (December 1996): 554–79.

Merrett, Robert James. *Presenting the Past: Philosophical Irony and the Rhetoric of Double Vision from Bishop Butler to T. S. Eliot.* Victoria, B.C.: English Literary Studies, University of Victoria, 2004.

Moreland, Richard C. *Learning from Difference: Teaching Morrison, Twain, Ellison, and Eliot.* Columbus: Ohio State University Press, 1999.

Nevo, Ruth. "*The Waste Land*: The Ur-Text of Deconstruction." *New Literary History: A Journal of Theory and Interpretation* 13, no. 3 (Spring 1982): 453–61.

Palmer, Marja. *Men and Women in T.S. Eliot's Early Poetry.* Lund, Sweden: Lund University Press, 1996.

Pathak, R. S., ed. *New Directions in Eliot Studies.* New Delhi, India: Northern Book Centre, 1990.

Poirier, Richard. "Pater, Joyce, Eliot." *James Joyce Quarterly* 26, no. 1 (Fall 1988): 21–35.

Raine, Craig. *In Defence of T.S. Eliot.* London: Picador, 2000.

Raine, Kathleen. *Defining the Times: Essays on Auden & Eliot.* London: Enitharmon Press, 2002.

Rainey, Lawrence. *Revisiting* The Waste Land. New Haven, Conn.: Yale University Press, 2005.

Ricks, Christopher. *T. S. Eliot and Prejudice.* Berkeley: University of California Press, 1988.

Schwarz, Robert L. *Broken Images: A Study of* The Waste Land. Lewisburg, Pa.: Bucknell University Press; London: Associated University Presses, 1988.

Shusterman, Richard. *T.S. Eliot and the Philosophy of Criticism.* New York: Columbia University Press, 1988.

Smith, Stan. *The Origins of Modernism: Eliot, Pound, Yeats and the Rhetorics of Renewal.* New York: Harvester Wheatsheaf, 1994.

Surette, Leon. *The Modern Dilemma: Wallace Stevens, T.S. Eliot and Humanism.* Montreal: McGill-Queen's University Press, 2008.

Vanheste, Jeroen. *Guardians of the Humanist Legacy: The Classicism of T.S. Eliot's Criterion Network and Its Relevance to Our Postmodern World.* Leiden; Boston: Brill, 2007.

Vendler, Helen. *Coming of Age as a Poet: Milton, Keats, Eliot, Plath.* Cambridge, Mass.: Harvard University Press, 2003.

Vericat, Fabio L. *From Physics to Metaphysics: Philosophy and Allegory in the Critical Writings of T. S. Eliot.* Valencia, Spain: Universitat de València, 2004.

Wellens, Oscar. "The Brief and Brilliant Life of *The Athenaeum* under Mr. Middleton Murry" (T.S. Eliot). *Neophilologus* 85, no. 1 (January 2001): 137–52.

Woolsky, Shira. *Language Mysticism: The Negative Way of Language in Eliot, Beckett, and Celan.* Stanford, Calif.: Stanford University Press, 1995.

Acknowledgments

Hugh Kenner, "Eliot and the Voices of History." From *Man and Poet*, Volume 1, edited and introduced by Laura Cowan. Copyright © 1990 by the National Poetry Foundation.

Cleo McNelly Kearns, "Doctrine and Wisdom in *Four Quartets*." From *Man and Poet*, Volume 1, edited and introduced by Laura Cowan. Copyright © 1990 by the National Poetry Foundation.

John Paul Riquelme, "Little Gidding' 3: Indifference and the Process of Reading *Four Quartets*." From *Harmony of Dissonances: T. S. Eliot, Romanticism, and Imagination*. Copyright © 1991 by the Johns Hopkins University Press.

A.D. Moody, "T. S. Eliot: The American Strain." From *The Placing of T. S. Eliot*, edited by Jewel Spears Brooker. Copyright © 1991 by the Curators of the University of Missouri.

Anthony L. Johnson, "T. S. Eliot's *Gerontion* and *Journey of the Magi*." From *"The Spectre of a Rose": Intersections*, edited by Mario Domenichelli and Romana Zacchi. Copyright © 1991 Bulzoni Editore.

Lee Oser, "Prufrock's Guilty Pleasures." From *T. S. Eliot and American Poetry*. Copyright © 1998 by the Curators of the University of Missouri.

Denis Donoghue, "Beginning." From *The Southern Review* 34, no. 3 (1998): 532–49. Copyright © 1998 by Denis Donoghue.

Ronald Bush, "In Pursuit of Wilde Possum: Reflections on Eliot, Modernism, and the Nineties." From *Modernism/modernity* 11, no. 3 (September 2004): 469–85. Copyright © 2004 by the Johns Hopkins University Press.

Joseph Jonghyun Jeon, "Eliot's Shadows: Autography and Style in *The Hollow Men*." From *Yeats Eliot Review* 24, no. 4 (Winter 2007): 12–24. Copyright © 2007 by Joseph Jonghyun Jeon.

John H. Timmerman, "The Aristotelian Mr. Eliot: Structure and Strategy in *The Waste Land*." From *Yeats Eliot Review* 24, no. 2 (Summer 2007): 11–23. Copyright © 2007 by John H. Timmerman.

Index

185